WITHDRAWN

A Song for You

A Song for You

My Life with Whitney Houston

ROBYN CRAWFORD

DUTTON

DUTTON

An imprint of Penguin Random House LLC
penguinrandomhouse.com

LIBRARY OF CONGRESS CATALOGING-IN-PUBLICATION DATA
has been applied for.

ISBN 9781524742843 (hardcover)
ISBN 9781524742867 (ebook)

Printed in the United States of America
10 9 8 7 6 5 4 3 2 1

BOOK DESIGN BY TIFFANY ESTREICHER

To my mom, Janet; brother, Marty; and sister, Robina, for your undying love. You are always with me.

To the most amazing beings, my children, Gillian and Jeremy. You make every day entirely brighter. You are my greatest love of all.

And finally, to my one and only. The one with whom I live adventurously, lay my head next to at night, and awaken to at daybreak. My endless love, Lisa. I still see your face from the first time we met and I draped my scarf around your neck. You are everything.

Contents

Introduction   xi

One   The First Time I Met
Whitney Elizabeth Houston   1

Two   Like an Angel   19

Three   Love = Love   33

Four   Separation Anxiety   53

Five   The Future Is Now   67

Six   Nobody Loves Me Like You Do   77

Seven   You Give Good Love   97

Eight   Introducing Whitney Houston   109

Nine   The Greatest Drug Tour   125

Ten   The Moment of Truth   137

Eleven   Tell On Your Damned Self   147

Twelve   Moving Fast at Twice the Speed   155

Thirteen   Can I Be Me?   165

Fourteen   From Sea to Shining Sea   181

Fifteen   I Will Always Love You   191

Sixteen   The Bodyguard World Tour   205

Contents

Seventeen   Four-Letter Word   209

Eighteen   The Trouble with Angels   219

Nineteen   Exhale   225

Twenty   SOS   241

Twenty-One   My Love Is Your Love   253

Twenty-Two   2000   263

Twenty-Three   California Dreamin'   269

Twenty-Four   Life   281

Epilogue   311

Acknowledgments   315

A Song for You

Introduction

···

Why now? Why did I make the decision to write this book when I could have remained silent for the rest of my days, keeping my memories all to myself? If you are a fan of Whitney Houston, you probably know my name. Google me, and you'll see my face at events and my name in articles.

Whitney and I met as teenagers and spent the next twenty-two years together as she became one of the most popular and beloved global artists of our generation. It was the relationship that would shape my young adult years, professionally and personally. Ours is a story of loyalty and trust—of two women who made a pact to protect and rely on each other. We shared a dream that became a journey, and that journey took us from East Orange, New Jersey, to New York City and then around the world, meeting superstars and heads of state. This is a story of manipulation, control, hunger for power, inexperience, race, AIDS, mental illness, the pressure the entertainment industry places on women, the bonds of family, and the importance of putting oneself first. Above all, it is a story of enduring friendship.

Some have said that I have experienced more than my share of loss. In examining my life, so many memories returned, both beautiful and painful. Writing this book forced me to confront the reality of death, and relive the losses of my mother, my brother, and my best friend. The process allowed me—drove me—to grieve, to face sorrow, something I previously worked hard to bury. But it also provided the opportunity to get to know my loved ones better, and to appreciate what I learned from each of them.

Believe me, I've done my best to stay out of the spotlight, keeping quiet while others painted their own pictures of me and of us. In the nineteen years since I left Whitney's company I have been pursued relentlessly to share my story. And since her death and that of her daughter, I have been saddened and frustrated by the way she and her legacy have been misrepresented.

I believe it is my duty to honor my friend and to clarify the many inaccuracies about myself and about who Whitney was. I feel compelled to remind people of her greatness, to lift her remarkable legacy. The Whitney I know was bighearted, determined, unselfish, private, hilarious, and confident in her gifts.

I hope to help readers understand and recognize fully the person behind that face, voice, and image. Yes, in the end it was tragic, but the dream and the rise were beautiful. I owe it to my friend to share her story, my story. Our story. And I hope that in doing so, I can set us both free.

One

....

The First Time I Met
Whitney Elizabeth Houston

In the summer of 1980 I rode my black Kabuki twenty-two-speed bike across East Orange. The phone had gotten me out of bed, but the wind in my face was waking me up. Coach Clark, my high school basketball coach, had called to tell me that she had a job for me at the East Orange Community Development center, and within minutes, I was out the door. I was starting my second year of college in the fall, and I owed it to Coach Clark to show. I raced to Main Street, the summer sun beginning to pulse in the sky.

I sped up to the glass-front building, jumped off my bike, and walked it into a dimly lit space crowded with people, tables, and chairs lined up against the walls. I found Coach Clark down the hall in the back, and she smiled, gave me a big hug, and then turned and handed me a stack of papers to distribute. Clark could have tapped anyone for the job, but she knew she could count on me.

I've always been vain about my hair, and in those days, I would wash it and then beg my little sister, Robina, affectionately called Bina, to braid it. Other times I'd set it on pink foam rollers; once I took them out, my coils would loosen, and by the third day my Afro would be amazing. It was day three, so I felt cute in my green shorts the color of grass, light green T-shirt, white Nike sneakers, and pristine white tube socks.

I walked around the room carrying a stack of camp counselor enrollment forms and clutching a bunch of pens. Then I came across a girl I'd never seen before. I didn't notice her at first because she was sitting in the back against the wall. But I paused as I handed her the paperwork: She simply stopped me in my tracks.

The girl wore a red-blue-and-gray-plaid silk blouse; slim-fitting knee-length shorts; and red-striped Adidas Gazelles. She had a gold watch necklace around her neck, and her sandy brown hair was pulled back, topped by a visor emblazoned with the Red Cross logo. Her skin was peachy brown, and her eyes caught the misty light.

"What's your name?" I asked.

"Whitney Elizabeth Houston," she said.

I found her response humorous, different. Who gives their first, middle, and last names? I asked where she lived, and she said Dodd-town, across from the McDonald's. My cousins lived right near there, and I often spent the night with them. I'd worked at that very McDonald's throughout my junior year of high school. Later that day, I learned she attended an all-girls private school and was a singer. Her mother had founded the Sweet Inspirations, background singers to big stars like Elvis Presley and Aretha Franklin, and her cousin was Dionne Warwick.

Before I moved on, I gave her one last look and told her I'd keep an eye out for her. I don't know why I felt the need to say that, but I did.

How had I never seen nor heard of her?

....

$Summer$ counselors took kids to participate in activities in various East Orange parks. I chose to work with kids aged six to eleven in Columbian Park, which happened to be near my high school, on the side of town where Whitney lived, so coincidentally she chose the same. I worked the morning session, so by midday I was free for basketball and able to run full-court games with others at Columbian in the afternoons. Whitney was scheduled in the slot after me, so I'd pass the campers on to her and go do my thing. When I'd come back from playing ball, she'd be dismissing the campers and we started spending time together.

I'd just turned nineteen and Whitney was about to turn seventeen. I had no idea where things with her were going to go, but I did know that the summer of 1980 was shaping up to be some kind of wonderful. Whitney Elizabeth was sweet and low-key but alluring. She carried herself with outward grace and confidence, yet underneath she was like every other young woman at that age. She was strikingly beautiful, but she didn't feel that way, always picking apart her looks. I couldn't understand where all this insecurity was coming from.

One day early on in our friendship, I rolled up to her mother's midsize white Cape Cod house. As I pulled up in my mom's car, there she was, standing in the doorway just above the steps, slender in a T-shirt with a cotton sweater tied around her neck. Sure that she could see my face, I smiled. She was wearing the worst pair of jeans I'd ever seen. They were narrow at the top and wide from the knees down. I'm certain she saw me grinning as she walked toward the car, because once inside she said, "What?"

I measured each word, careful not to offend. "Wow," I said. "Those jeans. They're okay . . . but . . . Why are you wearing them?"

She pressed me and finally I blurted out, "We gotta get you some jeans."

"Well what kind of jeans do I have to get?" she asked.

"Some straight-leg jeans."

Whitney proceeded to tell me that her torso was too short, that her waist was too high, and that her knees turned inward, making her knock-kneed. She went on and on, and it bothered me to hear her speak about herself like that. Just the month before, Whitney had told me, she and her mom were standing on the corner of Fifty-Seventh and Seventh Avenue in front of Carnegie Hall when a man approached them and said, "A modeling agency upstairs is looking for a girl just like you." Click Models had signed her that very day.

Now, sitting in the driver's seat, I said, "You're a junior model. Haven't you seen Cheryl Tiegs, or the Charlie commercial with Shelley Hack in those dark toothpick jeans with a stride that must be at least three yards long? That's you!"

Whitney smiled and seemed to relax. Her smile was like rays of light. I was happy I could bring that out in her. Whenever I looked through my brother Marty's fashion magazines, I'd find a smiling Cheryl Tiegs, looking happy, confident, and fresh. People described her as the girl next door. Cheryl didn't live anywhere near my house, but Whitney did, and I wanted her to feel as beautiful as she was.

Moments later, we were on our way to purchase Whitney's first pair of slim-fitting jeans. These were the days of name brands like Jordache, Sergio Valente, and Gloria Vanderbilt. Most of the girls I knew went for the over-the-top pocket designs, but I never followed the trends. I was straight-up a Levi's 501, Lee, or Wrangler girl, shopping at Universal Uniform Sales on Broad Street in downtown Newark. I took Whitney to the Gap in Willowbrook Mall and picked out eight pairs of straight-legs for her to try. We settled on the darkest blue pair, long enough for her to have a little cuff just above her Gazelles. We grabbed a lighter pair as well, and after that, she wore those jeans all the time. The Whitney Houston that the world would come to know in shimmering gowns was, in reality, a simple, easygoing, comfort-seeking lover of jeans, T-shirts, button-downs, and sneakers.

....

This was a happy time for me, having fun with a new friend, working, and playing basketball. It hadn't always been this way, especially when I was young. During the time I was two to six years old, my family had lived in California. They were hard times for us, despite the fact that Los Angeles was supposed to fulfill my mother's dream of the white picket fence. While my father was still in the army, she followed her brother and his wife when they relocated from Newark. Daddy was in the service from 1958 to 1963, serving part of that time as a paratrooper in Vietnam. He never once talked about it with us. Shortly after being discharged, he joined Mom in Los Angeles. But her dream soon went awry as his infidelity and abuse began and he lost his job. Then there was the puppy.

The incident with our puppy was my first encounter with loss. On Christmas, when I was five years old, Bina, Marty, and I were opening our presents. Next thing we knew, our father reached into the pocket of his American Airlines jacket and pulled out a wiggly little light brown puppy. We screamed with joy.

The next day we played with neighborhood kids behind our building, the puppy frolicking and climbing all over us. Daddy came outside on his way to work. He climbed into his white Bonneville and just before closing the door called out to us kids to step aside. We did as we were told, but none of us thought to pick up the puppy and suddenly I saw the most awful thing: Daddy put the car in reverse and inadvertently crushed Pup Pup. He felt awful about it, calling to our mother to bring us inside so he could clean it up before heading off to work.

My parents moved into a single-level three-bedroom house with white stucco that sparkled in the blazing sun. My brother, Marty, had his own room in the front, and I shared the back room with my baby sister, Bina. I thought my parents were rich until one day my mother overheard me talking with a playmate about what we had and shouted out the window, "Be quiet. We're eating out of one pot."

One day when we got home, my mother told us to stay in the house. It was getting late and the news reported that there was rioting in Watts. Daddy announced that he was going out with my uncle to see what they could get, taking advantage of the chaos. My mother told him she didn't want him to go out.

"I don't want to be here all alone with the kids," she said. Marty was eight, I was five, and Bina, my parents' only California baby, was two.

"I'll be back," he said, and went out into the night.

Mom locked the doors and brought us into Marty's room to wait for my father's return. It was dark, but we could see black-and-white cop cars rushing down our residential street. We remained in Marty's room, crouched down, looking out the window. Looking for my father. Waiting.

"Dennis. Dennis should be here," my mother said aloud. She trembled when she was nervous, so her hands were shaking. I cuddled her to help her stay calm. When my father and uncle finally returned, the sky was still black. Their loot consisted of tires, a few radios, and an eight-track player. My mother was unimpressed but relieved, and we all slept in the same room that night.

My parents argued a lot about money and my father's infidelities, and he often abused her.

When I was six years old, my father roughed up my mother so badly with a metal vacuum cleaner attachment that when the police came, they called an ambulance to take her to the hospital. She returned home with a black eye and a huge scar on her knee that remained for the rest of her life. Once home, she called Marty and me to her bedside, asking, "How would you like to see your grandmother?"

A few days later, she sneaked my siblings and me out of the house in the wee hours of the morning and we flew back to Newark. By the time we arrived, my father was calling my mother on the phone, apologizing. He drove back east in his white Bonneville, stopping only for gas; she took him back, and the beatings continued.

My family lived through the Newark riots, too. My father stayed in the house this time. The National Guard stood with rifles outside our door, patrolling the halls and courtyard of our building, and we were not allowed outdoors after four thirty P.M., when streetlights came on.

All the images of boarded-up storefronts and burned-out buildings faded to the background when, not long after, I witnessed my father throw Mom to the floor and drag her body down the hall of the apartment. I can still see her face and hear her pleading, "Call the police," as her body and head disappeared from view. That made my mother leave him for the last time, and again we ran from him in the middle of the night.

Martin Luther King Jr. wrote, "A riot is the language of the unheard." Some might say my father's rage was born of the same anger and frustration with discrimination and plain injustice that led Los Angeles and Newark to explode, and while there may be some truth to that, I cannot accept it as an excuse. I will never forget the fear in my mother's voice and the look in her eyes when he erupted—kicking in doors, grabbing her and throwing her to the floor, hollering and screaming—while Marty and I pleaded for him to stop, and little Bina, disoriented and frightened, extended her arms for one of us to hold and comfort her. Most of Mom's visible scars went away over time, but invisible ones were imprinted upon her, my brother, my sister, and me.

Janet Marie Williams Crawford set about rebuilding her life by going to college, eventually earning a master's degree; and when I was eleven, we moved to a new place in New Jersey. Two years later, she was excited to find brand-new garden apartments in Kuzuri-Kijiji, at the time the largest housing development built by a black construction company. In Swahili, the name means "Beautiful Village," and Mom told all her friends about it. Most of them were also single women with children, and they moved in, too.

....

Growing up, I knew that I was a different kind of girl, and that was all right. While Bina spent her teenage years going to parties, wearing makeup, and flirting with boys, I wasn't into all that. The only part of my body that I felt at all self-conscious about was my skinny legs, which once led to some guy calling me "Miss Twiggy."

When I complained to my mother she'd say, "You walk on those legs, don't you? You run on those legs, and fast, don't you? You should be grateful."

On picture day, or whenever I wore my hair down, falling on

my shoulders, men would look at me with such desire I would cringe. Losers. I was a child. The minute I left for school I pulled my hair back into a ponytail.

I wanted to be nothing like my father, but you could look in my face and see I was my daddy's girl. On several occasions, grown men walking down the street, driving trucks or delivering mail, stopped me to ask, "You're Dennis Crawford's daughter, aren't you?"

My father was a standout high school athlete who led the state of New Jersey in yards as a tailback. When it became clear that my brother, Marty, had no interest in sports, I was the one who watched football with him and filled his glass from the beer bar—which I loved doing because it involved jumping up on a chair, pulling the lever forward, tilting the glass, and even taking a sip or two of overflowing foam. A Miami Dolphins fan, he explained to me that it took the Giants a long time to have a black running back and shared other observations on black players and sports. But I also inherited a lot of my father's competitiveness, and athletic ability and sports came naturally to me.

It was 1974 when I began my freshman year at Barringer High School in Newark. I'd tune in to WABC radio most mornings hoping to hear Queen's "Bohemian Rhapsody," a masterpiece that drove me wild. After school I'd walk home along Park Avenue for miles, using my bus fare for treats. In one area, where Newark meets East Orange, a lot of men would hang out drinking by Cooper's Liquors & Deli. They would say anything: "Hey, baby. Come here, you sweet girl." I kept walking. I'd also pass a diner where this woman sold delicious sweet potato pie that wasn't orange, because, as she explained, it was made with white sweet potatoes instead of yams. I became such a regular that as soon as I walked in the door she'd hand me a slice.

On Saturday mornings, I rose early and jogged from East

Orange all the way to the North Ward of Newark and down to Branch Brook Park and back. I rode my bike as far as my legs would take me, first on one with a black banana seat and later on my beloved black Kabuki with gold letters. I would go anywhere just to make my world seem bigger.

....

Looking back on my childhood, I remember feeling conflicted about the concept of love. I knew my mom and dad loved me, but the love between them was hardly inspiring. I knew I wanted something other than the paradigm my family had set up, and I found myself praying and striving for a different kind of life and a different kind of love.

Those prayers came true, in the way they do for teenagers, anyway, when I first saw Raynard Jefferson while I was sitting on a swing outside my house. As he walked by, we locked eyes. I was able to read his lips as he asked his cousin Drayton, "Who's that?" That's all it took.

I was fifteen, and Raynard was my first love. He was quiet and good-looking, was my height, and had sweet lips. He was the third and youngest child in a family of boys. We met not long after one of his brothers was murdered, and Raynard was still experiencing the loss. I'd come along just in time to help ease his sadness. He attended Seton Hall Prep, miles away in West Orange, so every morning I'd rise a little earlier so that I could see him off at the train station, which was five minutes from my house. Every afternoon on my way home from school, I'd stop at Raynard's, where we'd spend most of our time in his room on the third floor, reading dirty magazines featuring the best lovemaking positions and talking about eloping to California. Raynard was beautiful: He touched and treated me with kindness and respect. I loved and cared for him then, and my fifteen-year-old self always will.

Mom wasn't all that enthusiastic about my budding relationship, and she told me so. She said I was too emotionally attached and that Raynard reminded her of my father, though I don't know in what way. Nevertheless, she allowed me to make my own choices, and I chose to continue seeing him. When she asked if I needed birth control, my response was, "When I'm ready to lie down, I'll be ready to have a baby." Raynard and I made out all the time, but we never went "all the way," because I was fearful of becoming pregnant. When my mother became pregnant at seventeen, my paternal grandmother had insisted that my father, who was eighteen, marry her.

We experienced the consequences firsthand. Their marriage was meant to save both families' reputations, offer stability, and pardon the sin of premarital sex. Instead, for over a decade, my mother was disrespected, physically abused, and cheated on while bound to a man she would not have chosen otherwise.

Luckily, my relationship with Raynard stayed healthy, and I had plenty of other things to focus on, too. My high school was a hothouse for promising young athletes, and colleges recruited heavily from the football, basketball, and baseball teams. NFL Hall of Famer Andre Tippett was in my health class; I let him copy off my paper once.

I was an active kid—always with a bicycle or a basketball, and I ran everywhere—but I wasn't a jock. Marty—who played the clarinet, cello, and tenor sax—was my inspiration, and like any scrappy little sister, I wanted to be just like him. So I picked up the glockenspiel, which we called "The Bells," and found my place in the marching band. It was a full-time extracurricular, and on game days or at holiday parades you could hear our drum line from miles away. As the sea of royal blue and white approached, 250 strong, rocking side to side, we sent tremors up and down the sidewalks and through Newark Schools Stadium.

I was into my routine and didn't have any ambition to change it up until my sophomore year, when a trio of cool, older girls from the varsity basketball team cornered me in the locker room. They were talking about upcoming tryouts and were on a mission to recruit some new talent. They looked at me and said they'd seen me shooting hoops in gym class and that I should come check out the team.

"You're going to try out," the leader told me. It was not a question.

"Sure, okay." I smiled and grabbed my things from the locker room bench.

I gave it a long think and figured I had nothing to lose, so I showed up at the gym and made the team.

Coach Carol Yvonne Clark, who eventually got me the job where I met Whitney, first saw me playing against her team. Soon after, she drove out to my house and introduced herself. "I'm the head coach of Clifford J. Scott High School in East Orange. You know, you can really play. Have you thought about college? If you come to my high school you'll definitely have more exposure and a better shot at going to a college of your choice." She seemed pretty convincing to me, so I made plans to transfer to Clifford Scott starting the second quarter of eleventh grade.

When I shared the good news, the first thing Raynard said was, "I'm going to lose you. Please don't go." I was surprised, but he was right. I don't remember exactly how or when we began to slip away from each other, but soon after I transferred, it was over.

That year I lit it up! I scored over a thousand points my first season and led my team to win our division, though we fell short in the semifinals. My mother was working long hours and didn't have time to come to my games. My father was absent in general but spoke to me as if he knew what was going on in basketball. I assume he followed me in the Newark *Star-Ledger* and other New Jersey papers. He attended one of my county games, and when he met me afterward, he said, "You need to be meaner."

After graduating, I went on to play in the famous Rucker Park league in Harlem and traveled around the country with the New Jersey Big Heads, the best basketball players representing the state. It was a great season—I was playing as well as ever, and I met my close friend Val Walker on that team.

I was recruited to play at Seton Hall University, which at the time was a Division II school. I was leaning toward attending, but that summer Montclair State was hosting a summer-league tournament and players from all over the tristate area were showcasing their talents. I was one of the top scorers in the league that year, playing next to Val, who went on to claim All-American honors in college.

I was also recruited as a package deal with Val by C. Vivian Stringer at Cheyney State, one of the winningest coaches in women's college basketball history. In part because I had already attended a black school, I passed and chose Montclair State, which was Division I, ranked third in the nation, and had a big-time traveling schedule.

After years of playing hard and lighting up the board, I knew I was ready, but when the official season started, the coach didn't play me. Instead, she put me in for two or three minutes per game if I was lucky. My ass was glued to the bench. As the coach frowned, folded her arms, and paced back and forth in front of the bench in frustration, I wanted to stand up and shout in her face, "You dumbass, I'm right here!"

I was beside myself. I didn't understand, and angry tears stung my face after each game. Besides, when you sit that long, you almost forget how to play. Coach Clark and my mom came to one of my games, and they both thought the coach was racist. I don't think she was accustomed to dealing with black girls. I was the first girl of color to make the team, and I did so as a freshman no less.

My refuge was the black sororities on campus: AKA, Phi Beta Sigma, the Deltas. They were my big sisters, always cooking something, so they fed me if I was hungry and offered their friendship. In their company I felt supported and understood, and found the camaraderie that was lacking in my team experience.

To add to the insult, at the start of my second year I was used as a tool to bring in other black players: Tracey Brown, Sharon Ross, and Bonita Spence. We all got along, but by then I wanted out.

Thankfully, the coach at Monmouth asked me to join her team, and I left Montclair after the first semester of my sophomore year. The only problem was that I couldn't get a scholarship in the spring, so I decided I would get a job and save cash until the fall. Bonita Spence was from Atlantic City and told me casinos were opening up there and they were hiring. She said I could stay with her mother. So I headed down and was hired by Bally's Park Place as a security guard.

I started out roving the casino in a typical gray polyester uniform, but after three weeks, I was approached by a well-dressed man who, after introducing himself, said he'd been watching me and wanted me to join the detective unit as a plainclothes investigator. I got to wear whatever I wanted—or whatever was necessary. Sometimes I could get away with nice slacks and a blouse, but if I was posted at the bar, I had to look like all the other women and dress the part. They gave me a per diem so I could easily blend in, and I would sit and chat with customers, drinking watered-down cocktails.

The detective unit was located underneath the loading dock entrance behind a solid door that housed an office equipped with a mass of video cameras. It was my job to look out for card counters, catch solicitation, and compare customer faces against a catalog thick with mug shots. Sometimes I would be dispatched to a particular casino lounge where a wanted person had been seen on a monitor. There were other times I would put on headphones, listen to conversations in a bugged hotel room, and write down everything I heard. I worked sixteen-hour shifts and slept during the day, and the long and late hours meant that I never had time to spend my generous paychecks. I liked the duties of the always-on, detail-oriented work.

Six months later, I returned to East Orange with a large stash, so I didn't need the summer job at the Community Development center, but it never hurt to have more cash. Plus, I owed Coach Clark a lot, so when she called asking for a favor, I didn't even blink. I was there. Little did she know her early-morning call would change my life forever.

....

Within a few days of meeting at the summer job, Whitney and I went out to lunch. We walked out the door and got about forty feet before she pulled out a cigarette from her breast pocket. I suppose I wore my surprise on my face.

"Yeah, I smoke," she said, then pulled out a joint, too. Now I was shocked. She did not look like someone who got high.

"Oh, you something else, huh?" I said. Whitney laughed and put the joint back in its place.

I had smoked a bong a few times in college, but that was the extent of my experience with drugs. In high school, my English teacher sent me to the back of the class for talking. After sitting in the last row across from a kid who was dividing up bags of weed, I was set up with a small franchise. I sold marijuana in little pink bags to the cheerleaders, made $300 but quit after two weeks. Customers and money came fast and easy, but I was afraid I'd get caught—that my hardworking mother would come home and find out I'd gotten busted.

....

You can call me Nippy," Whitney said. She explained that her father had given her the nickname, which came from a mischievous character in a comic strip.

I kept learning more about her. I never saw her with him, but Nip said she had a boyfriend named Craig whose mother was an original member of the Sweet Inspirations.

I wasn't seeing anyone at the time, though I was having a problem with a girl on my basketball team who was very possessive. We'd shared a couple of kisses, but I didn't think there was anything more to it until one of my roommates clued me in; I was blind and oblivious to what was going on around me. Anyway, Mom didn't care much for this one, either, and was vocal about her displeasure: "Robyn, this girl is trying to weave a web around you," she said. I remember responding, "But, Mom, if she wants to iron my uniform, I'm going to let her!"

It didn't take me long to understand what Mom was seeing.

This girl was controlling, and I needed to find a way to get her to loosen her grip sooner rather than later. I went to visit her one day that summer when she was staying in an apartment on the other side of my complex and she refused to let me leave. She kept blocking the door, so I was there for a few hours while expecting Paulette, another Big Heads teammate, and Val to come fetch me to play ball. Finally, she stepped away and I ran outside. She grabbed my arm and I swung around into a brick wall, leaving a bleeding knot on my head.

I told Whitney about the situation, and she said, "Don't worry, I'll get you out of that." I didn't ask her what she meant; we left a lot unspoken about things like that. But she did it. There was never any confrontation, and the girl simply faded away, as Whitney and I grew closer.

....

Other people could look at us and tell we were tight, but something more was growing between us. We became inseparable. If we weren't at my house, then we were at hers. Her room was a wreck. Stuff was all over, clothes were piled on the floor, her bed sat perpetually unmade, and book bags, school uniforms, and purses were strewn everywhere. One time when I was in her room, we kept hearing this crunching sound. We traced it to a mouse in her bag eating Lay's potato chips.

A few weeks after we met, Nippy invited me over. We took our time strolling through the neighborhood, and when we got tired, we went inside and sat next to each other on her living room floor, backs against the sofa. We talked and talked, and then all of a sudden, we were face-to-face.

That first kiss was long and warm like honey. As we eased out of it, our eyes locked, my nerves shot up, and my heart beat furiously. *What's gonna happen next? What will she say? Suppose she's upset?* I just didn't know, but clearly something was happening between us.

And then she said, "If I knew when my brothers were coming home, I'd show you something."

It was totally badass. Nip could get you into all kinds of trouble if she had the opportunity. Just like my mom said when she met Whitney for the first time: "You look like an angel but I know you're not."

Two

···

Like an Angel

Whitney wasn't the type of person to walk around singing all loud and showing off what she had. She wasn't like that at all. But that first summer that I knew her, when she was in the house, in the car, or sitting on her front porch, she sang every song on Chaka Khan's new album, front to back, especially "Clouds," "Our Love's in Danger," and "Papillon (a.k.a. Hot Butterfly)," which included Luther Vandross, Whitney, and her mother, Cissy, who was a legendary background singer in her own right. Whenever those tracks came on, Whitney would sing all the background vocals, holding her Walkman headphones to her ears as if she were in the studio. In public, she was more reserved, allowing only a lyric or two to come out softly now and then.

Music was in every part of her body; she loved it, craved it, and said she was going to be a professional singer. This had been her mantra since she was twelve. She was singular in her focus, outlining all the steps she needed to follow to get where she needed to go. She worked on getting a band together and building a repertoire of songs to showcase her talents. There was something intoxicating about being with someone wholly herself. Whitney Elizabeth Houston was something else.

Whitney loved telling me about her first time in the recording studio with Chaka Khan, singing background. Chaka heard her vocals and stopped the session to tell Whitney, "Move closer to the mic." Whitney felt she'd been anointed, so we'd be in her backyard and that girl would be going with that Walkman on:

Chanson papillon, we were very young
Like butterflies, like hot butterfly.

"Listen to Chaka! Look where she goes." She was teaching. "Watch how they go now. Listen. Right here, right here."

She'd play the track over and over, and I was her willing student. Whitney explained that Chaka's phrasing was brilliant and that her voice was like an instrument. When she was up high, she sounded like a trumpet or emulated the sound of a tenor sax. Whitney was also blown away by her enunciation.

"This is a Catholic schoolgirl. You can understand every word she says."

The prior summer, Val had proclaimed her love for Chaka, but I didn't get it back then. Now I listened closely, and sure enough, every word came through clear as a bell. Whitney deconstructed every line, and I came to understand Chaka's gifts.

"People don't appreciate Chaka enough," Whitney was fond of saying.

Along with breaking down the genius of other singers, Whitney took great pleasure in schooling me about her mother's recordings. She clearly had played each album over and over and knew every note her mother sang. Whenever a record that had her mother on it was playing, Nippy spoke with the reverent tones reserved for one-name stars like Aretha. Even though it was backing vocals, Whitney acted as if Cissy were singing lead. "I want you to hear my mother's whole thing," Whitney said one day, and she played me every last song her mother appeared on, proudly demonstrating why Cissy was paid triple scale.

Daydreamin' and I'm thinking of you
Look . . . at . . . my mind . . . floating . . . away

I'd always found the opening of Aretha's "Day Dreaming" hypnotic, but following the listening session with Whitney, I realized Cissy's voice was responsible for the sweetness. And I still have every album she was on and can isolate her voice on songs like Donny Hathaway's "I Know It's You," Chaka's "Roll Me Through the Rushes," and Luther's "You're the Sweetest One."

After hours of immersion in Cissy's discography, Nippy gave me a copy of her mother's self-titled album, because "Things to Do" was a song that I particularly enjoyed. I looked down at the cover photo of a smiling Cissy Houston dressed in an orange mandarin-collar shirt, bursting through ripped gray paper, and tried to reconcile the woman with the voice like glass with the mother who Whitney said made her feel small.

Over time, Whitney told me all about her mother's years with the Sweet Inspirations and shared stories about how they had to go through back doors and kitchens to perform at venues in the segregated South because black people were barred from entering through the front. Whitney said her mother frequently gushed about how handsome Elvis was and said he was a kind man who took great care of them. One of Cissy's most cherished possessions was a gift he gave her, a piece of jewelry.

Like most black families, mine was into music. My father listened to Johnny Mathis and Phyllis Hyman; my mother was a huge fan of Tony Bennett, Barbra Streisand, and Morgana King. My brother, Marty, was big into Black Ivory, Dr. Buzzard's Original Savannah Band, Motown, and club music because he loved to dance. When I was twelve, Marty, my cousins, and I even had a group called the 5 Shades of Soul. Until basketball won all my attention, we sang Bloodstone's "Natural High" and the Five Stairsteps' "O-o-h Child" at family barbecues and in competitions around Newark.

Whitney started bringing me around her cousin Felicia and her "cousin" Larry, who was really just a close friend. They were like the Three Musketeers. In their church choir, they performed medleys, so sometimes they would pick a song on the radio and sing it together.

I told Whitney I'd always wanted to be in a church choir, but that never happened for me. When I was small, we used to go to the Kingdom Hall downtown, where my great-grandmother was an elder, but they didn't sing and they didn't praise. There was no rhythm and no real celebration at all. My mother, a spiritual seeker, spent years going to different houses of worship hoping to find a place she belonged. As I child I went to church, but in my teens I was so busy with basketball I rarely made it. Bina and Marty followed Mom farther on her quest. The most important thing to my mother was that her children understood there was a higher power, and we did. We didn't play gospel music in our house, but if you listened to Aretha Franklin, you heard the gospel; there was no way around it.

Singing in the choir was important to Whitney, but there were

times when she really didn't want to go to her family church, saying it was "fake and filled with hypocrites." One night when we
were supposed to meet, she called and confided in me that her
mother was making her go out with their minister, Reverend Dr.
C. E. Thomas, and his son. Whitney felt as if it was a double date
designed to cover for her mother and the minister, who was married. I never saw him coming out of Cissy's bedroom, but I did see
him sitting at her kitchen counter in his undershirt.

Whitney said she wasn't comfortable going, but Cissy told her,
"That's what daughters do." Disturbed, disappointed, and irri-
tated, she went. When I saw her the next day, she said, "He liked
me, but I have no interest in him."

To my knowledge, it never happened again.

Even though it was summertime, Whitney was in church at
least three times a week. She had practice on Thursday nights, and
no matter where we were or what we were doing she would jet.
Her mother was the ministress of music and ran the choir rehearsals. Whitney was always on time. She was Cissy Houston's daughter, so she had to be. I understood. In my mind, choir practice was
like basketball practice: If you're late, you hold up the entire team.

Whitney, Larry, and Felicia talked about their songs and solos
as if they were preparing for a game. And in a way, they were; in
East Orange and Newark, these choirs were as popular as basketball teams. Choirs would compete with or visit different churches,
and Whitney was a main draw for the Junior Choir of New Hope
Baptist Church. There were nearby churches that had star singers,
too. Less than five miles away on Chancellor Avenue, a very young
Faith Evans was singing at Emmanuel Missionary Baptist Church.

....

When she and her cousins were finished strategizing about their upcoming concert, Whitney said, "Robyn, I want you to come." New Hope Baptist Church was having its music service and everyone knew that their choirs threw down. The congregation was used to visitors, but this was a particularly popular program and it was sure to be packed. I was the only one Whitney invited and was excited about that and the opportunity to hear her sing.

Though I no longer attended church regularly, I was familiar with scripture, and I believed in the Good Book. My brother and sister were baptized along the way, but somehow I never had holy water poured on me. I suspect it was because I was traveling to away games or practicing, so I was rarely home on Sundays. Still, I had wanted to know the Word for myself, so when I was fifteen years old I read from Genesis straight though to Revelation, and it felt as if I was transported backward in time. The scathing depiction of Sodom and Gomorrah left a deep imprint, and every time I sinned, I knew I needed Jesus to show me His kindness and mercy. I believed that His story was true, and that He quite possibly did all the good deeds and miracles that the Book said He did.

Whitney knew the Bible like the back of her hand. She told me about women in the Bible who I hadn't remembered, like the stories of Ruth and Esther, who stood up for the people of her kingdom and went before the king. There were some powerful women in the Book, and she knew them all. As for Jesus, she loved Him and found Him to personify everything that anyone should aspire to be.

I answered yes to Whitney's invitation right away, but it created two dilemmas. First: I would have to wear a dress. My mother always believed that when you go to church, you dress for God. I had to represent. Blessedly, it was summer. I damn sure wouldn't have wanted to wear stockings. I hated stockings. I dreaded wearing a dress, but it was a worthwhile sacrifice to hear Nip sing for real. I went into the back of my closet and found a simple lavender short-sleeved pullover that flared out a little at the bottom, and it was comfortable enough. The next time I willingly wore a dress would be at my mother's funeral.

Second: I was entering into her mother's world. Excited as I was about hearing Whitney sing, her church was really her mother's domain, and I wasn't too happy about that. Each time I came to the house to pick up Whitney, I could feel the hostility coming from Cissy all the way from the car. Before I met her, Whitney warned me that her mother never liked anyone she brought around.

"My mother can be harsh, but that's who she is," she said.

When Sunday came, I borrowed my mother's car and drove to New Hope Baptist Church, which sat down the street from the notorious Baxter Terrace housing projects. The redbrick church's interior was a bit run-down, but worshippers from the struggling to the well-off found their way there that first Sunday in August. It was filled to capacity.

I didn't want to sit too close to the front, but I didn't want to be too far in the back, either, because I wanted Whitney to see me, so I sat in the seventh row slightly left of center. The hard wood pews made me sit upright, at attention. I was acutely aware that I was in Cissy Houston's house. This was where she and her siblings first came together as the Drinkard Singers before she formed the Sweet Inspirations. A small brass plaque that read "Lee Warwick" reminded me that New Hope was also the church home of Whitney's cousins Dee Dee and Dionne. The whole family had come through that church. It was intimidating, and I felt like an outsider.

Reverend Thomas spoke and asked for any new members or guests to stand up, so I did. As he welcomed us, I couldn't help recalling what Whitney had told me about him and Cissy.

Introducing the Junior Choir, he said, "People want to hear me preach, but the Lord likes to be praised."

The church said, "Amen."

A sea of young people in black and white rolled in from the back and came down the aisles to the front of the church. Whitney passed by, but she didn't see me. She was wearing a black straight skirt and a white button-up shirt, had swept up her hair in a small bun, and was made up in her Fashion Fair foundation and a light pink lipstick that looked natural. Once she took her place in the pews adjacent to the pulpit, she looked at me but didn't smile. She had her game face on. She was focused. It was the smirk on Larry's face that helped me relax. They were just kids, so even in their seriousness they were silly, and after a minute, I could see Whitney, Larry, and Felicia cutting up, quietly joking with one another while fifty girls and boys took their places.

Whitney's mother stood before the choir dressed in earth tones that softened her appearance. Her brother Larry Drinkard, the organist, wore big, thick glasses that made his eyes look tiny, but he could play!

Cissy said, "Okay, y'all. Now, everybody ready?"

The choir rose up and sang. Some of the songs were familiar to me but I didn't know all the words. You had to be going to church regularly to know all the words. Their voices were so powerful, the choir sounded like a giant speaker, and I felt the rumbles in my chest. A few people in the congregation started keeping time by tapping their hands on the sides of their legs; others joined in with a soft double handclap. For a while, that's how Cissy clapped, too, and then she led her choir. Her left hand was in the air while her right moved up and down directing voices to rise or lower at her command. They were killing it.

Then Larry, Felicia, and Whitney made their way to the front. Felicia sang alto, Larry falsetto, and Whitney alto and soprano, creating a lovely blend. Their voices were welcoming, and for a moment I wanted to go up there and join them, but it wasn't the same as hearing them sing along with the radio. Their singing had a force that wasn't present when they were playing around. When they began to sing "Oh Mary Don't You Weep," the trio snapped and clapped. Whitney and Felicia swayed back and forth trading lines:

Mary . . .
Oh, Mary . . .
Oh, Mary, don't you weep
Tell Martha not to moan

The church said, "Amen."

The threesome separated, and Whitney stepped forward, now wearing a floor-length white robe. Before she even opened her mouth, I heard murmurs; members of the congregation were bracing themselves. There was stillness, and then she approached the mic, closed her eyes, and began singing the first few words while the piano played softly:

When Jesus hung on Calvary,
People came from miles to see . . .

"Sing, Nip," said Larry.

"Go 'head, Nip," Felicia added.

Even Reverend Thomas called out, "Sing, Whitney."

And then something just swept through the whole place. Whitney's face was radiant and her mouth moved with urgency, her voice rising as the words came out. She started to sway gently and the congregation clapped in time.

She'd opened high, and as her voice rose she brought us higher. People couldn't contain themselves. Nip was in the spirit, and folks started praising and catching the Holy Ghost and moaning.

"Woo."

"Praise the Lord!"

Her singing was open and vulnerable, angelic and powerful. On that day, I sat in that church and I watched that little body stand there in that white robe and fill the place with her voice. She held on to her sway; it wasn't even a rock, it was just enough to shift her weight from left to right. Easy. Gentle. She enunciated every word as she opened and closed her mouth. Her hands stayed pretty much by her sides, she stood firm, and the expression on her face would change with the lyrics. Her eyes were closed and people were hooting and hollering and falling out.

> They said, "If you be the Christ,
> Come down and save your life."
> Oh but Jesus, my sweet Jesus,
> He never answered them,
> For He knew that Satan was tempting Him.
> If He had come down from the cross,
> Then my soul would still be lost.

Whitney's singing grew more and more insistent. Midway through, she partially opened her eyes. She scanned the room and looked in my direction before closing them again. Whitney was in that moment, too. She was in it and you could tell she was in it. She was delivering that day.

He would not come down
From the cross just to save Himself;
He decided to die!

Whitney was pleading with us to understand how grateful we should be that Christ had suffered, erasing our sins and giving us new life. Now, I'd spent many Sundays in church, but this was a completely new experience for me and I felt a kind of deliverance. I didn't need her to convince me that there was a higher power— I already believed that—but I felt nearer to God and closer to Whitney.

I rose out of my seat and just stared at her. I had thought I knew her, but here I was witnessing a different side. All of a sudden, in that moment, I realized that Whitney Elizabeth Houston *was* something else, something special; there was greatness and power pent up inside that body.

I sat down and saw a woman ecstatically running between the aisles vocalizing her praise in a language of her own and heard other people speaking in tongues.

Whitney hadn't moved. She just kept on singing. She was the quiet in the storm of her own creation. She was amazing.

I wasn't looking at the people around me, but I could feel them. You could feel the energy in that room and that she was behind it. She was singing those words just like they needed to be sung. Whitney brought the song to a climax using her full voice, then gave everything she had, lifted us up, and held the final note for what felt like forever while the whole church vibrated.

HE DECIDED TO DIE . . . JUST TO SAVE . . . ME!

When she was done, while the last reverberations of that impossibly long note still hung in the air, Whitney opened her eyes, then calmly turned around and went back to her place in the choir loft. Someone handed her a fan and she dabbed her face with a white tissue, drying beads of sweat across the bridge of her nose and on her forehead.

The church was still feeling it, though. One woman had passed out, and two rather large and strong white-gloved nurses were fanning her to help bring her back. Tears streamed down the faces of many women and some of the men. It's a miracle the walls didn't just open up and let everything fall. She was a wonder.

....

After the service, Whitney waved me over to the side of the stage. Larry joined us and told me that I looked nice, and Nip smiled at me. I followed her down the stairs to the basement for the reception, and for a minute she seemed tiny, at odds with what I'd just witnessed.

"Wow, Nip, what does that feel like for you up there?" I asked. "People were so moved."

"Oh, I don't think about that. I don't look at them. There's a clock at the back of the church, and I set my eyes on that clock and then I close them and just do what I got to do."

"But you could feel it!" I insisted. "There were people falling out. People were rising to their feet."

"They should be moved. They should be." She said this not in a boastful way but with conviction, as if to say it wasn't about her, it was about the song.

But I knew different. While Whitney was singing, I had stood up to get a better look at what I was seeing and feeling. I wanted to get close to her. She had the power to move people through song and she knew it. And that day, standing in that church, I felt the power. There was no denying she had it, and there was no doubt in my mind that I was in the presence of greatness.

She asked if I was hungry and sent someone to fix me a plate. There were so many people and everybody wanted to talk to Whitney, but it wasn't like anyone was looking for an autograph then. She was theirs. Larry and Felicia were chitchatting with other members of the Junior Choir.

A woman handed me a Styrofoam plate filled with fried chicken, greens, mac 'n' cheese, and a piece of cornbread. I thanked her, moved over to a corner, and ate standing alone. I didn't mind waiting.

Three

....

Love = Love

That Sunday after church, I walked with Whitney and Larry to his car and she whispered to me, "We're spending the night at Larry's place."

I drove home and threw off the dress, changing into shorts and a tee. Whitney picked me up in a taxi. Though the rearview mirror was equipped with a little fragrance tree, nothing could cover the driver's body odor, so, laughing, we hung out of the window to breathe.

I liked Larry; he spoke quickly, somewhere between a stutter and a laugh. When we arrived at his brick apartment building on Munn Avenue in East Orange, he greeted us and then left, saying, "Okay, girls! Y'all make yourselves at home." At last, we were alone.

Larry's bachelor pad, as Whitney called it, was a studio apartment with a bed, a kitchen, and a little sitting area. We made ourselves comfortable, ate some Roy Rogers, and lit a joint that Nip had brought. When we settled in on Larry's love seat, she picked up a Bible and started reading under the low light, going straight to the sections about Jesus, covering every story that mentioned his name. She'd stop reading and say, "He's so cool, isn't He? I want to meet this man." Then she'd take another hit or two, maybe three or four, and pass the joint to me. We were a little cramped on the love seat, so we pulled down the Murphy bed.

I was a little nervous. I wanted everything to go right with her. I wouldn't push her to do anything. I wanted her friendship. That was what was most important. I didn't know if Whitney would disappear or if it was too good to be true, but what we had just happened out of the blue of a summer, and I wasn't even expecting it. I thought, *Here's the friend that I prayed for.*

But I was learning that when Whitney wanted to do something, she just did it. And this time was no different. We watched some television and soon began to kiss. We took off our clothes and for the first time, we touched each other. Under her T-shirt, Whitney wore a bra, flesh colored—but not the color of her flesh—that unhooked in the front with a faint click.

She was just as I imagined after that first kiss. I still remember the taste of her mouth. Whitney smoked Newports like they were candy but didn't smell like cigarettes; somehow the faint hint of tobacco was sweet on her mouth. I explored her body and mine by touching. Caressing her and loving her felt like a dream.

Whatever energy we had between us all that time was expressed through our bodies that night. It was free and honest. It was tender and loving. We both wanted to touch and explore each other, and we did until we fell asleep in each other's arms.

....

1 awoke first and looked over at Whitney sleeping. As I began to smile, I noticed blood all over the white sheets and on my hand. I shook her and was relieved that she awakened. Both of us sat up searching, but we quickly realized that the source was Nippy's monthly. I recall making light of the situation. I could imagine being in her shoes and feeling embarrassed. At moments like these, she seemed really small, almost childlike. I led and she fell into place, allowing me to take control of the situation.

This was a man's home, so there weren't any pads or tampons to come to the rescue. I told Whitney to wrap the sheets around her like a toga-meets-diaper and to stay put. Then I ran out to the store and grabbed what she needed. When it was time to leave, we stuffed the sullied sheets in a bag and tossed them into the building's incinerator.

....

We were together that entire summer. We could not stay away from each other. We didn't share what happened with anyone, but our connection was undeniable. You could feel it. At the church that day, I knew I was in the presence of something powerful and great, but even before that, there was something about her that made me feel as if we were meant to walk side by side. We were partners. I didn't know how long it was going to last, but I knew we were meant to be.

We never talked labels, like *lesbian* or *gay*. We just lived our lives, and I hoped it could go on that way forever. From a young age, I loved beautiful people. Sometimes the beauty that captured me came in the form of a male, and sometimes it came in the form of a female; either way worked for me.

Our affection for each other had blossomed undetected but in full view. Like other girls, we sat close to each other or held hands. Sometimes Whitney sat in my lap while we talked in the park, or sat between my legs on the ground, resting her head on my thigh. Nearby, another pair of girls might adopt a similar posture, doing hair or lying across each other telling secrets. So many girls were physical with each other, playing at being grown women, trying out seductions. Some, like us, experimented with drugs. And all of us attempted to reclaim our bodies after being told as children to keep our legs together, our knees shut, to stay away from the attentions of men, while being groomed to one day court the same.

That summer Whitney would come to my league basketball games, or we'd go for a drive together, or we'd hang out at my house or hers. Often, with little notice, Nip would come by and we'd go to the beach. She swam like a fish and loved the ocean; I could take it or leave it. Those days of arriving at the beach, running fearlessly straight into the water without testing the temperature, were long gone for me, and sitting in the sun crammed side by side with what seemed to be thousands of people wasn't my idea of fun. But it was heaven for Nip, and as long as we were together, I was down for whatever.

My mother was working, but if I could borrow her car, I would drive Whitney into New York for modeling appointments, called "go-sees." More often, though, she'd get on the bus and go to the city by herself. Sometimes we would catch a train to the beach, or take the bus across the George Washington Bridge and walk down into Sugar Hill, Harlem, to buy a dime bag.

On Thursday nights, I would speed in my mother's car to

deliver her to New Hope for choir practice. At other times, I'd crawl through rush-hour traffic in the Lincoln Tunnel as Whitney changed out of her jeans and into a dress, all the while praying for green lights going up Tenth Avenue to Sweetwater's nightclub, where she sang in her mother's act. She told me what it was like sitting at the board with producer Arif Mardin. The way Whitney talked about music was passionate and definite.

Some weekdays she went to the city with her mother, who was working with producer and composer Michael Zager. He was always saying how great Whitney was, and had featured her on his dance tune "Life's a Party" when she was fourteen. Other times, we would go to the home of her first musical director, John Simmons, so they could talk about songs and putting a band together.

When John began working with Whitney, he found out that she not only could sing but had a sensibility beyond her years and a vast understanding of music, and even at her young age, she somehow knew how to use her voice to make whatever she wanted to sing hers.

John, a good-natured, supportive, patient but no-nonsense professional, was the person who Whitney could depend on and trust to prep, pace, and challenge her musically and vocally. In the early days, before she was signed, I would go over to John's East Orange apartment with Nip and could see the two bond immediately, selecting songs for showcases, while sitting side by side at his keyboard, singing different parts of a melody, modulating and arranging the music with peaks and valleys, focused, but with smiles and giggles throughout. If John got excited about something, he would do a little trot, make a high-pitched squeal, and spin around.

Johnnie—as Nip called him—had tremendous respect for her. In an interview with an Italian television station during the Moment of Truth Tour, he said, "In the States, there are a lot of singers who are just R&B or just jazz, or just gospel. And I think that she covers all of it."

At a rehearsal one day, Whitney and I came upon a small room with a piano. She sat down and said, "Sit next to me, I'm going to play something for you." I listened.

She played a few chords. Smiling, she said, "You don't know it?"

"Hold on, I'm trying to," I said. "Just give me a minute." Whitney played and then started singing.

The first time ever I saw your face . . .

She told me that the first time she saw me she thought I was beautiful.

....

One night when we were hanging out, Whitney said she needed to go home to take care of something. I'd brought my sister, Bina, with me, so we all went, and it turned out she had a bunch of dishes to wash. I felt bad for Nippy because at my house all the kids had to help out. My brother cooked because my mother was working all the time. Whitney's brothers didn't have to do shit. The dishes would be piled high, and though she had modeling jobs and was working on her singing career, dishes were waiting in the kitchen sink when she got home. She was the girl. You could tell she was frustrated. I would offer to help and she'd say, "That's okay." She didn't make a big deal about it. Even when her brothers stole the money she earned from modeling, she didn't protest.

Bina was tired and sat down on the sofa, and I sat next to her. We were in the living room, but we could see the kitchen and chat with Nippy while she worked. It was a little chilly inside, and the sofa was deep, so Bina took off her shoes and put her feet up, covering her legs with her coat.

Mrs. Houston entered from the hallway, big and tall, in pajamas and a bathrobe, with rollers in her hair and a scarf wrapped around her head. I'd seen her directing the choir that day at the church, but we'd never actually met.

I was duly intimidated, but I wasn't prepared. Whitney had warned me that her mother wasn't going to like me, but I hadn't been worried. All my friends' parents loved me. Bonita's mom hadn't hesitated to let me stay with her while I was working in Atlantic City. My high school friend Paulette's mother suffered from migraines, and I loved her so much I would put my hand on her head to take the pain from her. I didn't know what I would have done with that pain had it worked, but I believed I could handle it.

Mrs. Houston was looking straight at Nip, but then she saw Bina and me, sitting in the low-lit room. She turned her formidable backlit silhouette in our direction and said to my sister, "Get your damned feet off my sofa!" It was enough to make Bina cry. Nippy had told me that her mom was rough, but based on that first conversation, she struck me as just plain mean.

"That's Robyn and her sister, Bina," Whitney said, trying to smooth things out.

"Oh, well, don't put your damned feet on my sofa," Cissy replied.

....

Nip loved going down to the shore and usually we went by train. I didn't love just sitting on the beach, because one time I suggested we rent a rowboat instead of our usual sunbathing and occasional dip. I paddled us out until I grew tired. It was beautiful and tranquil, and for a moment there was nothing for us to do but enjoy the gentle rocking of the boat. After a while, I asked Whitney to take a turn on the way back. She had the nerve to say, "No, this was your idea, I ain't rowing shit!" We started arguing, and when I tried to make Whitney take one of the oars, she let it slip through the hole and into the water. By this time we were full-on yelling at each other. A man who had been watching us went by in a huge sailboat, shaking his head as if to say we weren't going to make it. I watched him move out of sight, then realized that Nippy's standoff had given me a rest, so I used the single oar to bring the floating one closer, fished it out of the water, and rowed us back to shore.

If Mrs. Houston wasn't around, we were in her backyard in the pool, Whitney jumping around like a nut, bobbing in and out of the water, singing, "*Oooh you make my love come down!*" But most of the time we stayed away. We were constantly on the go. We'd go out to the park, and Whitney would take her tennis racket and hit a handball against the wall while I practiced basketball. Sometimes we'd hang out with Felicia and Larry or stop by my cousin Cathy's house, but it was always better when it was just the two of us.

We spoke about musicians, mostly reading liner notes, album jackets, and music publications like *Billboard* and *Pollstar*, and took note of producers. Sitting in her living room, we'd analyze Quincy Jones's claps, and Whitney talked about background singers with whom she would have loved to sing during a session. I easily identified which musicians played on one album or another. I further developed my musical ear with Whitney, after years of listening to records like Marvin Gaye's *What's Going On*, Quincy's *Body Heat*, Heatwave's *Too Hot to Handle*, Donny Hathaway's *Extension of a Man*, and Change's *Miracles*, and listening to MFSB and Love

Unlimited with my brother, Marty. On the radio or watching television, I knew that Luther Vandross was the one singing *"Be all that you can be in the army"* and that Phyllis Hyman's voice was behind the Mastercard jingle.

....

You could tell Whitney and I were tight. It wasn't all about our sleeping together. We could be naked. We could be bare and didn't have to hide. We could trust each other with our secrets, our feelings, and who we were. We were friends. We were lovers. We were everything to each other. We weren't falling in love. We just were. We had each other. We were one: That's how it felt.

Our relationship remained between us, although we both believed God was there, too. If you're a believer, God had to have been there. We safely hid it from everybody else; it was our secret, but we couldn't hide from Him—or whomever God is. Despite our understanding of what religion might say about our love, neither of us expressed any guilt or judgment; we were immersed in getting to know each other. That's what was important.

Sometimes we'd go to a hotel. Usually, we couldn't stay for more than one night because we didn't have that kind of money, even with my stash from the casino and all the modeling Nippy was doing. She didn't like the modeling world or how they treated her, but she liked the money. Sometimes we'd go to Asbury Park and stay in a little beachfront hotel near the Stone Pony, where Bruce Springsteen was the boss of the shore.

....

$\mathcal{O}urs$ was a typical teenage relationship, with, I guess, the exception of cocaine.

The first person to give me a hit of cocaine was a friend of Whitney's stepbrother Gary. I was over at her house sitting on the porch and Gary and his friends were there and had some blow. His friend Kelly asked me if I'd tried it before, and I said I hadn't. He said, "Do you want to try it?" and I said, "Yeah." I took a little hit, and then I took another one, and nothing happened—until about five minutes later, when I felt myself rising above the steps.

While I was floating high, Whitney came out of the house and looked at me funny. Kelly said something like, "Robyn's feeling nice." She was looking at me, she didn't say a word. We all got up and went for a stroll down near the train tracks, and Whitney told me that she was fourteen years old when she first tried cocaine.

A few days later, Whitney and I did coke together for the first time. We bought some from an older guy—handsome, well dressed, and driving a sky-blue Mercedes. We bought a little and left. That's how we did things—get it and go. From then on, it became our thing. We had limited funds; we mostly relied on a local guy who would sometimes give us marijuana and a little blow.

One day Nip wanted to stop by her house and grab a few items before going to the beach, so we took a cab over there, and I waited in the car. When she came out of the house, she clearly wasn't happy. Someone had taken her stash. This wasn't the first time that something of hers—weed, coke, or money—had gone missing. Someone was stealing from her in her own home, which was totally messed up. So the plan changed—the beach was out and NYC was in.

On the bus into Manhattan, out of the blue Whitney said, "Let's go to my cousin Dee Dee's." I'd met Dee Dee once before at her mother Lee Warwick's house in South Orange. Another Warwick cousin, Barry, was there, and for years after, whenever he was visiting, the three of us would hang out. As we sat at her mom's kitchen table chatting, Cousin Dee Dee emptied the tobacco from a cigarette onto the table. Then she mixed in some hash and put the mixture back into the cigarette shell, twisting the end closed. After she lit up and took a few tokes, she held it out and Nip and I each took a puff. That was some strong stuff! You had to be a cigarette smoker to handle that combo, I thought.

Nip told me that Dee Dee had a ton of talent and easily could have had a successful career but she was just too crazy. There was the time Nippy watched her onstage singing background for Dionne, visibly bored—huffing, puffing, and rolling her eyes. Contrary to what has been said, Whitney loved Dee Dee. She spoke fondly of her cousin and maintained close ties to the Warwick family even after she became famous.

Just as I remembered, Dee Dee had a totally cool disposition, a big laugh, and bright white teeth, and was funny as hell. Dee Dee had the lights low in her Upper West Side apartment, so I couldn't see much, and it looked as if she hadn't been out in a minute. Though we arrived in the afternoon, she was dressed for bed in cream silk pajamas. As we sat talking, she asked if we'd do her a favor and move her Cadillac to the other side of the street. When we returned to the apartment, we told her that there were at least a dozen tickets on the windshield.

Then Dee Dee had another favor to ask. Her bright idea was for us to drive the car to Jersey and park it at Nip's house. That sounded good to us—we were more than delighted to help her out. So we drove to East Orange, and when we turned down the radio, we could hear a sound like bells coming from the car.

Apparently, someone had helped themselves to the rims and the rim locks were dangling as the wheels turned—creating a constant jingle that sounded much like Santa was coming. I can still hear Mrs. Houston as we walked into the house: "Who the hell's car is that, and you two look like you've been working on the damn chain gang!" We couldn't have cared less. We had wheels! Or I did, at least, since Nip didn't have a license and the last time I'd allowed her to get behind the wheel, she'd slammed into the back of a car on the George Washington Bridge.

Later that day I drove the car to Washington Heights with Nip riding shotgun to complete our mission to cop. Getting in was easy; the problem was getting out safely and with the goods. We clearly didn't look like Harlem gals, so we had to be careful who we talked to. We parked the car and a nice-looking Latino guy around our age came our way and took us into a building and up three flights of stairs.

The building seemed vacant, but we could see bodies lurking in the shadows, lookouts in the hallway corners. He led us into an apartment where a man was sitting at a table with a scale, a lamp, and lots of white powder. Two other guys hovered nearby. I scanned the scene: a grayish, cloudy film filled the room, kind of like it was a dead space suspended in time, like you could get lost in it and left behind. I remember thinking that we must be out of our minds going up there. My mom would have had a coronary! These guys could have raped or killed us, or both, but all I could think was, *I won't be able to live with myself if something happens to Nip.*

As I was thinking about how to back out of the situation, I caught a glimpse of Whitney sitting in a chair across from the dealer, already making the purchase. She looked so young and innocent, and I bucked up quick and went to her side. She got it to go, and go we did.

As we walked back to the car a trio of young men approached Whitney. "Eh, *mami! Mami,* I know you. Come here!" they pleaded. By this time, Whitney was beginning to do national ads for products like Scope mouthwash. Her name and face were getting out there, so I decided then and there that if we ever did a drug run again, I would go in alone.

The next time we went I told Nip that I was going up by myself and that I wanted her to stay with the car. "Soon as we get there," I said, "I'm going to get out of the car and you should immediately get behind the wheel. If I'm not back in ten minutes, drive off, make a right at the corner, and then another right. The next block will be Broadway. I'll catch up to you there." It usually took about ten to fifteen minutes tops to score, and I felt better knowing that if there was any trouble, Whitney would be safe in the bustle and bright lights on Broadway. We talked about how we didn't want to call too much attention to each other because we were two girls, and we rehearsed what we'd do if someone tried to mess with us. We planned to think good and fast on our feet and say something like "My brother and his friend are around the corner." Luckily, it never came to that—the angels were working overtime.

It wasn't all about drugs, but we were enjoying ourselves. Sometimes we overdid it. "This shit," I said after a particularly long night of partying during one of our hotel stays. "I don't like doing it all day. The world is passing us by."

"Ain't nothing going on out there," Whitney said.

....

One time that summer, Whitney and I went to a gay club, a completely new experience for both of us. I couldn't have told you where to find any kind of club because that just wasn't my thing. But we got the idea into our heads, so we drove around and found one in Asbury Park. We walked up the wooden stairs and entered an intimate space that looked out over the beach. The interior was like any dive with wood paneling and a jukebox, but we felt comfortable. We played pool, listened to the music—which was honky-tonk—danced, and then slipped into the bathroom to do a few lines.

Whitney and I held hands and got close on the dance floor, but once we started kissing, we left. We made it to the car but couldn't wait long enough to get back to the hotel. I parked the rental car alongside the water, and before long a cop knocked on the window. We were in there naked, but the windows were fogged up so he couldn't see much and just urged us to move on.

Whitney was uncomfortable with her body, but I thought she was beautiful. I used to tell her, "God must have put you together piece by piece." Every inch of her fit together so nicely to make her beauty whole. Her legs were slender and shapely. I would tease her and say they looked like baseball bats because they were strong and smoothly shaped at the thigh with calves that tapered at the ankle. And her megawatt smile lit up her face. Even when she was sad that smile of hers was like a switch flipped on in a dark room, instantly flooding it with light.

Whenever I spoke like this, Nip would simply say, "Thanks, Rob," or sometimes look at me as if I'd just said something that she'd never heard, chuckle, and jokingly say, "You're so crazy, Robyn," or stare with that sweet, innocent expression she always seemed to maintain.

....

As summer drew to a close, I prepared myself to say goodbye and begin school at Monmouth. I was packing to leave when she phoned and said that she wanted to come visit me. I was relieved. Clearly there was something about me that made her feel comfortable and she wanted me to be part of what she was doing. I didn't know exactly what my role would be yet, but I was sure I could fill it, that whatever it was, I was made for it.

Once I got to school, we spoke every night on the phone, and Whitney ended our calls by saying, "I wish you were here." Larry would bring her to visit me, and the connection was still there. I missed her, too, but needed to focus on school and the team.

My dorm room was a sliver of a space, with a twin bed on one side. If I took two steps away from the bed, I could probably touch the opposite wall. It was pretty tight. Larry would drive Whitney up before tryouts and during the off-season, but she slept over only a few times. I didn't have a car, so Bonita or another teammate who did would take us to the store to get something to eat and then the two of us would go our way.

While I was away at Monmouth, I didn't do blow. I'd occasionally smoke pot with a bong that belonged to one of the guys on the men's team, but that was about it. But after I finished midterms, someone was going around with these little light blue pills. I took one and remember calling home and talking to my mother, crying and laughing. I ran and hid with another female, because we thought a girl on the team was chasing us and was going to kill us. Whatever those pills were, I didn't like them.

My mother immediately phoned Whitney and asked her to call me because she didn't know what was wrong with me, and she wanted to get to the bottom of it. Whitney called me right away. I told her what I'd done, and she told me to get in my room and close the door. I did just that. Or I tried. I saw a person's head squeezing through the keyhole, but Whitney's advice played in my head, so I shut my eyes and eventually fell asleep.

....

I got into a new rhythm with my basketball team. A freshman by the name of Barbara Rapp from Pleasantville, New Jersey, was a white girl who played like a black girl. Rapp was tall like me and could handle the ball. Rosie Strutz was the power forward—that was a given because she was from the area, and she owned that spot. Bonita, or "Bo," a lefty, was the point guard, and Rosie's sister Tammy started as swing guard. Now, Rapp was good but she wasn't going to start at the guard position ahead of Tammy, the hometown favorite. That left Rapp and me battling for the small forward position. I had to let her know she wasn't starting over me. I loved a great challenge, and so did she, so we pushed each other during practice. I won the small forward spot but Rapp was the best utility player ever. She could do it all. We had a great team that year and a winning season. I love those ladies.

Everything was going well until the day we had to play my old school. I was anxious and asked Whitney to be there to support me.

The game was close throughout and came down to the wire. Bonita and Rapp fouled out, and we were forced to put in a guard who hadn't played at all. We had no time-outs left with just seconds on the clock—ten or fewer. Having played a pretty solid game, I was in my head and decided it was best to keep the ball in my hands.

Someone took it out and tossed it to me, and I started dribbling the ball with urgency, heading toward the basket. I could see Tracey and her team waiting lined up on defense at the other end of the court. All of a sudden, my teammate Dee Dee Phillips appeared in my path, palms facing outward, asking for the ball. This is exactly what a guard should have done, but I waved her off. She hesitated for a moment, then turned to run; I glanced up at the clock and realized that the ball was gone. I stopped, turned, and looked to see it in the hands of an opposing player I'd just blown by. Two easy points to seal a win for them and a very hard-to-swallow defeat for us.

I fell to the floor. The gym was buzzing with emotion and the court was hot. Reality set in and I was exhausted. We were so close. After gathering myself, shaking hands, and getting some hugs, I saw Whitney coming toward me, wearing a taupe three-quarter-length shearling and oversize glasses with brown rectangular frames.

"It was a good game, anyway," she said. And it was.

....

That fall Whitney had started her senior year at Mount St. Dominic Academy. She wasn't happy about having to go back to school, but her mother said she couldn't pursue her music career until after graduating. Whit hated school and wearing the uniform. She had flunked out during her freshman year because she cut classes and didn't do her work. Each morning she rose and put on her uniform as if she were headed to school but spent part of the day in the Dunkin' Donuts down the street instead. A friend of hers would find her there at the end of the day, sometimes arguing with the guy behind the counter about how best to make a strawberry shake. If her mother was away doing session work or performing in Manhattan, Whitney circled back home. When she got in trouble, though, Mr. Houston pleaded with administrators and was able to get her back in.

....

While we were still visiting each other, finding time alone was becoming difficult, and we needed our own space. We were sneaking around in hotel rooms, my dorm, her mother's house or mine. Someone could have walked in on us, but it never happened, until the time my mother came home.

I was home on break, and after messing around, we cuddled up, talking in bed naked like a grown couple. Suddenly I heard the front door open and close. Nip jumped up and ran to hide behind the door to my room, which was slightly open. The sound of footsteps got closer and closer. My room was directly across from the bathroom, and through the crack in the door I could see whenever someone walked by or went in. I quickly pulled the covers up to my neck with only my head peeking out.

Mom sat down on the toilet with the door open, looking straight at me. I could hear her tinkling as she asked why I was in bed. All I could think to say was that I wasn't feeling well, which wasn't a lie because right then I was feeling pretty sick to my stomach. Picture this: Whitney Elizabeth Houston bolt upright behind the door in her birthday suit, and Mom staring at me from the toilet. It was a perfect visual split: Whitney in line with my right eye and Mom with my left.

It was a disconcerting sight, but I had to zero in on Mom so she didn't notice my darting eyes. Finally, Mom got up, flushed, washed her hands, and took a few steps toward my room. I was sweating, and my heart was pounding so hard I worried Mom could hear it. I was praying and was certain that Nip was, too. Mom stopped in the doorway, eyes on me; lifted her arm; and pushed the door slightly. Then she backed up and walked down the hall and out the front door.

Needless to say, Nip and I dressed in a hurry and headed out for the rest of the day, and into the night. What would have happened?

My Mom wasn't into embarrassing people, especially her children. I suspected that she knew something was going on but she was giving me the benefit of the doubt, or respected me enough to just leave it alone. I don't know why she didn't probe or look behind the door. My mother was the kind of parent who trusted her children, and even when she did not approve of a certain behavior, she felt it was important to allow us to learn for ourselves.

Four

Separation Anxiety

In the summer of 1973 I developed a mysterious illness. Almost overnight, weird swellings sprang up on my feet, my legs, and my abdomen. My mother took me to the doctor, but no one could figure out what was wrong. Weeks turned into months, and the undiagnosed condition spread all over my thirteen-year-old body, becoming acute enough to land me in the hospital for almost the entire summer. My mother, the sole breadwinner, reluctantly left me in the care of the hospital for most of the day, stopping by before work with games, cards, books, and magazines—anything to help me pass the time and distract me from scratching my skin, making things worse. In those magazines, I discovered a world that I believed reflected my future: cities and countries to travel to, fine hotels to stay in, the best cars to drive, and special things I could acquire.

I used to say, "Mom, I'm gonna buy you a house in Rio Rancho.

I'm gonna have a Camaro or maybe a Firebird." My brother and sister never talked like that. They were never looking for something else, something more. I was. All the time.

My mother wanted things to be better, too. A year before that, she had furnished our newly constructed three-bedroom apartment with new, modern pieces. My father had cluttered our old home with used, mismatched furniture from relatives. Mom often called him "a satisfied man" who didn't want much. I wanted to make my mother's life better because she had worked really hard and been through hell. Once I paid $112 for a sixteen-carat gold necklace with an amethyst, which was her birthstone, and she told me to return it. I tried buying her other gifts and she would make me take back every last thing. When I began touring and making real money, I'd bring her back leather handbags from Italy, Hermès scarves, and other luxe pieces, which she happily accepted.

The mysterious swellings went away, only to return periodically when my mother traveled for her job as a consultant for an electronics company. I could tell she'd asked Marty on the phone how I was doing when I heard him say, "Swollen."

Mom soon left the consultant job so she could spend more time with us and dedicate herself to her education. In the interim, she worked as a counselor at a drug rehab center and at an adult school where she helped students earn their high school diplomas. She attended Caldwell College, which shared a campus with Mount St. Dominic Academy. Years before we would meet, Whitney and I were frequently in the same orbit.

My mom was so wise and so strong. Looking back, I don't know how she made it through the stormy times to raise us, work, and put herself through college *and* graduate school. She finished her BA in psychology at Caldwell and went on to earn her master's degree in counseling from Trenton State. She was well respected by her colleagues, championed by her students, and described by her friends and family as an angel.

My mother was a good woman, so I couldn't understand why she never found a decent man. Some of the men she dated weren't very ambitious or seemed unworthy to me; others were married. I knew the Ten Commandments, and it didn't jibe with what I was seeing.

....

The summer before I left for college, a year before I met Whitney, I would ride my bike to the Orange projects with my teammates. We would play Orange High School girls under the floodlights and whup their asses until late into the night. Other times I'd play one-on-one with Val for hours. My mother rolled back my curfew to ten o'clock after I came home at one in the morning. I protested: "Mom, I wasn't getting into trouble. I wasn't doing anything but playing basketball."

"That's too late," she said. "You play basketball in the daytime."

The curfew didn't last long. I eventually wore her down and convinced my mother that I was safe.

We rode our bikes in a pack of five girls. Eventually we would branch off—three would go to the left and the other two would go right. Even if I had been alone, I knew how to stay out of the path of trouble.

Those street smarts stayed with me as I got older, and when Whitney and I were together, I would look out for her the same way. One time, Whitney had to bike home from my house at nearly midnight because we didn't have money for a cab. I mapped the safest route to follow and she called me when she got home without incident. She stayed on the line while I stretched the long cord from the kitchen into my room and got under the covers with the phone. We talked into the wee hours. All of a sudden, the line went dead, and I peeked my head out to see my mother standing there with the cord dangling in her hand.

"Your power has been cut," she said.

I told Mom everything. When she got home from work and wanted to know something, she'd ask me. I never lied, even if it caused me trouble, and I'd frequently take the heat for Bina because she was younger and probably following my lead. When I was feeling down about myself, Mom would tell me, "You're beautiful, and you have a strong, confident presence. You should be aware that that can be intimidating to some."

The relationship between Whitney and her mother baffled me: It was so different from what I'd experienced with mine. Whitney only had that summer counselor job where we met because Cissy said Whitney needed to learn some responsibility. Whitney proved herself to be responsible, but her brother Michael, who was also a counselor that summer, rarely showed up for work. For some reason his fellow counselors covered for him by signing him in.

In their home, I don't recall Michael being taken to task for failing to follow through, but Whitney was always under scrutiny. She told me Cissy's own mother died when Cissy was only a girl; she left South Side High School during her sophomore year, and when she was eighteen, her father died. I wonder if she never gave Whitney a break because for most of her life there had been no one to do the same for her.

When Whitney was young, Cissy's good friend "Aunt Bae" would watch the kids when she was on the road, so Whitney did have Aunt Bae's children to hang out with, but no friends from school. Her life was organized around going to church, choir rehearsals, and her mother's recording sessions.

Whitney wanted to go to Cicely L. Tyson Community School of Performing and Fine Arts, a public school in her East Orange district. She was trying to find herself and her tribe. Her mother told her the girls there wouldn't like her and that they'd be jealous. Mount St. Dominic was mostly white. One time she was at a sleepover at a classmate's, and when the girl's father came home, he said, "What's that nigger doing in my house?" Whitney called her mother to come take her home. She said the sting of that ugly word made her feel awful. The racial environment remained the same throughout her years there. During her senior year, a classmate asked Whitney to sing at her wedding. She was excited to do so, but the girl's Italian American parents wouldn't allow it because she was black.

Her grandfather John Russell Houston Sr., who passed away five years before Whitney and I met, didn't show his granddaughter much love, either. He was partial to his other son Henry's children. Nip explained, "One day I was at the park playing with my cousins and when my grandfather came to fetch us, he said that before going home he was going to take us for ice cream. But then he took them and intentionally left me behind. When I got home, I was upset and told my father what he had done to me. They got into such an argument my dad threatened to kill him." Nip continued, "I was a child and didn't understand why he did that to me."

"Do you understand now?" I asked.

"Sure. My skin was darker than the other girls' and my hair wasn't long."

"What color skin did *he* have?" I asked.

"He could pass for white," Nip responded. "He never liked me. He was a mean motherfucker."

....

Nippy couldn't wait to graduate and did the bare minimum to get by. The only class she spoke about was Sister Donna Marie's religion class, because she enjoyed the debates. Whitney, firmly rooted in her Baptist beliefs, had a direct relationship with God and an aversion to confession. "Why should I go sit down and talk to some man behind a curtain about my problems?" she asked. "How much sense does that make?"

I honestly have no idea how Whitney graduated. On one hand, she was a disinterested student, and on the other, she already knew where she was headed. Back in those days, it was rare to see a black girl on the cover of *Seventeen* magazine, but in 1981 Whitney shared it with a young white model, and afterward the nuns took to calling her "Miss Seventeen."

She was doing just enough to get by in school; no one was telling her that she wasn't going to amount to anything. She had her mind made up already. College wasn't even a thought, and she said, "Going back to school would be my worst nightmare."

Following Mount St. Dominic tradition, as a junior Whitney had chosen a first-year named Michelle Zakee as her "little sister," which meant Whitney was supposed to look out for her. She did so by buying her lunch almost daily, teasing, "Damn, girl, you don't have lunch money again?" They went on to become lifelong friends.

Almost every morning before Michelle and her mother left home to pick up Whitney for school, Michelle would sneak a call—and when Whitney answered in a hoarse whisper, she always sounded as if she was dead to the world.

"Girl, you're still in bed!" Michelle would exclaim. "We'll be there in ten minutes."

Cissy never helped Whitney get ready for school, and years later

Michelle told me that her mother pretended not to notice but felt for Whitney's struggle to get out the door unassisted. More than that, it angered her that on the rare occasion Cissy took a turn driving the girls to school, she dropped them off late.

....

Once Whitney proclaimed her devotion to singing, Cissy began bringing her to the studio for session work, and she spent her teen years among studio musicians, standing next to her mother, learning how to sing background. During the summers of her youth, Whitney often went on the road with Dionne, which was another sort of education. She had the gift, and the seeds were there, but her time in the studio and touring was her accelerated degree. She wanted to be ready.

But Whitney couldn't talk to her mother—not about school and not about her feelings. As the youngest child, she was the only one still living full-time with her parents. She told me that her stepbrother Gary had a brief stint playing with the NBA's Denver Nuggets but was dismissed from the team and sent home. Though I didn't know either of them, her brother Michael had played on Clifford J. Scott's varsity basketball team while I was there and had gone on to Fairleigh Dickinson.

Nippy was Daddy's girl and Cissy's daughter and caught in the middle of her feuding parents. When they confronted her about her failing grades during her freshman year, she unleashed years of anxiety and anger by screaming, "I hate being here in the middle of the two of you!" Soon after, Mr. Houston moved out and into an apartment in north Newark.

Whitney had conflicting emotions concerning her family and felt that they were always putting her in the middle of their issues and dramas. When she shared some of the stories with me, I suggested she try again to open up to her mother the way I did with mine.

"I can't talk to my mother. She knows best," she said sarcastically.

"You should try," I said.

"I could never tell my mother about how I'm feeling."

"Well, would you talk to someone else?" I asked, and told her that my mother had sent me to counseling when I was younger.

....

One time before my parents were officially divorced, my father showed up at our apartment looking for Mom. When he discovered she wasn't home, he flew into a jealous rage. As he circled around in his car looking for her, I prayed Mom would make it home before he could get to her. My brother, my sister, and I watched out the window, and as soon as we saw her coming, we yelled down to her to get inside. She made it, but as soon as she closed the door, my father arrived and tried to push it in. Marty added his weight and I heard the lock click into place. My father went to work on the heavy metal door, and once he kicked that door in, he dragged my mother around the apartment holding a hammer to her head.

"Daddy, that's not right!" I yelled, but he acted as if he hadn't heard me.

"Call the police!" Mom told Marty. My brother picked up the rotary phone and tried, but his hands were shaking and he couldn't get it right. He couldn't have been more than thirteen. I snatched the receiver from him and dialed myself.

My great-grandmother Alvina Crawford, who lived across the courtyard from us, came in and said, "Sonny, you done gone too far." He finally released my mother. The police arrived and told my father to leave, but he wasn't arrested.

From then on, I was always the one who would stand up in the middle of some trouble. That's what I knew how to do. It was just the way I grew up—always having to get in the middle of some drama. When I was twelve, Mom arranged for Marty and me to attend two weeks at summer camp. It sounded great: We were promised lots of swimming and other sports and a chance to see something new.

As we left from city hall in Newark, I enthusiastically waved goodbye, but when we arrived at camp, I refused to get off the bus.

"Honey, you've got to get off," the driver said.

The counselor who climbed aboard the bus was sympathetic and patient, so after about thirty minutes, I finally got off, but once I reached the last step, I froze again and wouldn't let them walk me into the camp.

"Call my mother," I said.

When she was on the line, I agreed to go into the office, where I told my mother I didn't want to be there. Mom said, "Robyn, it's going to take me over two hours to get there. Why don't you spend the night and see how you feel in the morning."

"Mommy," I said, "come and get me."

Marty had already gone to the boys' side of the camp and was clueless about what was happening. I was too worried to stay. I didn't know what would happen to Mom in my absence.

After that, Mom was concerned that I was too attached to her and perhaps seriously scarred by my father.

I told Whitney that the weekly counseling sessions I went to were really helpful in allowing me to feel more comfortable and less worried. She said it was good that I went, and Whitney then fell silent, going deep within her thoughts.

....

These thoughts stuck with me, and by spring semester of my third year at college, I was having trouble in my sociology class. We were studying juvenile delinquency, drug arrests, and petty offenses, and a correlation was drawn between single-parent families and these outcomes. I didn't connect much with the professor, which was my first challenge since it was an intimate class of maybe twelve students. According to her, if you came from anything other than a two-parent household—"the norm"—you were put in another category. I didn't think it was fair to those of us who didn't fit into that norm. I knew people who came from two-parent households who were a mess, and children of single-parent households who performed very well. I would bristle at these and other designations and participate in open class conversation to challenge them.

I said, "I've been there. I've been to an all-white school and I know what they have access to." Whitney also used to say there were more drugs in Mount St. Dominic alone than there were in the city of East Orange. Those girls had money for cocaine or whatever they chose.

If it wasn't about drugs, then it was about broken homes, and I just wouldn't fall in line. My professor would say, "These are the statistics." And I would respond, "Who's taking the statistics? They haven't been to my house." My mother told me that I could be and do anything that I wanted; no one could stop me from moving forward but me. But in that same breath she also said, "Don't be foolish, this is a white man's world, pay attention."

I can't explain why I was even willing to put anything bad into my body. Anyone who knew me from high school or my years in college knew that I did not indulge. But I guess I was so taken with Whitney in those early days, I just went with the flow. We knew that the use of cocaine was not something we should get comfortable with but must have convinced ourselves—if only in our heads—that we would do it for only a short time.

If Whit felt like talking, she talked *a lot*, and fast; and when I was high, it would almost make my head explode. We'd start with a game of Uno or Spades—those games could go on forever. We'd talk music and scripture for hours and before long, I would nearly cry with frustration because she would not stop talking. I continued to read the Bible on my own. I knew there had to be something more than what life had presented so far and it bothered me that the creation of human life was so amazing and yet finite. We are supposed to enjoy this journey but not hold on too tight to anyone or anything because inevitably, it all goes away.

In the beginning I enjoyed taking a few hits, but coming down from cocaine was always bad. I hated it. I felt like a vampire running from daylight and avoiding people. It took days to fully recover, and I found myself shriveled up, dry mouthed, and blinking uncontrollably, with a crusty nose and insomnia.

We knew that everything we'd talked about as far as show business was starting to get real. We agreed that we couldn't take cocaine along to where we were going, though we weren't ready to give it up entirely just yet.

I thought we were in control, but we were doing it enough that one day Mom told me my face was shaped like the devil's. Apparently I was getting much thinner, and it showed.

I finished my sophomore year at Monmouth and headed home for the summer, returning in time to learn that Nip was going to her senior prom with a family friend named Richie. He was good-looking.

"Don't worry about Richie, he's gay," she said.

On prom day, Cissy was beaming and gushing over her daughter, calling her "my princess." We'd been hanging out, and I stayed for a while as she got ready. Whit looked lovely in a lavender-and-white two-piece floor-length gown with wide fluttery sleeves and a long sash tied around her waist in a bow.

Whitney was traveling for fashion shoots as far away as Santo Domingo. She thought we might have more time together if we were both modeling and took me to meet her agent, who said she might be able to book me for runway in Africa. That was much farther away than the Dominican Republic, so modeling was a dead end for me.

It was much better for me to be around New York anyway. Since Nip didn't have a license yet, I would drive her to go-sees, Sweetwater's, or wherever else she needed to be. There were always people visiting backstage after the shows at Sweetwater's. Luther Vandross, Phyllis Hyman, industry people. I'd be in her dressing room off to the side watching. Cissy was usually upset about something: Maybe the drummer played too loud, or maybe someone handed Whitney their business card without going through her mother. Whitney was always very gracious and sweet and looked at every visitor as if she was really listening, when all she really wanted was to change into her T-shirt and jeans and leave.

My mother came to some of those early shows, and after one of them she was dining at a table near where Cissy sat with her church friends using the F-word like other people say *excuse me*. My mom told me that she was leaving and, on her way out, whispered, "And she calls herself a woman of God."

While Mom didn't appreciate our late-night phone marathons, she really liked Whitney. Many times she said that she didn't know how she'd turned out the way that she did. Whitney was responsible and her brothers were not. She was lovely when she spoke, while her mother's mouth was foul. Whitney was respectful and polite, with a disposition that was likeable and engaging.

One night backstage at Sweetwater's, a man from the music industry came over to praise Whitney and talk to us. When he said, "You're both so beautiful," Cissy whipped her head around and pronounced, "No one should be looking at anyone but my kid." We thanked him for his kind words, excused ourselves, and left.

Five

The Future Is Now

In the fall of 1982, I headed back to college to finish out my senior year. But halfway through the semester I decided that I needed to take control of my future—and that future started with my decision to leave college.

My basketball team was nearing the end of the regular season, right before the start of tournament time. The WNBA didn't exist, so it wasn't like I was working toward anything significant by playing college ball. It was a different time, and I knew that coaching wasn't for me. Also, the coach who'd recruited me, Joan Martin, had stepped down. Her replacement was a guy who bellowed, "I'm your father; I'm your boyfriend; I'm your coach; I'm your everything." I knew he meant well, but I no longer felt inspired. My mind was elsewhere.

During one of our late-night conversations, I asked Nippy what she thought about my leaving college. She replied, "That's a decision you'll have to make on your own." I knew she was suppressing her true feelings. Almost every previous call had begun and ended with her saying, "I wish you were here."

I thought about it and decided to leave Monmouth before the fall semester was over. I informed my mother, who said that I was ungrateful and that I'd received a scholarship only to toss it out the window. I couldn't argue; she was right. Janet, who had worked so hard to lift herself and to give her children opportunity, wanted to see at least one of her children graduate from college. After telling my mother, I called a meeting after practice and told my team. We had played nineteen games and I was probably the leading scorer. It was a difficult conversation.

Finally, I told Whitney. "Are you sure?" she asked, but she could barely contain her excitement.

No one else understood my decision, but it made perfect sense to me. I believed in my friend and what she was trying to do, and moving back to join her cemented that commitment. So I said my farewells, packed my bags, and left college just over one semester short of a degree.

It wouldn't be easy, of course. Nip and I needed money, and her modeling gigs weren't putting enough cash in her pocket to live on. I drove her to local jobs, and she traveled to places like St. Barts for catalog shoots. She hated how the fashion world treated models— as if they weren't real people. Sometimes the photographers and stylists would stand there discussing the setup for a photo as if she weren't sitting right there, saying things that were insensitive and hurtful. After one shoot, Nip came home in tears, her head a sticky mess from all the product applied to her hair to make it comply to the photographer's vision. I played it down, told her not to worry, that I would take care of it, and I washed the styling gunk out until her hair returned to its natural cottony-soft texture.

My first morning back home, Mom was in my face. "If I'm getting up to go to work, you will, too!" I told her that I was helping Nip launch her career, which was like a full-time job, and that I was reading books like *The Road Less Traveled* and thinking a lot. Of course, Mom didn't buy it. Neither did my uncle Robert, who'd practically laughed in my face: "You think this girl is going to make it big, huh? That only happens in the movies, child." My mom just listened. She'd always believed in me, and I think that deep down she even wanted to believe in my and Whitney's dream.

But I gave her reason to doubt: She saw the signs. In the months after I left school, there were too many times I was silly from weed or distant and cold when I came home high on coke. I often stayed out all night without the courtesy of a phone call.

One morning, when I got up, Mom was sitting in the living room waiting for me.

"Robyn, I want to talk to you. Sit down," she said in a soft but firm voice, her eyes never leaving mine.

When I sat across from her, she asked, "Where were you last night?"

"We were just hanging out," I said.

My mother pressed me about my recent behavior, and I confessed that Whitney and I smoked marijuana and did coke. She wanted to know where we got the stuff, and I said we went to different places, but mostly from a guy we knew in East Orange.

"What's Cissy's number?" When I hesitated, she demanded, "Dial her number." I did what I was told, hoping the whir of the rotary phone would slow things down.

As I sat next to Mom on the arm of the sofa, I listened to her half of the conversation and became more distressed with each word. I wished I had been able to warn Nippy and was worried that she would now be in hot water because of my big mouth.

"Cissy, this is Janet Crawford, Robyn's mother. Do you know what these kids are doing? Robyn says they're doing cocaine and smoking marijuana. Now, I'm not blaming your daughter, because I've raised my children to have minds of their own. But what I will say is that Robyn was not doing this before she met your daughter. Are you aware?"

By this time I'd melted down into the sofa. When Mom hung up, she didn't utter a word, didn't even look at me. She got up and went to her room. The silence was deafening.

Nippy called me later and we met up to discuss what had happened. I told her my mom knew and there was no way around the truth. I had to own up. I said it was time for both of us to shape up and that Janet Crawford wasn't playing! It took me a few moments to realize Nip hadn't told me anything about Cissy's reaction.

Finally, Whitney took a deep, slow drag on her Newport and said, "My mother spoke to me." She did not seem the least bit concerned. In fact, she was nonchalant about it.

When I returned home, a man and woman were sitting in the living room on kitchen chairs. They introduced themselves as drug counselors from the rehab center where my mother used to work. They offered me a seat in my own home. The man asked me what I knew about cocaine, where I got my drugs from, and if I knew what else was in them. He warned that sometimes cocaine is cut with substances that could make the drug even more dangerous. I dismissed him and said I knew and trusted the person who gave it to me. The woman asked, "How often do you do it?"

"Not that often. I enjoy just doing a little bit and I plan on stopping soon!" I continued to make light of the situation. I remember saying, "Believe me, I know what I'm doing." I didn't take it seriously at all. In fact, I was practically giggling and joking about it. Whitney and I even stayed out that night.

When I went to open the door the next day, my key didn't work. Mom had changed the locks. She was sending me a message and wanted to be certain it was received. I felt ashamed and knew I deserved what I was getting. I called my mom and told her I knew she was disappointed in me and that I was disappointed in myself, too. I told her I would be safe and find somewhere to stay while I got myself together. Suddenly, I was homeless. I needed food to eat and a place to sleep, and it was important to me that I handle it on my own. It was summer, after all, and that would make it a bit more tolerable. At least that's what I hoped.

I was able to find places to stay. A guy who coached a summer-league basketball team had an extra room in the front of his house. I didn't eat there; I just slept, made up the bed, and slid out. After about a week or two of that, I slept in a car parked in Nip's backyard. She had her license by then and told Cissy the rental was hers. Overnights could get pretty chilly, but as soon as her mother left the house, Nip would call me inside. One time, Cissy came out and walked around the car. I hid beneath the blankets and stayed as still as a log of wood, and it worked. Miraculously, she didn't see me.

This vagabond lifestyle wasn't sustainable, so I went to Newark airport and filled out a job application. Then, after three and a half weeks out of the house, I apologized to Mom for my behavior and said I was getting my act together. Mom was relieved and tearful when she let me move back home. She didn't bring up my drug use. A few days later, I heard from Piedmont Airlines, and soon after, I was gainfully employed as a ticket agent. I had a six-month contract as a part-timer with an early-morning shift, starting at four A.M. and ending at ten A.M.

I liked the daily routine and responsibility, but the shift was rough. I didn't have a car of my own, which meant I had to be out of the house by three A.M. for an unpleasant walk down to the parkway to catch a ride with a coworker. I was struggling to keep myself alert and available after work for Nip, who was the reason I'd come home in the first place.

As far as party time was concerned, we were so busy that we were lucky to be off for a day or two. But if we had a little downtime, she'd ask, "Wanna get some?" and we'd get a gram—maybe two. Though neither of us said it directly, my mother's confrontation had had an impact and our priorities shifted. We became more focused on the dream and what we could accomplish. Whitney would often say, "Cocaine can't go where we're going."

I was ready to get my own place but didn't make enough money working at the airport. Whitney and I would wait for our mothers to leave and take a cab from one side of East Orange to the other, climb into bed, and make lists of songs Whitney wanted to record. She'd grab her Walkman, playing things like Al Jarreau's albums *Breakin' Away*, *All Fly Home*, and *This Time*, and sing the songs note for note wearing headphones, gesturing with her hands, pacing the floor, and sweeping her head from left to right as if she were in front of an audience.

I kept a notebook so that one day, when Whitney Houston was famous, I'd be able to look back and say, "Okay, remember you said there's this song that you wanted to do?" That's exactly how "I'm Every Woman" came about. She always had ideas, but I was there to recall them for her and take the steps necessary to make them happen. At times like that we felt closer than ever.

....

On Dionne's recommendation, Whitney signed with a management group called Tara Productions. Her team featured three men:

Gene Harvey, Seymour Flick, and Steve Gittelman. Steve's father, Daniel Gittelman, was the owner. The buzz about Whitney was spreading. Valerie Simpson, of the songwriting duo Ashford and Simpson, saw Whitney performing with her mother at Sweetwater's and called Quincy Jones to say he had to sign Cissy Houston's daughter. But Quincy said he already had a female artist he was working with: Patti Austin, whose records Whitney loved and listened to all the time. Music publisher Deirdre O'Hara repeatedly suggested that Arista A&R man Gerry Griffith go hear Whitney sing. He finally did and was blown away, phoning Deirdre to tell her she was right, and then advised his boss, Clive Davis, to sign her immediately. He arranged a showcase for Clive to see Whitney at the Bottom Line.

Simultaneously, Elektra Records president Bruce Lundvall attended another showcase and was simultaneously courting Whitney. In fact, her only solo recording prior to signing a record contract was "Memories," a track on jazz fusion band Material's 1982 album for Elektra records, *One Down*. Bill Laswell was the group's founder, front man, and producer, and a bass guitarist known for his diverse musical influences, from avant-garde to funk to world music. Tenor saxophonist extraordinaire Archie Shepp also plays on the record. Before she even stepped into the recording booth and opened her mouth, Bill Laswell told Gene Harvey that she wasn't right for the record—maybe because he thought she was too young to interpret the song. Things became tense, until finally Gene insisted that since they were there, Whit at least should be given an opportunity to lay down a vocal.

When "Memories" was released, *Village Voice* critic Robert Christgau called the song "one of the most gorgeous ballads you've ever heard."

Clive attended a second showcase, after which Nip told me that he sat in the front at a table with two or three other people and just watched, expressionless, while tapping his foot. When she was done, he got up and left without saying a word. It wasn't until Gerry told him that she had done the song for Elektra that he moved quickly to sign her. Arista called and Whitney was faced with a big decision: whether to sign with Arista or Elektra. Her mother and manager both wanted her to go with Clive.

She and I talked a lot about Clive's roster, which included Phyllis Hyman, Barry Manilow, Dionne, and Aretha. Arista was a label of legends and Whitney chose to sign with them. But if Quincy had been at the table, I believe she would have gone with him.

Whitney finally had what she'd been working so hard for. "I signed my deal today. Now it's time to get going." I could hear the relief in her voice, and the pride, but Whitney wasn't the type to praise herself and be overly excited about things "You did it," I said. "The next thing is to find producers," she announced.

Shortly after, Whitney came by my mother's apartment and said she had a gift for me. She placed a box in my hands, and inside there lay a slate-blue Bible. She said that we shouldn't be physical anymore, because it would make our journey even more difficult. She also said she wanted to have children one day, and living that kind of life meant that we would go to hell.

"You know what we shared," Whitney added. "You know how I feel about you and we will always have that."

I told her I didn't want to go to hell, either. But I also knew that if Whitney had said she wanted to keep our relationship going, I would have gone ahead with that, too, because Whitney was the kind of person I wanted to love. There was no reason not to. I wasn't totally blindsided that day; in the recent past, we'd talked about how our relationship might affect her career. By this time, we were feeling the pressure. People knew we were tight and were starting to ask about us. We were so connected we could communicate without talking.

"If people find out, they'll never leave us alone," she said.

I knew what the church and the Bible said, and I loved her anyway. The love I felt for Nippy was real and effortless, filled with so much feeling that when we talked about ending the physical part of our relationship, it didn't feel as if I was losing that much.

....

After Whitney and I had that talk, the only thing that changed was the physical intimacy. We remained best friends and companions, and we continued to be there for each other every day, on every level.

We started looking in the papers and found a recently built condominium complex near Woodbridge, New Jersey, just south of the Oranges. Seven oh five Woodbridge Commons Way in Iselin felt safe and offered easy access to restaurants, shops, and Route 1. It was a straight shot to Newark airport and the turnpike heading toward the Big Apple.

My mother was concerned about our ability to take care of ourselves. She knew that our cooking skills were way below par. But she was never one to stand in the way, so on moving day she gave us Spam and a couple of other canned goods and recipes, and wished us well.

Next, we went to Whitney's house to gather her belongings. Her mother steered clear of us until we got into the car. As I turned on the engine, Cissy came out to the front porch. She held up a feminine product and hollered, "Don't forget your douche bag." Nip shed tears as we drove off. I was merely moving on from my house, but she was running from hers.

We moved into a first-floor apartment in a tasteful mint-green building with tennis courts directly behind our patio door. It was good sized, and the layout was nice: kitchen, living room, two bedrooms, and bathroom. Nip had her room; I had my room. Often I'd end up sleeping in her bed, because we were already hanging out in there. And if we got high together, I didn't like leaving her alone. I didn't want anything to happen to her, and it felt safer being together.

As for our furniture, well, it was basic. We had unfinished-pine platform queen beds with drawers underneath, an ironing board, and one sorry floor lamp that we carried from room to room. We managed to scrape together enough to purchase dishes and pots and pans from a home store, as well as our big splurge, a Technics turntable, a Hafler receiver, and a pair of really good speakers. We were going to make things happen; she had the dream, and I was going to help her fulfill it.

I kept the Bible she'd given me on top of my headboard. In order to embrace God and honor our love for each other, we cemented our sentiments on its endpapers. We each wrote a page about our love, pledged that we would always be honest and loyal, and left our past there. We signed it on February 13, 1982. We knew that God understood what we felt and that we had a bond that no one could penetrate. It would be our secret, and it would hold us together.

Later that year, Whitney went into the studio for her second solo recording ever, making a guest appearance on the record *Paul Jabara and Friends* with a ballad called "Eternal Love." That day, we met Martha Wash and Izora Armstead, the duo originally known as Two Tons O' Fun. Those large sangin' mamas, now called the Weather Girls, were there recording their smash hit "It's Raining Men," which appears on the same album.

Six

Nobody Loves Me Like You Do

On June 23, 1983, about a year after we moved in together, I sat in our living room in front of the TV waiting for Whitney Elizabeth Houston to appear on *The Merv Griffin Show*. Clive Davis relaxed on Merv's couch as if he was visiting a friend, talking about how he'd "discovered" Nippy. At this point, I'd met Clive once or twice at Sweetwater's. He would bring industry folks to hear Whitney sing as part of his master plan to create buzz by introducing her as his new "discovery." He was cordial enough to me, but I could see he was laser focused on making her debut a commercial success.

Back in the day, if I loved an artist enough to buy their album and not just a single, I'd study the artwork, logo, and credits listing who was who and who had done what. So I already knew Clive's artists. A lot of them were popular and female: Phyllis Hyman, Angela Bofill, Aretha Franklin, and hometown favorite (and

Whitney's cousin) Dionne Warwick. In my mind, it was fitting to refer to the label as a home for legends. Unlike most music executives, Clive was highly visible in the media and his name was also synonymous with acts like Janis Joplin; Barry Manilow; Bruce Springsteen; Sly & the Family Stone; Earth, Wind & Fire; Patti Smith; the Grateful Dead—the list went on and on. His successes across all music genres solidified his reputation as "the man with the golden ears."

Having seen Clive in action schmoozing with people after witnessing Nip do her thing, I shouldn't have been surprised that he was holding court on Merv's couch. Ever the promoter, Clive knew how to draw out the intro and build expectations, but in this moment, he was making me crazy. I wished he'd hurry up so Whitney could come on!

Finally, Merv introduced Whitney, who was practically sparkling; she looked almost as sweet as she did on the night of her prom. She was stunning in a purple off-the-shoulder top with puffed sleeves, and her long black skirt and high heels made her look even more statuesque than usual. Watching her introduction on the show, I felt the pressure that was on her. She seemed a little nervous, standing at the mic, rubbing her hands together and clasping them in a way that reminded me of my mother. But her body relaxed as she started to sing "Home" from *The Wiz*, her voice soaring as she powerfully delivered the words. Somehow she made it all seem easy, natural. No strain at all. I couldn't see the audience, but I could tell from the silence that she had them. She sang with conviction:

And I've learned
That we must look inside our hearts
To find a world full of love

Like yours
Like mine
Like home

Home became a long note held at the end of the song. Most singers would have been spent, but Nip even added vibrato.

When Merv came over from the couch, Clive and Whitney embraced, celebrating a shared moment of victory. "You won't forget that name," Merv proclaimed. "Whitney Houston."

Merv Griffin invited Nippy back onstage to close the show, this time with her mother. Together they sang a medley of songs from the off-Broadway musical *Taking My Turn*, which Cissy was appearing in. Whit deferred to her mother in the duet, holding back, giving only what the songs needed, staying in her place while her mom was out front.

When Nippy came home, I gave her a big hug of my own and insisted that she tell me everything.

"I know you could see my mother back there leading the band," she said.

"That was her?" I laughed. She was right. I could feel the tempo was too slow, then saw a body appear in front of the band, arms moving up and down as the tempo quickened.

Whitney said the band had been dragging on "Home," so Cissy went out and started conducting to get them to pick it up. It worked, and Whitney was able to lock into the groove. Sometimes when I think of Nip and those early days, I'll search the web for that appearance, and there's Cissy moving her arms up and down behind the sheer iridescent-blue curtains that obscured the band.

....

Although things were looking up for Whitney and her music, the past year had been a hard one for my family, especially for Marty. The summer before, he'd been in an accident.

He had joined the armed forces and was a bomb loader stationed at Seymour Johnson Air Force Base in Goldsboro, North Carolina. He was driving home from a sweet sixteen party in his Fiat hatchback with three women who lived in his neighborhood squeezed in among the equipment he'd brought to DJ. He stopped at a corner and began inching out to see beyond the cornstalks blocking his view. The coast was clear, but suddenly a drunk driver came speeding down the road. The point of impact was at the hinge of the driver's-side door, so the car door was flung open, sending Marty flying as the car tumbled over and over.

When Whitney and I returned from a day in Atlantic City and got the news, my mother had already left for the airport. We scrounged together $100, filled up the car with gas, grabbed Bina, and drove straight through to North Carolina with orange juice and Mary Janes for sustenance.

I spent some time on that ride thinking about how far Marty had come since we were kids. He had always been an inspiration to me. He was the eldest of the three Crawford kids and the man of the house. Growing up I was never hassled about my preference for athletic wear and running with the boys, but people sometimes asked me, "What's up with your brother?" He had no interest in athletics even though he could outrun everyone in a game of Catch One Catch All while wearing a maxi coat.

"He's just into music," I would answer.

"You're tougher than him," was a common observation.

Marty was an artist and performer. He would hook up my sister, dressing her in elaborate ensembles, like one of his shirts fashioned as a dress, belted around the waist with a necktie and finished off with coordinating tights. He'd alter my best practice shorts to fit him tighter, then wear them out dancing. Girls loved him because he was cute, was a gentleman, and could Hustle, but he never dated anyone.

Mom adored and cherished him, and so did all her friends, but this turned out to be a double-edged sword. When Marty clearly demonstrated he wasn't like most other boys, the blame fell on her: What did she do wrong—was it dressing him in corduroys instead of jeans? My dad in particular came up with all kinds of explanations, whether it was "being around women too much" or being coddled by Mom.

Dad's attempt at correctional therapy was yelling at the top of his lungs in Marty's face, "Who's the boss—me or your mother?" Marty would meekly respond, "You are, Daddy," and as soon as he said it, Dad would punch him in the chest and call him a punk. My dad was keenly attuned to homosexuality because his older brother was gay. The few times we visited Uncle Dickey's house, my father was happy to take a plate of his home cooking and seemed to love his older brother. But my father was incapable of extending the same tolerance and understanding to a son who didn't reflect him.

Though I was like him, my father never called me a tomboy. My mother always said I was a Crawford. I inherited my father's looks, athleticism, and competitive nature, while soft-spoken and artistic Marty and quiet and brainy Bina took after my mother's side.

Once Mom got us away from my father, Marty began to thrive. He was handsome, with big, beautiful, sad eyes, and all the ladies liked him. He was awarded a music scholarship to Florida A&M University for his accomplishments in the orchestra and marching band. But not long after Marty went away to school, he got sick: He and a few other students contracted hepatitis B. Marty told us it was from dirty dishes. Soon after that, he left college and came home complaining about the harsh treatment of band initiates. "They beat you with a stick," he said. Marty didn't talk much about his short college experience, at least not to me, but I knew it was painful for him.

When we arrived at the hospital, we hurried into the emergency room waiting area. Whitney was steady and held my hand. "Whatever happens, I'll stay with you," she said.

I found Mom sitting in the waiting room, relieved to see us. She guided us through the corridors toward his room, saying Marty had significant internal and external injuries and was in a coma. He had initially been rushed to a hospital that didn't have a neurology unit, so he was then medevacked to Pitt County Memorial Hospital, where they found no evidence of brain damage.

I gathered up my courage and entered his room. It was hard to see my brother lying there like that. His lungs had collapsed, and he was all bruised and swollen, with a broken arm, jaw, and ribs; tubes going into both sides of his torso; and dried, bloody patches smeared on his face and body. They had to reconstruct his nose. Despite all of that, Marty looked as if he was radiating life—his skin had an orange glow! At that moment I just knew he would be okay. And I said so. My mother called my father and suggested he come to North Carolina to check on his son. He showed up for one day. Mom put us up in a hotel, and after a few days she and Bina went home while Whitney and I stayed behind for a week, went home, and then returned again.

By then Marty had been moved to a naval hospital in Portsmouth, Virginia. It had been about three weeks and he still remained in a coma. After a few days, I called home and told my mother Marty would awaken the next day, a Wednesday, and he did. We asked him if he wanted anything and he said, "A cheeseburger and a strawberry shake." His jaw was wired shut, but he had a little opening, large enough to fit a straw, so I said, "I don't think you can eat the cheeseburger, but we'll get you a shake."

His motor skills needed work and he could barely walk. He got a little stronger, and one day Whitney wheeled Marty outside the hospital where there was a pretty nice view of the water, and we gave him a toke on a joint.

Six weeks after the accident, Marty was recuperating in my mother's living room. He wrote in a journal a lot and was frustrated and angry, but I didn't know all that was behind it. My mother called my father again to tell him Marty was home and discharged from the air force, but also to ask for help because her credit card bills were high from the hotel and travel. Dennis Crawford didn't come up with a dime. "Even in an emergency he isn't good for anything," Mom muttered, and went down the hall to her room.

When she was out of sight, Marty blurted, "Robyn's only good in a crisis." Stunned, I stopped what I was doing and waited for him to explain what he meant. When he didn't, I broke the silence with a concern of my own.

"Do you think Whitney and I will still be together when she makes it big?" I asked.

"She'll probably get tired of your ass," he snapped. He'd seen Whitney and me kiss once, but we never talked about it. Whitney's multiple trips with me to North Carolina and our living together made it clear she and I were close. His words baffled me and stung, but also sounded a little jealous and mean. I had never seen Marty with even one person who seemed to care for him the way Whitney did for me.

Once he recovered, Marty returned to Seymour Johnson, where because of the injuries he sustained, he could no longer be a bomb loader. Instead he was put in charge of "the tool shed." This new position gave him a view of his crew on the flight line, where he used to be. Marty was precise about the tool line, instructing personnel to thoroughly clean all instruments before returning them to their proper slots.

Nippy and I decided to pay him a surprise visit for his twenty-sixth birthday so we could celebrate with him.

Surprises always made Marty smile, and boy did he deserve a good one after all he'd been through. At first he didn't believe us when we called and told him we were there, but after we described a landmark or two, he giggled and called the front gate. He always took an interest in whatever we were up to and found Whitney and me pretty funny, nicknaming us "Nippy and Nappy!"

We had a fun visit, meeting some of his fellow airmen and friends. Over the weekend, Nippy developed an attachment to a stray Angora kitten that Marty had taken in. The cat, only a few weeks old, was named Misty. He had been feeding her milk through a tiny plastic bottle with a nipple, and Nip stayed up at night and through the next day holding and feeding her. When it was time to leave, she asked Marty if she could take Misty with us. Of course he said yes.

We decided to return the rental car in North Carolina and fly home. Since I was still working for Piedmont Airlines, I was able to get a jump seat, so we had only to cover the cost of Whitney's ticket. Nippy hid Misty inside her bag and cradled her like a babe. Midflight we discovered that Misty was loaded with fleas, so Nip wrapped her tightly in a complimentary airplane blanket and then left the blanket behind for the cleaning crew. (I know—terrible!)

When we were home and settled, we had to figure out how to get the fleas off Misty, as they were quickly spreading all over our apartment. (Payback from the plane!) We had wall-to-wall carpeting and could see little black spots here and there on the light gray weave. I'd sit on the sofa and spot them on my white socks, feel them biting my ankles, shoulders, and neck. Nip would sit on the floor with Misty on her lap, picking the fleas off one by one and killing them between her thumb and pointer fingernail.

Nippy loved that cat, and I did, too, but after a week, I'd had all I could take of the fleas. One day, as Nip was sitting with Misty, doing her flea fetching and plucking, I felt one of them bite me on my arm and spotted several crawling up my shirt. I shouted, "I can't take it anymore! We have to do something about this *now*. This is too much! Either this cat has to go or I have to!" Very calmly, she looked up at me and said, "Pack your shit." She loved her some Misty. We finally took her to the vet, where we found out that she was, in fact, a he, and we renamed him MisteBlu.

....

Not long after the *Merv Griffin* broadcast, Clive called saying Jermaine Jackson wanted to record with Whitney. Apparently, Clive had shown him a video of Whitney's performance, and Jermaine said that he "had to work with her." Nippy was excited about collaborating with a Jackson. My understanding was that Dick Rudolph (Minnie Riperton's husband and collaborator until her death in 1979) was originally tapped as a producer for Whitney's first album, but that deal failed to materialize, so Jermaine ended up filling the producer role. When Whitney shared the news, it didn't make much sense to me, because Jermaine Jackson hadn't done anything on the producing side with anyone remotely as promising as Whitney Houston, but what did I know? He was a Jackson; she was the new singer on the block. Arista thought they would jump-start her career by pairing her with an established artist. So they flew her to Los Angeles and scheduled her to record a few duets.

She was gone for a week and a half, which felt really long. I was alone except for MisteBlu, who sat with me on the couch at night while I waited for the phone to ring. I could tell right away that more than just recording was going down. Whenever Nip and I spoke, she wasn't at all focused on herself or her career—every call was "Ji" this and "Ji" that. She barely asked me anything about things at home, and when she did, it was brief, and then we'd move back to more Ji talk. She called a few times from the studio to play me what they'd recorded, but all I could focus on was the two of them laughing and whispering in the background.

I didn't feel like I should call her, even though I had the phone numbers for the studio and her hotel. I didn't want to wake her too early or interrupt anything. There were a few times I did phone around the time that I thought she would be getting ready for the day. She'd answer and quickly say that she was about to go to the studio and would phone when she got there. Of course, that would turn out to be hours later.

Whitney had said that she would always be there for me and needed me to be there for her, and I believed she meant it—that we both felt that. Now I felt her slipping away.

I lay on the floor of our living room in the dark, letting the tears flow down my cheeks. I was alone.

After she returned, Whitney said that in her opinion Jermaine had a better sound to his voice than his brother Michael. She had three songs for me to hear: "Nobody Loves Me Like You Do," "If You Say My Eyes Are Beautiful," and "Don't Look Any Further." They were cool, though Jermaine's voice was no match for Nippy's, especially on my favorite: "Don't Look Any Further." Whitney's vocal was out front, as if she were a jet burning up the runway and Jermaine was left behind at the gate. "Girl, you're gonna blow out your vocal cords if you keep singing like that," Jermaine told her. He decided not to include that duet on his album and "Don't Look Any Further" was snatched up, recorded, and released featuring Siedah Garrett and Dennis Edwards of the Temptations.

A week or two after her trip to Los Angeles, Nip and I drove over to Arista to have a meeting with the department heads and staff. We went down the agenda of artist-related stuff, and when Jermaine's name came up, an executive at the label pulled me aside and told me that Jermaine didn't want Whitney riding on his coat-tails. *Ain't he dreaming*, I thought. The long-anticipated 1984 Jackson Victory Tour had recently been announced, and I guess Jermaine was really feeling his Jackson power around this time.

Back at home, even with this new emotional distance, Nip and I still talked into the wee hours, and I'd sometimes fall asleep right next to her in her bed. She never slept in my room, though, and if the middle of the night found her there, Whitney would rouse herself long enough to stumble back to her own. I was wounded by her new relationship and disappointed that she wasn't talking to me. I mean, this was a Jackson! That was huge! Didn't we tell each other everything? I thought being truthful with each other was paramount. I could live without being romantically involved, but I had trouble facing the walls that were going up.

....

After a show at Sweetwater's, Whitney changed into street clothes and was putting on her shoes when an acquaintance of

Cissy's came into her dressing room. While he was talking, Nip shot me a look that let me know she wanted to cut the conversation short and get out of there.

"Oh, you two can communicate without talking?" he asked. Whitney and I looked at each other, guilty as charged.

"That's good," he said. "Girls, y'all gonna be fine. You just have to be careful with the three M's: men, marriage, and marijuana." Whitney and I burst out laughing and thanked the man for his advice.

It seemed funny at the time, but now the first M was becoming a real problem. As long as we remained loyal, I didn't have an issue with it. But when she chose not to talk to me about her relationship with Jermaine and left me to wonder and figure it out on my own, I began to feel like ours was not a true friendship at all. It also concerned me that I couldn't get her to leave the house to go anywhere but the club because she preferred sitting in her room waiting for the phone to ring. It was as if she'd forgotten all about herself, the music, and me. I tried to imagine myself in her shoes, but I couldn't. She had said we were supposed to be a team, but that's not how it felt.

I knew I was having a hard time, but apparently, I wasn't aware of quite how hard. One afternoon while Whitney was driving us somewhere on the highway, I asked her a question and was met with total silence. Suddenly, without thinking, I raised my right arm and swung it toward her head, making contact. Whitney lifted her elbow to shield herself, but my arm still hit her shoulder, causing the car to swerve a little. *You've lost it*, I said to myself. Then aloud, I said, "I'm sorry. Pull over and I'll walk home." Whitney asked me if I was sure before she made a U-turn toward a shoulder near a gas station. She was hesitant to drive away, but I motioned for her to go. Don't get me wrong here! Whitney didn't appreciate that shit at all and her face said so. I felt horrible and shaken about losing control and needed some time alone.

What I had done wasn't only wrong, it was dangerous. We were on a three-lane road and Whitney had been driving in the middle, but luckily no one was next to us. We were three-quarters of a mile from our place, which gave me thirty minutes or so to think as I walked. I had never lost my cool like that before. Even on the basketball court, I never pounced on someone for pulling a dirty move.

By the time I reached home, I knew it was time to explain myself, to lay bare the agony of what I had been feeling while she was in LA and to point out how distant and preoccupied she'd been since she returned home.

When I entered Whitney's room, I plopped down beside her on the bed and apologized again. I was honest in saying that I could sense they were sleeping together and was determined to get through it in spite of the pain. Then I came straight out and asked her to talk to me about where her head was and about what had happened in Los Angeles. She began calmly recounting her first meeting with Jermaine. He told her he was obsessed with her beauty and spellbound by her voice. With the help of his buddy Marcus, the two of them sneaked away to a hotel on three occasions.

When she finished, I couldn't say a word; my emotions were bouncing off the walls. She wasn't telling me anything I hadn't already suspected, but the fact that she chose not to tell me and then forced me to drag it out of her? That burned. Up until that point, Whitney had included me in all her plans and dreams. But now she was not the same person. Her enthusiasm for her career had been displaced by this new fixation on "Ji."

I got up, went into my room, and began throwing things against the walls and turning over furniture: my bed, my dresser, anything I could get my hands on. I didn't stop until I got too exhausted to go on. The room was a total disaster, and when I looked up, Whitney was standing in my doorway. Our eyes locked and she said quietly, "Now clean it up." I took a nap, and then I put it all back together.

It made sense that at some point we were going to be with other people, but this thing with Jermaine hurt like hell. I had to find a way to move on emotionally, too, and that was that. Before I went to sleep, I made a pledge to myself to find love and adventures of my own.

The next week I fielded calls from Jermaine, who always spoke in that low and soft Jackson voice.

"Speak to Whitney?" he'd say.

"Hi, Jermaine," I'd respond. "Hold on."

His "Speak to Whitney" was more cordial than Cissy's "Speak to my daughter," but both greetings left me cold. When she and "Ji" spoke, I could hear the hum of Nippy's voice moving up and down in confidential tones that had once been reserved only for me. But I didn't hang around listening to her conversations. That would have been pretty pathetic, so I gave Nippy her privacy.

By now, Whitney had filled me in on more of the backstory: According to Jermaine, he was unhappy in his marriage with Hazel Gordy, was planning to get a divorce, and would soon be single. I said, "Nippy, is that what he's telling you?" I was good and mad. Here this Jackson bro was using Whitney's talent to boost his career while simultaneously messing with her head *and* cheating on his wife. I tried to tell Whitney how distracted she had become, all because this guy couldn't sing that well, produce that great, or keep his penis in his pants. I thought she needed to understand the situation and the effect it was having on her (and on me). But Whitney was smitten and there was no talking to her.

Her only complaint about him was his hair, which "Ji" was wearing like a slicked, combed-back Afro. I'd never seen anything like it. Whitney said, "When I touch his hair, it's hard as a rock!"

The Jacksons had all given up their signature 'fros for Jheri curls and relaxers. When Nip asked him what he used in his hair, he said it was something his brother Michael gave him. That didn't seem to intimidate her. She told him, "Well, you should stop using what Michael gave you!"

Determined to put on a brave face, the next time he called, I was even nicer: "Hey, Jermaine. How are you? She's right here." I passed Nip the phone, and he asked her to pass it back to me.

"I love your friend," he told me.

"You do, huh?" I said. "I guess we'll see about that." And I handed the phone back.

Months later, they performed "Nobody Loves Me Like You Do" on *As the World Turns*, a popular soap opera. Whitney's eye makeup was a little heavy, but she was beautiful as always, and her hair was close cropped, bringing out her facial features. Any other viewer probably thought the looks she gave Jermaine were part of the emotional interpretation of a gifted songstress. It's true that Whitney would come to be known for her unparalleled ability to translate sentiment into song, but I knew those looks intimately, and she wasn't acting at all. Jermaine was trying to play it cool, but Whitney's true feelings—like her voice—overpowered his performance. I took some solace in the fact that she had sung him under the table. But now they were lip-syncing, and, God help me, I had to endure this process on set watching take after take after take 'til the cake was baked.

I wasn't going anywhere, but it was clear that I needed to protect my feelings. Ever since that conversation about ending our physical relationship, I had figured she would have guys hot on her tail, perhaps get married, and possibly have children—I could totally see it—but I hadn't anticipated that witnessing any of that would hit me like a ton of bricks. I tried to focus on myself and decided to reach out to some of my basketball and college friends and spend more time with my family.

Sometime between late '84 and mid-'85, while Whitney was on a promotional tour with Gene Harvey, I went out dancing at the Paradise Garage in New York for Marty's birthday along with his friend Robert. Right before entering the club, we each took a tab of mescaline—my first time doing both. Once we were inside, the music was so loud, I felt my heart racing, pumping in time with the beat. My brother leaned over to tell me he and his friend were going to hit the dance floor, and as they walked away, they disintegrated as if someone had said, "Beam me up, Scotty." I sat down on a riser feeling overwhelmed, confused, and lost—as if I was in a tunnel. Suddenly I heard someone calling, "Robyn? Robyn Crawford?"

It was Flo, a point guard on a New York summer-league basketball team and an acquaintance of my friend Valerie.

"Robyn," she sighed. "You're fucked up, aren't you?"

I tried to tell Flo that I had been there with my brother until he disintegrated. She asked, "What does he look like?"

"He looks like me," I told her. That wasn't very helpful, but Flo promised she would stay with me until we found him. She took me up to the rooftop patio for some air and that was better. I have no idea how long we were up there, but it was daylight by the time Marty found me.

When I got home, I fed MisteBlu, and as he ate, it sounded as if there was a microphone in his bowl. I got in the bed and prayed to God in the name of Jesus: "If you will please, Lord, just get me through this, I will never take mescaline again."

....

The Jacksons were finally coming to Madison Square Garden in the summer of 1984. When Jermaine arrived in NYC, he told Whitney that he'd call her after rehearsal and get her some tickets. Now even I started to get excited. Though I was for Michael, I grew up loving all the Jacksons—including Tito—and my girl had a hookup! We were going to see the Jacksons up close and personal!

But the dates came and went. Jermaine never called, and we never went to the show. The phone conversations slowed down big-time after that, and eventually they stopped altogether. Whitney didn't know what to say, and I didn't, either. I tried to make her feel better by saying she was worrying over the wrong Jackson. After all, most girls had Michael on their walls, not Jermaine. Hell, even she admitted that as a young girl she had intended to marry Michael when she grew up. "You're so crazy, Robyn!" She laughed, but I wasn't kidding.

The following weekend, Whitney decided to travel alone to Antigua. I was at home when Jermaine called.

"Speak to Whitney?"

"She's not home," I said.

"She's not?" he asked. "Did she leave a number?"

"Yep," I said. "But she didn't tell me to give it to you."

After she and "Ji" were over, Whitney sent me some mixed messages, especially when it looked as if I might have some things of my own going on. As a part-time airline employee, one had to work various stations in order to qualify for full-time status. I was now in operations, loading and unloading luggage and driving carts to and from the aircraft to the baggage claim conveyor belts, and guiding aircraft on the tarmac. One of the Piedmont pilots took an interest in me during a weekend layover one night, as I was guiding his aircraft in to a stop.

After the crew unloaded the plane and I walked back indoors, a supervisor told me the captain wanted to have a word with me. He was a nice-looking, cocoa-skinned man, probably in his midthirties, who made a charming first impression. He told me that he was based in Greensboro, North Carolina, and staying at a hotel not far from Newark airport for the weekend. He invited me to come by for a bite or something. *Hmm,* I thought. *Maybe this is a good opportunity for me to do something for me, or maybe not. We'll see.* I took his number and told him I would call him. Remembering Jermaine, I decided that if I paid him a visit, one of my first questions would be "Are you married?"

The next day, Nippy was lying low at the apartment, and I told her that I might stop by the hotel after my shift to see the pilot who'd spotted me out on the tarmac. She gave me a quick "Okay," and I was out the door. Once at the hotel, I called him from the lobby and asked for his room number. I had no reason to be afraid of him, especially since I made it clear that my people knew where I was, and all the crew members were staying there as well. Anyway, it turned out he was married with two children, and I told him I had a rule against that. He was understanding about it and said he appreciated my company. I wanted to get out of there and suggested we go for a ride, and we ended up at a casual dinner. I called Nippy from the restaurant and told her we might swing by the apartment. She sounded as though she didn't care if we did or not, so we did.

Shortly after arriving, I was in the kitchen grabbing a drink when I called out to Nippy—and she entered with a foul attitude that filled the room. She glanced at the pilot, gave him a dry hello, and in one dismissive wave, turned and went back to her room. He and I looked at each other with the same stupefied expression. We left quickly, and I giggled a little bit when he asked why my room-mate was so mean. I said she wasn't really, and that she must have been tired.

We went back to the hotel, where he invited me to stay and watch a movie. I said, "I'm happy to stay for an hour, but I'll have to leave after that." When it was time for me to go, he begged me for just a kiss. I obliged, but before closing the door behind me, I told him that he should be kinder to his wife and family.

When I returned home, I asked Whitney, "What was up with that? He thought you were mean!" She said she didn't care what he thought. Then she took a beat, apologized, and said, "I just don't want him in here."

At least she was honest. I never saw the pilot again.

Seven

You Give Good Love

Before she'd even begun recording her first album, Whitney was in demand. In 1983 she was asked to record the single "Hold Me" with Teddy Pendergrass. Teddy had been the lead singer of Harold Melvin & the Blue Notes, whose 1975 song "Wake Up Everybody" was a key release from Philadelphia International Records, Kenneth Gamble and Leon Huff's CBS label, backed by Clive Davis. After that, Pendergrass went out on his own, releasing a string of platinum albums. His powerful baritone was versatile: As a soloist, his tunes ran the gamut from hot and heavy ballads to more introspective songs like "You Can't Hide from Yourself."

In 1984, Pendergrass's album *Love Language* marked his return to music after a near-fatal car accident two years earlier that had left him paralyzed from the neck down. Teddy still could sing, and Whitney carried her part. "Hold Me" would eventually be included on Whitney's first album as well. Finally the time had come to record songs on her own.

....

First up with an original tune for Whitney was Kashif Saleem, the producer of Evelyn "Champagne" King's number one R&B hits "Love Come Down" and "I'm in Love." We first met Kashif when Clive brought him to Sweetwater's and were a little thrown by how Kashif looked. Based on his music and name, we both had a vision of him as the funkiest man on the planet, and here was this regular-looking guy before us. He looked like Michael Jones— the name he was given at birth.

Kashif's mild-mannered appearance was almost as much of a surprise as when we met Kenny G. Whitney and I had just gotten off the elevator on the ninth floor at Arista heading to Clive's office when his door opened, and out he walked with a young man about five feet eight. Clive gave Whitney a welcoming hug and intro- duced us to Kenny G. As he and Clive resumed their conversation, walking toward the elevators, Whitney whispered, "Ain't this some shit. Kenny is white?" His *G Force* album cover is an inverted image, like a film negative, showing Kenny G sporting an Afro and wearing sunglasses and a polo with the collar turned up, so we had no idea. Incidentally, Kashif also produced most of the songs on his breakthrough album.

At Sweetwater's, Kashif extended an invite to his new home in Stamford, Connecticut, formerly owned by Jackie Robinson and his wife, Rachel. Kashif said Mrs. Robinson would be there on Saturday, so Nippy accepted his invitation to hang out with him and meet black royalty.

As promised, when we arrived that afternoon we were introduced to Mrs. Rachel Robinson, a beautiful, light-skinned, petite woman, her salt-and-pepper hair pulled back in a bun. I'd seen pictures of her with Jackie and their children in magazines, and now here she was right in front of me. I said hello but was speechless after that. All I could think about was her husband and what I had learned about the challenges and the obstacles that they had to endure to stay together. And now he was gone.

When I tuned back in, Kashif was chatting about his involvement with Rachel's charitable organization while Whitney looked on, listening. Kashif told us he never had a family of his own, having grown up in foster care in New York City. He had a rough upbringing and was horribly abused at a young age. By some miracle, he discovered music and taught himself to play multiple instruments. His final foster mother provided him with more stability, but in church, he'd get his hands slapped if he played anything other than sacred music on the piano. His foster mother died when he was fifteen, leaving him to fend for himself, until B.T. Express, the group responsible for "Do It ('Til You're Satisfied)," invited him to join them on the road. He'd been making music ever since.

He was an early adopter of technology, with a love for the Minimoog, a synthesizer that gave 'Shif his signature sound. Whitney took to calling him "the Professor" because of the look of concentration he wore on his face, sweating as he moved the levers on the mixing console, coupled with the way he pushed up his glasses, which were perpetually sliding down his nose, with his index finger.

Kashif had written a new song called "Are You the Woman" and talked to Clive about recording it as a duet with Whitney but was told it wasn't the right direction for her. I suspected 'Shif submitted the song during the Jermaine hookup and then ended up having to use it on his own record. In the meantime, he casually asked Whitney to sing background on a number of tracks he was readying for his sophomore album and she agreed.

"Hey, Professor, was that good?" Whitney would call out from the booth. "Professor, what you want me to do now?"

Usually the answer was "Another take. Another one just like the other," or "More breath," or "Sing 'huh' three times like panting—'huh huh huh'—for me." The studio was an intimate, comfortable space and sometimes I sat at the board beside him (though he jumped up a lot, moving and grooving) or in a chair off to the side near the console, my eyes on Nip, following the process but making sure she was enjoying herself.

Kashif was like a technician who loved experimenting with his keyboards, drums, and electronics, mixing vocals and sounds. Whitney sang background vocals on "Ooh Love," "I've Been Missin' You," and "Send Me Your Love" on that album. The vibe felt good in Stamford. We stayed for one weekend and then went back the next. Kashif told us to make ourselves at home, and we did. His chef concocted healthy smoothies and fed us lots of veggies, nuts, fish, steak, whatever we wanted.

Whitney was in the zone, having a blast playing around, improvising and adding her magic to each vocal line, tag, chorus, or sound effect. Her method was just as meticulous as her approach to singing lead. I sat there watching her go into the vocal booth and sing, come out for a listen to the playback, go back in, then come out again to have another listen. Whitney would ask, "What are you hearing?" or "How was that?"

She'd pause while thinking about his answer and then say, "I'm coming in to listen." Whitney knew exactly when she'd nailed it. She didn't need anyone to tell her when she got it. She could feel it. Even I could hear it, if I was paying attention—which I always was.

"Should I be charging him for this?" she said after finishing laying down background vocals for "Fifty Ways" on our second trip to Kashif's house. She was starting to feel as if he was taking advantage. A few times during the session, I could tell by the look in her eyes that she was done, but he seemed to be pushing her to give a little more nuance here and there. Up to this point, Nip had seemed cool about what he was asking and had gone along. But I knew she felt the song was a wrap and she was done. Michelle, Nippy's "little sister"—who, by the way, is five feet eleven—joined us on this trip. She too could see Whitney was becoming increasingly agitated. On the drive home, Nip talked about how much she had sung and how she deserved to be paid.

I sensed there had to be a solution, and it was my job to help figure it out. It was no secret to Clive that Whitney was working with Kashif in Connecticut, so we agreed that I would call Arista and speak to someone in legal who could steer me in the right direction. It was clear there was a lesson to be learned, but for now, I was driving back to Jersey with Nip's mouth in overdrive about Kashif's concocting some potion, using her vocals for his project. Or in Whitney's words: "Professor trying to be slick!" She was funny, and Michelle and I laughed our tails off. But then Whitney got serious, saying, "They did this same shit to the Sweet Inspirations! Atlantic has all of those tracks of B vocals in the vault and you hear them sampled on the radio today. Well, they're gonna pay me!"

The next time we saw Kashif was at a studio in Manhattan, where he introduced us to songwriter LaForrest Cope. Lala was talented and funny, with a beautiful spirit. We three bonded immediately. She sat down at the piano, played a few chords, then started to sing.

I found out what I've been missing
Always on the run . . .

Whitney leaned on the piano and broke into a smile, signaling that she connected with those lyrics. "Yeah! That's it!" she exclaimed. Lala modulated just a little bit and came back down to that chorus that hooked you in the simplest way. Inspired, Whitney went right into the booth, got behind the mic, and sang.

After "You Give Good Love" was released, syndicated columnist Ann Landers wrote a column lamenting pop music's move toward sex-laden lyrics. Later, in an interview, Whitney pointed out Landers must not have actually listened to the words. I agreed. It was about someone giving you love in the purest way. It was about the willingness to fully expose yourself.

I thought the issue with Kashif and the background vocals was settled after I submitted an invoice to Arista. But one day after speaking to her mother, Whitney asked me to tell Kashif she wanted to take her vocals off the songs or her name off the credits. I called to deliver the message. "Really?" he said with surprise. "But she sounds great." We went back and forth a few times about removing her name until Whitney, who was sitting next to me, said, "Let me talk to him," and, taking the phone, told him she wanted him to remove her vocals altogether. Kashif said he would.

Several months later, when *Send Me Your Love* was released, I called Arista and requested a copy. Whitney sat in an armchair, her legs resting on an ottoman, while I stretched out on the floor in front of the stereo. We listened all the way through and then Whitney said, "He didn't take me off." Kashif did replace her lead vocal tag in the middle of "Baby Don't Break Your Baby's Heart" with Lala's voice. But on other songs, he only pulled her vocal back, and he used her breaths for a drum sound on "Ooh Love." She is all through that LP and you can hear her giving those songs a lift and punctuating the hooks. This is especially true on "I've Been Missin' You," where he layered in another singer named Lillo Thomas. You won't find her name in the credits, but Whitney Houston set the tone and flavor for that track vocally. I know why he didn't take her off. He couldn't do it—she was killin' it.

....

Gerry Griffith at Arista found another song for Whitney, this one written by George Merrill and Shannon Rubicam, called "How Will I Know." Janet Jackson had passed on it for her *Control* album, making it available for Whitney. Enter Narada Michael Walden, who at the time was in the studio producing Aretha Franklin's album *Who's Zoomin' Who?* Narada received a call from Gerry urging him to work with Whitney. After he made some changes to the song, Narada tracked it in California and then flew to New York to meet Whitney and record. I watched her lay down her lead in one take. From that moment on, everybody called her "One-Take Houston."

Here's how it went down: A fat-ass instrumental track blared through the studio speakers while Nip stood inside a booth separate from the control room. Wearing headphones, she took a gulp of her usual Throat Coat tea with honey, then stepped in front of the microphone and was ready. Narada and the engineer were at the controls, and I stood or sat nearby, where I could see Whit and she could see me.

Her background vocals were always laid first, doubled and

sometimes tripled, and after that, they moved on to the lead and ad libs. We would never leave until she got a copy of what she had done. If it wasn't ready, I would hang around until it was—leaving with what was usually a rough mix of the track featuring what they deemed to be the best of her vocal passes. Sometimes she'd call and say, "Make sure you keep this ad lib," or push for a certain phrase that she felt worked particularly well. Occasionally, if a line or even just a word was used and she believed there was another take that worked better, she'd call them on it. But for the most part, she'd allow the producers to do what they were hired to do.

When she first heard a demo, she would get really quiet, pop a few Luden's Honey Licorice cough drops, and study the lyrics. If she felt it, it was on. What came out each time was original; it often left producers like Narada in awe, and fulfilled a songwriter's dream. She told me she had what she called "tricks." Her way of saying a word to make it fit within a sentence, interpreting the feeling of a song, phrasing, enunciating words—knowing when to go easy and when to attack. "You gotta know the tricks," she'd say.

Shortly after, Whitney put me on her payroll. "I won't be back tomorrow," I told my supervisor at Piedmont with a big smile on my face. We were trying to figure out my title when Whitney said, "I wish that I could be two places at once, but I can't. I can handle the inside. I got this. But I need you on the outside looking in." I understood what I needed to do. If she didn't want you there, you weren't getting in, at least not through me. I was ready for this role, being out front when needed, getting things done, asking questions, or doing whatever was necessary to make things better and easier for Whitney. She knew that I had her best interest at heart. I began organizing all correspondence from Arista, handling performance requests, and fielding calls from agents, songwriters, artists, television producers, high-profile personalities—you name it. Anyone wanting to do business or talk with Whitney got me first.

Rumors about Whitney being gay and having an affair with her assistant began swirling around the industry not long after I took on the role. Cissy was beside herself and phoned Whitney's father to express her displeasure over our running together. Cissy was more concerned about me than she'd been about her twenty-one-year-old daughter's involvement with a man twice her age. Clive had said Jermaine and his wife, Hazel, were separated, and that may have been true, but still he was married and an older man. Whitney hadn't had any real experience with relationships, other than taking a chance on the love she had for me.

Whitney took me to meet her father at his apartment in Newark. He lived in a modest high-rise building and worked as a housing administrator under Kenneth Gibson, the city's first black mayor. Her family had moved from Newark to East Orange when she was four years old, after the riots. Her father's mother, Sarah Elizabeth Collins Houston, lived above the Houston family's home. I had been upstairs with Nip a few times to see her grandmother. But most of the time when I visited, I would hear her dragging big, black orthotic shoes across the floor or calling downstairs on the phone, asking Nip to run errands. Whitney spoke proudly of her grandmother's years as a schoolteacher in Brooklyn educating mostly immigrants and minorities. She'd even thought of following in her footsteps before she discovered her voice.

"Robyn, you don't say 'off-ten,' you say, 'offen,'" Whitney would correct me. "My grandmother taught me that."

When John Houston greeted me, I could see that he was his mother's son. Nip, a total Daddy's girl, sat on his lap and put her head on his shoulder while telling him about life in the condo with me and about her burgeoning career.

When I looked at Nippy and her father, I was struck by how affectionate they were with each other and how safe she seemed to feel with him. It was also clear that she was able to speak with him much more openly and freely than she was able to speak with her mom. Whitney had talked to her father about how close we were, and it seemed he understood the importance of our relationship. But that day, whatever Cissy had told him about us was front and center.

Whitney told her father that she needed me because she trusted me. "Robyn understands me, and I want her by my side in this business. I know that she loves me for me. She's my friend—the sister I never had."

"Okay," her father said, nodding his head in agreement. "Why don't you two go out with a couple of guys to the movies?" I cringed, not believing my ears. *He actually wants us to stage fake-boyfriend scenarios*, I thought. He was old-school, with a Rock Hudson–throwback way of thinking, but I could not go along with it. I let Mr. Houston know right away that I wasn't down for playing that role. Even then, I knew that pretending to be someone that I'm not is a total waste of time.

Whitney used to say, "Don't worry about what people say. We know the truth." And that made us stronger, because it wasn't for anyone to know. We still had each other and cared for and loved each other whether we slept together or not. I hadn't stopped loving Whitney but nothing was going on. I didn't feel as though we needed to pretend.

....

Nip encouraged me to be out front. I joined meetings with the players at Arista and was welcomed by all. With Clive Davis, it was a different story. When I accompanied Whitney to meetings with him, he would say hello to me and close the door behind them.

The first few times he did that, I chatted with his secretary Rose, just in case Whitney needed to call me in for anything. But after it seemed that was to be the norm, I would make rounds through the building. There was always business to be done, and she was the prize horse in the stable. Though Whitney always shared their discussions with me, I did wonder why she never invited me to join her in Clive's office, but I never asked.

Eight

....

Introducing Whitney Houston

Nip's debut album, *Whitney Houston*, was set for release in February of 1985. I was the liaison between Whitney and the label, keeping track of everything. She consulted with me when it came time to write her acknowledgments; she told me she wanted to open with the Serenity Prayer: *God, grant me the serenity to accept the things I cannot change, the courage to change the things I can, and the wisdom to know the difference.* I don't know if she realized this prayer was central to twelve-step programs, but I didn't learn this myself until many years later.

Below the acknowledgments to her record company and her family, Nip wrote, "Robyn, What an assistant! I love you and I guess all you need to do is stay in my life." She ended with: "I hope this album will be enjoyed as much as I enjoyed making it."

I enjoyed being a part of her process, too, although I had lost all pride in my own singing voice after I met Whitney. The only time

I felt comfortable singing in her presence was if "little sister" Michelle, Whitney, and I were riding in a car, singing out at the top of our lungs. I felt intimidated in the face of Whitney's voice even though she often told people, "Robyn's got a nice voice. She don't want to do nothing with it, but she's got a nice one." She asked me to sing a part in the studio a few times, but I declined until the filming of the music video for "You Give Good Love."

That day, I stood behind Whitney while she was getting her hair and makeup done in her dressing room, watching her face in the mirror. "I already told them that you wouldn't want to do it," she began. "We have one girl who can fake it, but we need someone who really knows the words." She looked at me in the mirror with those eyes, wordlessly saying, *They fucked up, just do this for me.*

I never liked the spotlight. I was more comfortable in the number two spot behind the scenes, preferring to be, as Whitney put it, "on the outside looking in." But when something was needed, I was good at figuring it out and getting it done. So I put on an oversize eighties-style blazer, rolled up the too-short sleeves, and shimmied into the tight pants wardrobe gave me. When I complained about the jacket's fit and ugly check print, Nippy said, "Welcome to my world!" She wasn't crazy about the fuchsia catsuit they had her in, either, but off we went.

The other "backup singer" came through a temp agency, and for most of the video, the mic was placed in front of her face to mask any flubs, so I had to awkwardly bend down to it. I had no intention of telling anyone about the video, but a few weeks later, while we were visiting my mother, Whitney popped in a videotape and pointed me out, to my mortification and her delight. "Miss Crawford, there's Robyn right there! Look at Robyn, Bina. You see your sister? There she goes again."

Before releasing an album, Arista would hold meetings with

department heads to discuss the artist promotion plans and packaging, which included a look at artwork from photo shoots with samples mocked up for album covers and upcoming singles. Clive usually had the first word and the last. The photos for Whitney's first album were taken by Gary Gross, best known for his controversial nude photographs of ten-year-old Brooke Shields, and album covers like Lou Reed's *The Bells* and Dionne Warwick's *Heartbreaker.* When the artwork for the album cover was sent to the apartment for us to see, I was pleased that he had captured Whitney. She looked fresh, youthful, and elegant. Her hair was natural and smoothed back, her makeup minimal. The mock-up that would ultimately become her album cover featured a headshot with a salmon-orange border to accent her peachy-colored skin. She was wearing a simple string of pearls and looking straight into the camera, soft and strong. On the back cover, Whitney is statuesque in a white Norma Kamali bathing suit. She looks regal and at ease, standing tall on the beach, hands on hips, feet firmly rooted, her face lifted to the sun.

Not long after that shoot, an executive in the R&B department pulled me aside and told me that, although he and his colleagues disagreed, the general feeling around Arista was that Whitney's cover photos looked "too black" and not friendly enough since she wasn't smiling. I loved them and had made that clear to all concerned. That day, to get ahead of the game, I took home the final edited images that were still in contention so Whitney could sign off. Folks at Arista asked the photographer if he had more images, but Gross said the makeup was too heavy and wouldn't release them. She won this battle, but it was the first and last time cover approval would go so easily. On future album covers and singles, Clive would almost always insist she appear smiling.

Nippy and I were sitting in Gene's office on Fifty-Fifth Street going over her upcoming schedule when he informed us of a call he'd received from the record label. They suggested she have her hair done similarly to that of former Miss America Vanessa Williams, whose straight-with-a-flip shoulder-length 'do was standard-issue beauty pageant. I knew right away that this request hit Whit hard. She had conquered every step thus far to the best of her ability, and now they were telling her, "Here's what you don't have and are going to need to cross the waters." We were told that Whitney should get the weave in place prior to her European tour for press and photo shoots. Whitney's short hair was a little longer than it had been for her appearance on *As the World Turns*, but Arista was still pushing for a pretty big change. I didn't understand why this was necessary when she had gotten this far looking like herself. She'd even broken into the great white world of modeling with her natural hair.

Neither of us even knew what a weave was. We knew they existed, but we had no knowledge of the lengthy process, which requires braiding or sewing in fake or human hair. Gene sent us directly to the salon where Diana Ross got her voluminous hair. On the way over, I kept reminding Nip that this was a consultation and not a commitment.

But almost as soon as she sat in the chair, two stylists who had anticipated Whitney's arrival began talking over her as if she weren't there. I remember one of them saying, "She has almost nothing on her sides, so we could shave it." The whole thing felt kind of cruel from where I was sitting. "It" was Whitney's hair, part of her body, her person.

Looking around the place, I was drawn to a woman who seemed to be handling most of the clients. She was Amazonian in stature and had a heavy, purposeful walk that announced her movements around the salon. Her name was Carol Porter. I overheard Carol discouraging the use of chemical relaxers and talking about how to nourish and condition hair rather than beat it into submission. When she had a free moment, I went over and asked, "How can I make an appointment with you?" We ended up talking until Whitney's "consultation" was done.

Once back in the car, Whitney broke down and cried all the way home. "The weave will protect your hair from the hot lights onstage and make it much easier to manage while on the road," I said, sharing what I'd learned from Carol, trying to console her. Whitney laid her head in my lap, and as I stroked it feeling her own fine, cotton-soft hair under my hand, I hoped that Carol was right.

In preparation for the makeover, Whitney and I went shopping for hair. I looked at the menu in amazement: Asian hair, Hawaiian hair, Pacific Islander hair, Malaysian, Indian, and more. I was glad we had options and were able to find human hair that matched Whitney's hair color. After she spent the better part of a day getting straight extensions braided in, Carol cut and styled it. Once done, Whitney's hair resembled a lion's mane. She was a Leo, and I had come to see the lioness as Nippy's kindred spirit. Referencing a nature show we watched once at the apartment, I teased, "She's the one doing the work, hunting and providing for the cubs. That's you. That should be your logo—a lioness!"

Nippy thought for a minute, then said, "Make it happen." I sat down and talked with Donn Davenport, head of Arista's art department, while he sketched out my description on a sheet of paper until I said, "That's it!" Whitney now had a logo for her company, which she dubbed Nippy Inc. It appeared on all Whitney products, but Arista didn't want the logo to be too prominent, so the lioness image was so small on singles and album artwork that everyone thought it was a cat.

Up to this point, Whitney's management company had been

sending her $300 a week. Money was tight, and Nip called Gene and asked him if he could increase her disbursement to $400. He told her no, which was surprising given that he cared about his talent and was accustomed to working with strong women, having promoted stars like Nina Simone. Of course, Whitney wasn't happy with that response, but she didn't stand up for herself. Instead, she went quiet. I pushed her to call him back for an answer, but she demurred, saying, "I feel funny asking for something that's mine."

Performing, Whitney was a lioness, but offstage she was quiet and rarely roared. When I likened Nippy to the big cat, I didn't consider the animal's selflessness. At one point in the wildlife show, the lioness broke her jaw taking down prey yet still kept hunting for the benefit of the pride. I would soon learn that when it came to family, Nippy had a similar tendency. She was soft-spoken at heart and would much rather have avoided confrontation. But I wasn't afraid.

I suggested Nippy call her parents, but she was hesitant. So I picked up the phone and dialed. When Cissy answered, I passed the receiver to Whitney. She told her mom what had happened with Gene. "Your father will take care of it," Cissy said. He did. And so, in a move that would come back to bite me in the butt, I initiated John Houston's entrée into his daughter's business affairs.

....

Whitney's first album was released on Valentine's Day 1985. One morning soon after, I was home straightening up our apartment while listening to the radio and heard, "Next up is 'You Give Good Love.'" Whitney was asleep, and I ran into her room to wake her, turning the radio way up.

"It's on! It's on!" I yelled. She rolled over as I sat down on the side of her bed, grinning. When it was over, Nip looked at me and said, "Sounded pretty good, huh?"

"Yeah." I smiled. "Sounded great."

Nip was similarly cool at the Belmar beach one summer afternoon a few months later, when we heard that song coming from neighboring blankets on nearly every radio down the beach.

In those months after the album came out, we were so busy that we had little time to celebrate her first hit, but when we could, we would go out for long drives, and sometimes we'd find ourselves down the shore. Once when Michelle joined us, we brought along a bottle of Dom Pérignon that Clive Davis had sent for the success of her first single. As Whitney was about to pop the cork, I said, "Whit, you gotta shake it up and let it explode."

Nip looked at me and said, "If I shake it up like that, what are we going to drink?"

Tired of our back-and-forth, Michelle said, "Give me that bottle!" and drank straight from it, and the three of us passed it around. On the way home, we stopped along Route 35 in Monmouth County to race go-karts. Michelle's car broke down, and she was stranded on the track while Whitney laughed her tail off, yelling, "Michelle!" every time she whizzed by.

Being Whitney's assistant also meant accompanying her when she traveled. I was excited as I stood in line for hours to get my first passport so I could join her on a promotional tour in the European markets.

In preparation for the trip, Nip and I looked at her itinerary and laid out clothing for each performance, meet and greet, dinner, and interview. She would hold up pieces and say, "What do you think about this?" We assembled outfits with accessories and Whitney tried on each combination and did a fashion show for me, walking the narrow hallway between the front door and the back wall—where we'd set up our sad, tilting ironing board—as if she were on the catwalk. I'd laugh and give her thumbs-up or -down, and when our couch, chairs, and just about every surface was covered with clothing, we took turns ironing everything before it all made its way into her suitcases.

Nippy and I settled into the gray leather seats of the Concorde headed to London. She had made an earlier trip to Europe with Gene, but this was her first voyage on the supersonic jet. I never imagined this would be how I took my first international flight. And we sure didn't know that we would soon fly the Concorde the way some people ride the bus.

When the pilot announced we were ready for takeoff, I was completely unprepared for the 250 mph sprint down the runway, which felt three times as fast. The force was so great that my back was plastered against the seat and I couldn't lift my head. The cabin was a little claustrophobic, but the adventure took precedence. And I marveled at the fact that we would be in London in three and a half hours, as long as it took to drive round-trip from Fort Lee to Kashif's house in Stamford. The sky outside the window was so black that all I could see was a line of light coming from the jets, and I swear I could see the arc of the earth. We were flying at twice the speed of sound and it felt like it.

As we settled ourselves in, Nip grabbed the in-flight menu written in French and English and said we should definitely order the caviar, which came with egg, onion, and toast points—she said she'd had it before with Dionne Warwick. "It's baby fish eggs and sounds horrible, I know, but it tastes good." We threw down.

One of our stops on that first promo tour was a hotel in England. We walked into a huge ballroom filled with press, and Whitney went from table to table answering questions. At one large rectangular table, she was at the head, I sat to her right, and her manager Gene Harvey stood behind Whitney on her left. About ten reporters filled the other chairs, and a woman who was at the far end of the table asked, "How do you feel about the tabloids that talk about your personal life?" She tossed one such rag on the table and shoved it toward Whitney, who, with the reflexes of a cat, curled her right hand into a claw, stopped its momentum, read the headline to herself, and placed it back down on the table. Adopting a posh British accent, Whitney replied, "I don't have to tell you about your English literature." She then gave the tabloid a gentle shove back, and in her own voice added with a smile, "And I don't mean Shakespeare."

Ha! That's my girl, I thought as I followed her to the next group of reporters.

....

Whitney Elizabeth Houston was taking off, full speed ahead. We'd now been in each other's lives for five years, and it was clear that we were in it for the long haul. She had my back, and I had hers. She was in the lead, and I was there riding shotgun, keeping track of our ideas, looking ahead, staying focused, and following through.

We were still sniffing cocaine, but not very often. We were busy, and being busy was the best thing for us, especially Nippy. I loved rising early and getting a jump on things, whereas Nip was never an early riser. She could stay in her room all day until she got hungry for a snack and never feel as if she was missing anything at all outdoors. She used to tell me that I was too happy in the morning.

That year, after her album came out, Whitney was asked to participate in "Stop the Madness," a well-meaning but absurd anti-drug recording and music video PSA sponsored by First Lady Nancy Reagan as part of the War on Drugs. When she agreed to do it, I said, "You have to do the right thing now, Nip."

"I know I do," she replied.

"People are going to think you're drug free and you're not. It's not right to say one thing in public and do another in secret."

"I know," she said, following with her now-worn motto: "Where we're going, this can't go." The thing was, we were already there, and so were the drugs.

....

Having outgrown our first apartment, we moved into a luxurious high-rise building with a stunning view of Harlem in Fort Lee, New Jersey. Apartment 16-B was lovely and very comfortable, and Whitney hired an interior designer to style everything to our liking. The color scheme was lavender and cream with gray hues, and we had lots of oversize silk pillows in bright shades of blue, orange, red, and purple. By that time, I was making $300 a week and living rent-free.

Within a year of settling into the new apartment, in July 1986, we were preparing to embark on Whitney's first big tour. We desperately needed someone to look after the cats—MisteBlu and Marilyn, Nip's newest acquisition—whom she loved above everyone else. "They don't talk back," she'd say.

As part of Whitney's growing team, and as her newly titled "assistant," I knew when to talk back and when to stay silent, when to pass and when to take the shot. And as we faced weeks on tour,

I knew I needed to hire some help—ASAP. Now, Fort Lee was an affluent area, a place where lots of people had live-in nannies, au pairs, housekeepers, you name it. I didn't doubt that I'd find someone, but this person had to be next to perfect. I wasn't about to open up the newly big-time world of Whitney Houston to just anyone.

I got the ball rolling by asking one of Nip's managers if he could recommend someone. He told me about the woman who took care of his place, whose daughter lived with her and sometimes came along. He gave me the mom's number and I called.

I went to their house and met Silvia Vejar, who was twenty-three years old and about five feet tall, with big brown eyes, a kind round face, a medium build, and beautiful long brown hair. Silvia told me she was born in El Salvador and came to the United States with her family at age seventeen, speaking no English. Upon arriving, she enrolled in Fort Lee High School, and also attended night school so that she could catch up to her eleventh-grade class. She had her daughter at twenty.

I invited Silvia to the apartment for her second interview, and when she arrived, I realized that I had to make a run to the store, so I asked her to come along for the ride. In the elevator, I took a closer look at how she was dressed. She was wearing a light-colored, ankle-length, summer-weight cotton skirt with a loose-fitting T-shirt, an overcoat, and thin-soled, white canvas sneakers on her feet. The problem? It was freezing outside. I was staring at her, wondering, and then her eyes connected with mine.

I asked, "Aren't you cold?" She said she was. "Why are you dressed like that? Outside it's going to be even colder." She told me that she was a churchgoing woman, and that her church didn't allow women to wear pants. The elevator doors opened on our underground garage, which even in summer was chilly. We silently made our way to my Mercedes 560SL. I looked over at Silvia and said with a smile, "I don't believe God would want you to freeze."

She smiled and said, "I don't think so."

On the drive to the store, we discussed family, her leisure time, and what she wanted for herself and her daughter. Her accent was heavy. When she said *Miami*, it sounded more like *pajama*. Her English speaking and writing skills were rough, but I sensed an ability to understand and learn, and she seemed trustworthy. Not to mention, she was perfectly capable of caring for the pets, and, on top of that, she said she could do manicures, pedicures, and massages!

I really liked her and felt that Whitney would, too. Silvia lived nearby, was a responsible single mother, and didn't smoke or drink—which was huge. Now all I needed was a blessing from Nip.

The next day, when Silvia returned, I was showing her where things were kept, going over our preferences, and sharing how Whitney was accustomed to having things done. Just as Silvia began to tell me how she liked to work, Whitney entered from the back hall.

She extended her hand and said, "Hi, I'm Whitney!"

Silvia gazed up, smiled, and said, "Hi," and then giggled. "You so young!"

Whitney was wearing a white terry-cloth robe, her hair pulled back with a headband, fresh faced and makeup free. She smiled at Silvia and said, "Nice to meet you."

Whitney asked Silvia a series of questions: how old she was, where she lived in Fort Lee, and how old her daughter was. Still standing, Whitney asked if Silvia and her daughter would be comfortable living in the apartment until our return from the tour. Clearly we shared the same first impression. Silvia assured us that they definitely could and that no one else would be staying with them.

Silvia got the job. She would stay in the apartment whenever we were traveling, and upon our return, she'd work weekdays from nine A.M. to around five P.M. The directive I gave Silvia was simple: Whitney is the boss. We work for Whitney, and we answer to Whitney. I felt good about passing the baton and was confident that Silvia had the right stuff: honesty, ambition, humor, faith, and the desire to do her very best.

Whitney was scheduled to make her Carnegie Hall debut on October 28, 1985. That afternoon when we arrived, we learned that Reverend Al Sharpton had his people picketing Whitney because white promoters were involved with her show. Before the concert started, I went out front myself and saw Sharpton hitting the side of a white plastic bucket while a small group of middle-aged black folks walked in a circle holding mops and signs that read *Whitey Houston.*

"What do they want me to do? Why is this my battle?" Whitney wondered aloud. Most of the promoters associated with large venues in New York City were white and had everything on lockdown. I don't recall Michael Jackson or Prince ever being targeted with the same criticism that Whitney faced. Talk of a demonstration had been brewing for weeks, so much so that the NAACP issued a statement denouncing "any boycott planned at the New York City debut of rising black singing star Whitney Houston."

On top of the picketing situation, Whitney's brother Gary compromised that Carnegie Hall concert. Sound check came and went and by early evening, Gary, who was supposed to do a duet with Whitney in the Jermaine Jackson and Teddy Pendergrass numbers, was still nowhere to be found. I kept hearing the production team saying over the walkie-talkies:

"Anybody got a sight on Gary?"

"Negative."

You could feel the stress. Up until then, Gary had been barely cutting it singing background and, of course, should have been at sound check like everybody else to rehearse "Hold Me" and "Nobody Loves Me Like You Do." I asked Whitney, "What are you going to do if he shows up?" and she said, "I don't have time to be worrying about Gary." Which was exactly my point! Whitney had too much to focus on already; the show was sold out and the audience was packed with celebrities. I said to her, "You don't need those songs. Nobody's going to miss them. Plus, Gary was a basketball player. He knows that if you don't show up to practice, you don't get to play." Whitney agreed.

Gary eventually turned up for showtime. He'd clearly been on a drug mission, and it was obvious to everyone that he was high—looking dried out and ashy, clutching the black toiletry bag he carried everywhere. But Cissy didn't bat an eye. She told him he was going out on that stage.

Standing next to Whitney, I thought, *This can't be good*. I knew that he shouldn't be taking the stage in that condition. But Whitney didn't say a word. Just stood there silently, looking at Gary as her mother pushed him onto the stage. In that moment Cissy was more concerned with positioning Gary to get a recording contract than she was about her daughter's feelings, despite the fact that it was Whitney's name on the marquee of one of the most prestigious stages in the world.

There are moments in life that seem very small, but in the end, they come back to haunt you. This was one of those moments. Whitney knew exactly what was going on with Gary, and when her mother insisted that he go out onstage in that condition, she gave permission to Whitney to think that you could mess around and still get to perform your duties. At least that's what it felt like to me.

You don't do drugs, skip practice, and then get to step out on the platform—her platform. But instead of setting an example, Cissy handed out a pass. There was no lesson or moral, no repercussion.

....

Despite all the chaos, Whitney was shooting up the music charts. Her first hit, Kashif and Lala's "You Give Good Love," went to number 1 on the R&B chart and number 3 on the pop chart. "Saving All My Love for You" hit number 1 on both the R&B and the pop charts in the Uinted States and was her first number 1 pop single in the UK.

The album became the biggest-selling record by a solo female artist to date.

Whitney received Grammy nominations that year for Album of the Year; Best Pop Vocal Performance, Female; and Best R&B Vocal Performance, Female. But she was deemed ineligible to be considered for Best New Artist because of those earlier recordings with Jermaine Jackson and Teddy Pendergrass. Clive wrote an op-ed in *Billboard* magazine blasting the National Academy of Recording Arts and Sciences for denying this honor to an artist who released the first album by a female artist to yield three number 1 hits. "Whitney was a major event for our industry and for music itself," he wrote.

The Grammy Awards ceremony was held on February 25, 1986. Once again, I was home alone watching her on TV. The event was entirely a family affair, with Mr. and Mrs. Houston attending as if they were still a couple. Whitney came out to sing "Saving All My Love," for which she'd been nominated for Best Pop Vocal

Performance, Female. She made it gracefully down the steps that led to center stage, singing beautifully. That Grammy performance would earn her a Primetime Emmy award the following year.

She had me on the edge of my seat, right there, in our apartment, just as she had that very first time I heard her sing at New Hope Baptist. I hollered as if I was watching a game.

After her performance, Cousin Dionne and Julian Lennon came out to announce the winner of Best Pop Vocal Performance, Female. Lennon read off the nominees: Tina Turner, Madonna, Linda Ronstadt, Pat Benatar, and Whitney. Opening the envelope, Dionne jumped up and down then spun around when she announced Whitney's name. She gave her cousin a long hug, rocking her side to side. Whitney wiped a tear from her eye before making her speech. I cried, too, so proud of her and grateful to be a part of it.

Whitney called me from LA and I could feel her energy. She was full of pride about her Grammy. Barbra Streisand, whose song "Evergreen" Whitney used to sing in Cissy's nightclub act, and Marilyn McCoo, who had recorded the original version of "Saving All My Love," were both sitting right up front. Streisand, who famously suffered from stage fright, came up to Whitney after the ceremony and asked, "How do you do that? Aren't you nervous?" Without missing a beat, Whitney politely answered:

"No, I just do what I gotta do."

Nine

The Greatest Drug Tour

Whitney christened her first tour as a headliner "the Greatest Love Tour," an homage to what I still consider to be her most significant and everlasting song. When I first met Whitney, she was performing it in her mother's Sweetwater's show. Composed and written by Michael Masser and Linda Creed, the song was commissioned by Clive for a 1977 Muhammad Ali biopic titled *The Greatest*. George Benson made the original recording, but Whitney made it her own.

I was there when Clive brought Masser to hear her sing it. Michael wasn't a tall man and wore his reddish-brown hair in a style reminiscent of the Beatles. He gave a first impression of being shy and reserved, until he started talking about music or sat behind a piano. That night, hearing Nip sing, he was blown away. He would later produce the song for her album, but only after he and Whitney convinced Clive that the time was right. I was surprised to hear about Clive's doubts. Whitney had been singing it and taking everyone who witnessed it—including the composer and Clive himself—to another place, and still he had his foot on the brake. But Nippy stood firm.

After Whitney recorded "Greatest," we were told that the other songwriter, Linda Creed, was battling breast cancer. Whitney and I prayed for Linda, sending her strength and positive energy. *Whitney Houston* came out on Valentine's Day 1985. The first single, "You Give Good Love," dropped a week later, with "Greatest Love" on the B-side, and soon reached number 1. The second and third singles, "Saving All My Love for You" and "How Will I Know," immediately charted, too.

In March of 1986, Arista made the decision to release "Greatest Love" as the album's fourth single. Whitney had been performing it as the encore song in her show. As the song climbed the charts, Michael Masser asked Whitney to call Linda in the hospital to share the good news. She was glad to have the opportunity to talk with Linda and express all the love, admiration, and gratitude she had for her, and said it was an honor to sing and record such a masterpiece.

Within a month, "Greatest Love" had reached number 5 on the charts. I can't recall where we were when we were informed that Linda had passed, but the news shook us into silence. After some time, Whitney said, "This song better go." And I said, "It's going, Nip. Linda made sure of it." By May, it was Whitney's fourth number 1 single, and it would become Linda Creed's best-known work.

Back in 1985, Whitney had her first experience touring as the opening act for Jeffrey Osborne and later Luther Vandross. Jeffrey mostly drew a straight-up adult R&B following from his days with the band LTD. My mom was a fan, and I recall her frequently singing along with "Love Ballad":

What a difference
A true love made in my life.

But as my girl burned up the airwaves, I began to notice that the audience was more varied. The Whitney Houston audience included twentysomethings, middle-aged folks—black, white, and everyone in between.

Touring with Luther was a great experience for everyone. He treated Whitney and her entire crew as if we were his entourage, and I can still hear him stopping by her dressing room or in the halls asking, "Everything good? Y'all all right? Got everything you need?" He was a real showman who truly enjoyed doing what he loved for a living. His singers and band sounded tight and looked fabulous, as did Luther, known for his shimmery jackets by black couture designer Fabrice.

Whitney loved her some Luther Vandross, as a person, friend, and performer: "He really knows how to sang!" She knew every song and jingle he had ever done. When Whitney went on the road as his opening act, she marveled at his show and saw firsthand what it took to be a headliner. Luther was the perfect artist to take notes from when it came to showmanship and production. You were captured not only by the vocal harmonies and blends but also by the arrangements, which Whitney originally had been privy to in the studio watching her mom's work with Luther. On-stage, Luther generally used the same singers who recorded his songs in the studio—with the exception of Cissy Houston, whose flavor stands out on "Wait for Love," "Creepin'," "Better Love," "The Night I Fell in Love," and "Since I Lost My Baby"—"What's gonna happen to me / I don't know." In other words, if you listen to Luther Vandross, you're gonna hear Cissy Houston.

Luther's singers Kevin, Ava, and legendary backup singer Lisa

Fischer glided and swayed across the stage, glitzy, glamorous, and graceful, with spellbinding moves. Paulette McWilliams sang from a chair offstage, adding another layer. Luther's band featured the sounds of A-list industry musicians, like the funky thumping bass of Marcus Miller. His show was dazzling.

Soon after finishing her opening duties, Nip would quickly change and tell us that she planned to go see the show, and I'm not talking from the side of the stage. With the lights low, just a few of us—me, Nip, Felicia, and John Simmons—would creep out into the house so as not to call attention to ourselves. We'd find a spot on the second level of the arena where we could see everything, sitting on the floor in the aisle by a railing. There were never empty seats; the place was packed! Whitney would lean forward, resting her forearms on her thighs, watching Luther shine until a concert-goer inevitably recognized her.

....

Now it was time for Whitney to headline her own shows. The Greatest Love World Tour ran from July to December 1986, with thirty-five shows in the United States and Canada followed by concerts in Europe, Japan, and Australia. It was unbelievable. I worked on the tour book, T-shirts, hats, buttons, and sweatshirts, and designed my first piece of clothing: Whitney's varsity-style tour jacket with fire-engine-red leather sleeves and "The Greatest Love Tour" written on the back in silver with a single red rose floating high.

Whitney promoted Silvia to be her personal assistant, which would include accompanying her whenever she traveled. We also agreed on hiring Carol Porter as the hair stylist for the tour. Everything was falling into place.

Whitney was like a kid, wanting to have as much fun as possible. In our downtime, Whitney and I would have barefoot hundred-yard dashes down the long hotel corridors, betting dollars on who would get smoked! I won a couple, but she made sure that she was victorious most of the time by talking trash stride for stride. She'd get so excited, and I loved seeing her smile.

Sometimes there would be a hoop outside the back of a venue, and then Nip played defense against me with her head forward, her behind out, and her long arms draped around me—despite my insistence she was fouling. Though her two brothers played, Whitney didn't have any game. Her most memorable play in grade-school basketball was a breakaway layup scoring on the other team's basket. With her determination she might have gotten better, but Cissy said basketball was too rough for her baby girl and made her quit.

Twice, Whit rented an arena for dress rehearsals, and a bunch of us played touch football in the space. In one game, the last play was to hike the ball to Whitney; the entire line would go right, and she was supposed to take two steps behind us before darting off to the left. But instead, Whitney immediately shot to the left. It was as if she were running in slow motion, and then, wham— somehow she connected knee-to-knee with her accountant, who was the only person within fifteen feet of her, then toppled over, hurting her right knee so badly she had to be carried off the field. The injury left her unable to perform in heels for the duration of rehearsal.

After that, it was all about Ping-Pong games and water-gun fights. We traveled with two Ping-Pong tables, but wherever we went throughout the country, we couldn't wait to go to the local toy store and buy up every water gun they had. As many as fifty of us would engage in serious water fights, running through the hotels to refill our guns and then engaging in full combat around the grounds. Whitney carried a Rambo soaker and water balloons. Once, at a Tampa hotel, Whitney lost her emerald ring and the water battle stopped until one of the tour personnel found it in a stairwell off the ballroom.

Before we went overseas, Whitney was so busy she wasn't really using and only occasionally smoked a joint. But I quickly learned that once a tour was under way, there were drugs all around. Dealers would station themselves at every venue or hotel, ready to capitalize on the arrival of an entourage. The guys in production were the first to know where to go if you wanted something, because they were the first to arrive in each city. A band member dubbed it "the Greatest Drug Tour."

If Whitney and I wanted to indulge, her brother Michael was happy to hook us up. Gary was in trouble from the moment the tour started and was always lurking around, spewing negative energy, and then he would suddenly disappear. He'd borrow money from crew members, and when they tried to collect, it would fall to his sister to cover for him. I never once heard Gary congratulate Whitney after a show or thank her. Multiple times, I overheard him backstage saying he was in the studio recording or discussing getting his own record deal, which never happened. Many nights as we huddled up before a show in a prayer circle, holding hands and bowing our heads, Gary would stroll up last and Whitney, leading the prayer, would increase her volume and say, "And, Lord, protect us from this negative energy." Or "Lord, don't allow Satan to have his way. Armor us with your all-knowing, omnipotent power, oh God. We ask in your name, dear Lord—amen."

Gary freebased regularly on the road. He once holed up in the bathroom of Boston's Four Seasons Hotel and his wife, Monique, phoned Whitney's hotel room in a panic because she was so afraid of him. Silvia, whose room was connected to Whit's suite, phoned me saying she'd caught Gary and Michael getting high in her room, the contents of his black toiletry bag on full display. Silvia sat staring until they said she was blowing their high and eventually got up and left.

One time we went to an industry party and there were a few people sitting on a sofa talking. On the coffee table in front of them sat a bowl filled with cocaine. I had a little appetite, and it wouldn't have been a problem if I'd picked up a plate and spooned a few teaspoons onto it. But I didn't. After all, someone had to get up in the morning and get work done. Sometimes I had the urge to get high with Nip and Michael, or maybe by myself at night, but it was never my desire to get into a marathon with anyone. Having experienced my share of staying up all night, I knew the conclusion was always the same: folks looking crazy, hair jacked, eyes big and blinking rapidly, dry mouthed and tongue-tied, thirsty 'cause it's all gone and you're looking for ways to get more.

There were long days and late nights, but the work was exciting, so I tried to keep to myself more and more, curling up in my bunk on the tour bus, which usually rolled out from each city in the wee hours, around two or three A.M. If I was strong enough to resist temptation, I'd peek through the curtain, and if it looked as if it had been a bad night, I'd hold out a sandwich as folks straggled by. Everyone thought it was kind of funny, but I knew how they were really feeling. They were hurtin'.

At this point, Gary bothered me regularly, mumbling under his breath, staring darkly. One day, as I was about to board the bus, he appeared out of nowhere, stood in front of me, and yelled in my face, "You're not in charge!" Caught off guard, I walked around him and silently climbed the stairs. One of the singers said, "He's so crazy," and Carol added, "Scary, too!" I took a window seat, and as the bus rolled away, Gary was still standing on the sidewalk staring through the glass at me. I didn't have a clue how to react but I'd regained my composure, so as we drove by him, I stuck out my tongue.

At the top of every show, Whitney would say to the audience, "I'll make you a deal. You give me some of you and I'll give you all of me." And she did just that: She gave her all and was sweaty and spent at the end of each show. She enjoyed herself, but sometimes after a performance there would be a few folks who wanted something more from her. Once, when we were walking the long corridor of a venue in Virginia leading from backstage to the dressing rooms, we passed two young women in their twenties like us, and one of them loudly said, "Look, she don't know nobody," trying to call her out for not greeting them. Whitney, flanked by security, came to an abrupt stop, turned around, and walking right up to the one who'd spoken, said, "You're right, I don't know you."

At US stops, Whitney mostly stayed in the hotel. The crew would locate a restaurant and then she might join in, but most of the time she didn't want to go out. She was a homebody even on the road. Silvia and Cissy's friend Aunt Bae packed what they could to make her feel at home. There was a large case on rollers filled with Nippy's favorite comfort foods: Fruity Pebbles, Cap'n Crunch, tuna fish, Ritz crackers, and peanut butter. Wherever we stopped, Nippy would ask us to pick up coloring books and crayons for her, a relaxing pastime she enjoyed whenever she had free time. I used to tell her that she should sign them and hand them out to fans, but she probably did so only once.

Not long after I met her, Whitney said, "Stick with me, and I'll take you around the world." And now she was doing just that. This time, Whitney, Silvia, and I flew the Concorde to London while the rest of the crew were taking the eight-hour flight. Aunt Bae was upset about Silvia's flying with Nip while she wasn't invited. "Why are you flying on the Concorde?" she demanded. "'Cause Whitney said so," Silvia answered, looking a little like a kid standing up to a bully. When we arrived at Heathrow Airport, the three of us descended the airplane stairs and were met by paparazzi. "Follow me," Whit said. She looked ready for it in her sunglasses and brimmed hat, taking long strides with that walk of hers that verged on pimping—an international star.

The country I really fell in love with was Japan. Akihabara made Times Square look like it needed more lights! The way that place was lit up, it felt electrifying. I went out at both the beginning and the end of the day, and the energy was always the same, always buzzing. The music stores had all the latest audio equipment, electronic gadgets, and a vast collection of what seemed like every artist who'd ever released a record. Artists were so revered that you could find every little thing a singer or group ever recorded. I probably spent my per diem earnings solely on rare Chaka Khan, Rufus, Motown, and Philly sound recordings—all the classics.

As for food, there was no such thing as a California roll. Instead, I spent days eating tender, fresh sushi rolls in restaurants where you could point to the fish of your choice in the window. The presentation of everything was lovely—even a bottle of Coca-Cola was poured with a flourish over three perfect ice cubes. Some nights, when I was feeling a little homesick, I'd go downstairs to the restaurant at the Capitol Tokyo, where we were staying, and order spaghetti Bolognese. This wasn't necessarily what I ate at home, but given where I was, it seemed familiar. A lot of times I'd find Michael down there, and we'd ask the waiters in their beige coats for hot sauce to add to our pasta. For the most part Michael was good to me, friendly, easygoing, and affectionate. His disposition was similar to Nippy's.

Nobody was looking for cocaine in Japan. The closest thing I had to a habit there was the blueberry gum I bought in the hotel gift shop. Maybe it was because there was a language barrier, but instead of getting high, we spent time mingling with concertgoers after the shows. People bowed and called me Robyn-san.

We were in so many cities: Osaka, Yokohama, Tokyo, and on later tours, Sendai, Fukuoka, and Hiroshima. In Hiroshima, we made sure to visit a park that was a symbol of peace in remembrance of the war, the living, and the devastation of life caught in the path of nuclear bombs in World War II. We saw statues of adults, kids, toddlers, babies—everybody who had been going through their everyday lives before everything changed.

En route to one of our shows, the traffic in Tokyo was so terrible we had been at a standstill for long enough to be concerned. We called ahead to the Budokan arena, afraid Whitney wasn't going to make the curtain. They sent a motorcycle, and Whitney, without hesitation, hopped on the back and made it. Once onstage, she was in the zone: calm, cool, and collected. Most of the people probably couldn't speak a word of English, but they all knew her songs.

Our next stop, Australia, was magical—the climate, the water, the beach, the people. We played touch football on the front lawn of the parliament house in the capital, Canberra. Melbourne's weather and walkability reminded me of San Francisco. The audiences were mostly white, but we made a point of meeting and breaking bread with Aboriginals. We traded beautiful, elaborate handmade belts and bags for swag and tickets to the show.

The exchange rate for the US dollar was very favorable, so

cocaine seemed like a bargain. One night after a show, I was sitting in Whitney's room, and Michael said he was going out to get some and would be back in five minutes. When he finally showed, it was eleven o'clock the next morning. Getting high at that point just seemed crazy to me. I had a thirst for being outdoors instead. I also was ready to go home.

I missed my car and bed, eating bags of chips instead of crisps; I missed sweet potato pie and I missed my family. When the tour was officially over and we came home to America in time for Christmas, we kissed the tarmac.

Ten

The Moment of Truth

While we were on tour, Clive had started working on songs for the second album, *Whitney*. Whit was back home for a stretch, but her plan to rest had to be scrapped because Clive insisted she ride the wave of her unprecedented success.

Starting in December 1986, we made several trips to Narada Michael Walden's Tarpan Studios in San Rafael, California. It was a beautiful, calming space, and Nip was happy to be there. Whitney and Narada had a great vibe. While she was in the booth, he would close his eyes and press the palms of his hands together, holding them at his heart. A beautiful, contented smile would cross his face. His approach, like his demeanor, was gentle, and he handled the board with subtlety, pushing the levers up or down gradually. Nip called him "Peace, Love, and Happiness."

Just as she did on the first album, Whitney always left with a cassette tape from the day's recording so she could listen overnight and return to the studio the next day ready to jump in. Her background vocals alone would liven up any party. I had watched Whitney sing countless times in church, at rehearsals, at performances live and in the studio, and she never ceased to amaze me.

I was always paying attention, my eyes on Whitney. Because of this, Narada sometimes asked for my input. "Sit here, Robbie," he'd say, using Whit's nickname for me. "Listen to this one. Did you hear the difference?"

She would do a take and Narada would say, "Perfect, now do another one, just like that." Even if her pass at a line was perfect, he had the patience to see what possibilities could unfold during a session, and Whitney had the stamina to do one take after another; she would work until they both were satisfied. Narada, always sensitive to energy, occasionally would turn around and ask, "How is she, Robbie? She okay?" When we completed the recordings, he said Nip needed a getaway and recommended Kona Village Resort on Hawaii's Big Island. Off we went for two serene, television-and-phone-free weeks, gorging on fresh fruit and sharing our room with the geckos and iguanas.

Narada produced more songs and had more hits with Whit than anyone. "I'm Every Woman," the anthem penned by Nick Ashford and Valerie Simpson, was originally delivered by Chaka Khan, on her debut album, with none other than Cissy Houston on backing vocals. Because she trusted him, Whitney phoned Narada to produce it. She instructed, "Don't change it. Do it just like the original. And keep Val's piano." After that initial recording, David Cole and Robert Clivillés of C&C Music Factory were brought in to create dance remixes. As David was also a native East Oranger, Nip agreed to go into the studio with them to record additional vocals for the clubs.

....

𝒪𝓃ℯ day I needed a break, so I asked Michelle to accompany Whitney to rehearsal at SIR in Manhattan, and Whitney drove to the studio in her silver Range Rover. On the way back, traffic was at a crawl, and another car tapped her car door while they were inching into the Lincoln Tunnel. Whitney got out of her car and started cursing the other driver out. Michelle yelled at her to get back in because it was just a little tap. Then the driver, who had started to apologize, suddenly said, "Oh, shoot. You're Whitney Houston." This snapped her to attention, and she quickly got back in the car and they drove away. Even after her successful debut album and world tour, it was still a surprise sometimes for her to be recognized.

After that incident, she became a little hesitant about going out and being spotted, but I convinced her that if she went to the Short Hills mall around eleven A.M., there would be only moms and babies there, so most people wouldn't recognize her. They were so used to seeing Whitney all done up, and she never looked like that day to day. You really had to look at her closely—like that driver had—for her features to come into focus. She wasn't hiding, but she wasn't declaring herself, either.

And then there were people who still didn't recognize Whitney at all, even up close. One time, she was at Neiman Marcus in Beverly Hills with Silvia and wanted to look at a bracelet. She waited while not one but two white men behind the counter assisted another customer, who was also white. Silvia asked if someone could help them and was told to wait, so she went over to a young man working at another counter and asked him for assistance. He pulled the bracelet out of the case for them, and after a few minutes, he said admiringly, "You're Whitney Houston." All of a sudden, the two salesmen were available, but Silvia wasn't having it.

She told them, "Oh, now you want to come over? Before, you thought you could just ignore us because we are a Spanish girl and a black girl? Now you find out the black girl is Whitney Houston, so here you come." Whitney, who had been quiet up until then, asked the young man who had helped them, "Do you work on commission?" He nodded, and she said, "Go get your manager. I want to buy it from you."

....

Around this time, Robert De Niro became an admirer of Whitney's—one she had trouble shaking. The first time he called, we were in London shooting the video for "How Will I Know." Peter Barron, then head of video production at Arista, told me De Niro wanted to take Whitney out to dinner. At nearly midnight the following day, after a sixteen-hour shoot, I answered the phone in her hotel room and heard, "This is Bob De Niro. Can I speak to Whitney?" I relayed the message, and she looked at me and said, "No." A few months later at a music industry event in New York, a stagehand came to Nip's dressing room to say that Robert De Niro was holding for her on the backstage pay phone. "He must be crazy," Whitney said. This time she took the call and I don't remember exactly what she said to him, but she did let him down gently.

One afternoon, Mr. Houston called with some "exciting news" about an amazing house he'd found for us. It turned out to be more surprising than exciting: Neither Whitney nor I had mentioned any-thing about wanting to move. Our apartment was a stone's throw from Whitney's office and a bridge away from Harlem, and we were both perfectly content. Mr. Houston insisted that we at least ride over to the property to look at it. After an interminable drive, we ended up in a part of New Jersey I'd never been to before. The house was newly constructed, and you could tell. There was no landscaping, and while there was an outdoor area that looked like the perfect place for a pool, one hadn't been installed.

The house was modern, and unique, with its round rooms and floor-to-ceiling windows that flooded the space with natural light. She seemed at home, even happy, as we walked the property, which was surrounded by sandy dirt. When she asked me what I thought, I told her I liked it but that it might be too far from the city—far from everything, actually. Mr. Houston defended the decision, saying that Whitney was getting too famous and needed privacy. She didn't dispute that, so she bought her first home for more than $2 million.

I was surprised by the change. We would be giving up the convenience of living moments from the city. Sure, with a two-bedroom condo I felt we could have used some extra space, but not a twelve-thousand-square-foot house that we had absolutely no idea what to do with.

....

After we'd been home for a while, Carol took out Whitney's weave. Under her care and direction, Whitney's hair had grown so much under the weave that it now almost skimmed her shoulders. I was glad to see how long and healthy it was and hoped this meant the end of her hair concerns.

I was standing there in her new kitchen. Whitney came out of her room, and Cissy, who had come over unannounced, took one look at her daughter and said, "You took your hair out? You look like a damn man.

"What are you going to do when you have an interview or something?" Cissy continued, oblivious to the wounded look on Whitney's face. Whitney remained silent, so I said, "We thought she would give her hair a chance to breathe and let Carol condition it now that showtime is over."

"What are you going to do when you have to do something?" Cissy said, ignoring me.

Whitney looked me in the eye and said, "Well, that's true, I will have some things to do."

"You just came off the whole tour. You do what's best for you," I said. To my mind, that meant maybe to hire a trainer and follow a regimen, to learn to take care of herself and maybe get involved with something other than singing, like rest. After some time off the road, I was starting to see that idle time was not Whitney's friend.

"You can't be walking around looking like that," Cissy insisted.

At that time, my own hair was still shoulder length and I didn't like to get it wet. Whitney, who swam like a fish, used to say about me, "Robyn's hair governs her life," and she was right. Like many black women, I acted as if water was the kiss of death. Eventually I would cut it all off and free myself, but Whitney was now moving in the opposite direction. After Cissy's pronouncement that day, it seemed that a weave became a permanent feature.

Meanwhile, rumors about Whitney and me were flying as high as her career. At that point, Whitney and I hadn't been physical for several years, so the whole thing was pretty ridiculous to me. The speculation initially made us tighter, because we knew our truth. Whitney often wanted me by her side, and she didn't want anyone new jumping on her bandwagon. "I already have a friend. I don't need any more." Our bond was cemented, and we kept what we'd shared close. Her mother didn't like it at all and told Whitney, "It's not natural for two women to be that close."

Every time I went to the supermarket, I saw at least one tabloid magazine with my face on the cover. I tried to ignore the gossip, but the Houstons couldn't abide it, least of all Cissy. With her, I learned to just roll with things.

I had nicknamed Cissy "Big Cuda," short for "Barracuda," because of the aggressive way she carried herself. It got to the point where I'd put on this bright-eyed look and cement a smirk on my face whenever she started talking. I wasn't trying to be disrespectful, but I was no longer a child and didn't need her affirmation. I just wanted to keep the peace. I knew at some point the time would come for me to push back, to stand up for myself, but not yet.

Having been recorded at head-spinning speed, Nip's second album, *Whitney*, was poised for release in June of 1987. One day before the album's release, I was at Arista for meetings, and the head of R&B promotions told me that radio stations were calling up in gossip mode asking what the story was between us. During interviews about her new album, out of nowhere they would ask Whitney something like, "So . . . are you dating anyone?" She politely diverted such conversations by saying her private life was her own, but they'd ask anyway. The first single off the album, "I Wanna Dance with Somebody," was an instant hit, and even after that huge source of buzz was out, an interviewer would drop a non sequitur: "So, is there someone special in your life?"

After a radio interview, we'd get in the car and Whitney would say, "Really? Are *you* dating anyone, motherfucker? Did you get laid last night? How was it?" That's what she wanted to say to them. We laughed and let it roll off of us. They did the same thing to Dionne, after all, and other women were usually subjected to this, too. When *Whitney* was released, she became the first woman to debut an album at number 1; her second album was making history, but even that wasn't the main focus.

The tabloids were one thing, but when Richard Corliss of *Time* magazine decided to include the rumors in a big article that ran in July 1987, it seemed to make this a standard line of questioning, even for reputable publications. I was present listening to the interview, and Whitney called me over to the reporter and asked me to share my thoughts on all the speculation about our relationship. "I tell my family, 'You can hear anything on the streets, but if you don't hear it from me, it's not true,'" I said. I was still trying to figure things out about myself, so I wasn't ready to declare anything to my family, let alone to the public.

Whitney added, "People see Robyn with me, and they draw their own conclusions. Anyway, whose business is it if you're gay or like dogs?"

I didn't like it when she talked like this, and we discussed how she might best handle herself in situations like these, but she never wanted to find the time to sit down and prep for interviews. And this rumor had stamina. When she compared homosexuality to bestiality or spoke so rigidly about herself as a man's woman, it seemed to me as if she was desperately trying to throw off the hounds. Her protests were too much and sometimes unkind. However, she was 100 percent right that whomever she was sleeping with was her business. When the *Time* article came out, Corliss described me as "severely handsome," which felt like a low blow. My mother didn't like it, either, and told me, "You're a beautiful woman," reassuring me as she had done when I was much younger.

"You okay?" Whitney would frequently ask after we'd run a paparazzi gauntlet or left a press event where someone scrutinized our relationship for the millionth time. Once we were back in the car, she'd tightly squeeze my hand, as if making sure I was still there. She wanted to reassure me that no matter what people were saying about me—about us—we were steady, that I was important to her and worthy. Her shout-out to me on the liner notes for *Whitney* read, "Robyn, you are my friend and you are also quite an assistant. Be strong for you are a child of the Almighty God and you walk in his love and in his light. I love you, Whitney."

Eleven

Tell On Your Damned Self

Whitney was a little strange: As open as she could be with me, she was also very private. She loved her quiet and spoke only when she wanted to. But when she was in a mood to talk, there was no stopping her. Some days she spent more time talking to Jesus than she did to me. I would hear her in her bedroom, but I was careful not to listen in on such a private act. I knew she was alone, in prayer, but sometimes she sounded so animated—the way you speak to another person—that one day I asked her, "Nip, who were you talking to in there?" She gave me a surprised look and said, "Jesus. Who do you think?"

There were times when I would be in that big, empty house, bored, just waiting for a sound. I might hear Whitney moving around a little, but the true indicator was the click of her double doors opening and the muffled sound of her shuffling in the white terry-cloth hotel slippers she loved to wear out into the long tiled hall leading to the kitchen and returning with her usual snack of a bowl of cereal.

Whitney was not a morning person, and if she worked all night, you'd be lucky to see her rise before late afternoon. She was a homebody who enjoyed swimming, lounging by the pool, watching television, playing with MisteBlu and Marilyn—and, above all, listening to music. I was usually up early, dressed and ready for action. When Nip finally surfaced, in her pajamas, I'd immediately launch into what I'd been doing while she slept. She would put her index finger to her lips, silently shushing me.

Whit and I talked about how we needed to change our bad habits by replacing them with good ones. I suggested bike riding and then jogging. One day she agreed, and we went out for a run down the road near our house. When we finally made it to the last corner of our half-mile run—which really was more like a half-jog and half-walk—the plan was that we'd sprint to the finish. But instead, Nip said she was tired and thirsty and wanted a cigarette.

As a housemate, Whitney was boring as hell unless some music got down. Once she got the music going, though, the show was on and she'd come alive. Silvia and I enjoyed the energy generated by Whitney's playlist: Chaka, Stevie, Change, Walter and Tramaine Hawkins, Andraé Crouch, the Winans, and Fred Hammond. Or we'd all sing along with BeBe and CeCe, René and Angela, and El DeBarge, the music blaring through the house and outside, and then soon we three would be in the pool!

....

Our cooking skills had not improved much and, constantly on the go, we needed to eat healthy to keep up with the demands of her schedule. So, I suggested we hire a chef. Whit gave me the green light and then told me a few days later that she needed to hire Aunt Bae for the job. She had taken care of Whitney and her brothers when their mother was on the road, and now Cissy said Bae needed money, so Nip felt she owed her. "I really don't want her in my house; she's nosy and will just report back to my mother what's going on. But she can really use the money. It'll be all right," Nip said.

Though she kept her word by hiring Bae, Whitney would allow only Silvia to bring a tray with a prepared meal to her bedroom or to her hotel suite when on the road. Once, when we were on tour, Bae was staying at another hotel and was cooking meals and bring-ing them over to Nip's hotel, where Silvia and I were also staying. The room phone rang, I answered, and it was Bae saying she was coming up with the food. I told Nip who it was and was about to give Bae the room number when Nippy said, "No. Tell her Silvia will come down to get it."

Of course, Aunt Bae and Cissy didn't care if that was how Nip wanted things to go. They seemed to feel that they should be the closer ones. And this would set the tone; if they didn't like some-thing that Whit said, wanted, or did for herself or someone else, even if it was crystal clear that the decision came directly from Whitney herself, Silvia's ass was always grass—and I would never be clear of the mower, either.

In the midst of the first tour the previous year, Nippy Inc. had moved to a new building. The space was gutted and renovated, and the new, largest office was meant for Whitney. Cissy threw a fit when she saw she didn't have an office. So, to keep the peace, Nippy gave her own office to her father, and her mother took the one originally designated for her father. The boss was now in a much smaller of-fice next to mine. By the time we completed the move to the new office, John Houston had become president and Cissy was anointed vice president, though she was rarely present. From then on, unless we were traveling, touring, recording, or doing another artist-related activity, I went in every day, with or without the boss.

After the release of *Whitney*, I took on an even greater role with requests, scheduling, and special projects. I was also handling scripts, traveling to LA with Whitney for meetings with writers and producers, putting together TV and radio spots for tour announcements, hiring photographers for album covers, documenting tours, and working closely with creative teams on televised specials and endorsements. All requests for Whitney Houston came through me; you name it, I was on top of it.

But my hands were tied when I didn't know financial details. John Houston would not share anything regarding contracts or money with me. This frustrated me greatly: I was representing Whitney, and not knowing exactly what the fine print said made me look weak and Nippy Inc. look disjointed. I didn't have the juice to make big decisions or weigh in effectively, and if Nip wasn't around, I had to go to John and ask questions—which he hated, asking me why I needed to know. Still, I kept at it because I really wanted to learn as much as I could. Nippy's career was going up, up, up, and I felt the need to strategize in a way that would keep us ahead of the game.

....

One evening, Whitney and I went over to visit Michael and his wife, Donna. The four of us were doing coke. It was getting late. Nip knew we had work the next day, and I wanted to go home, so I kept asking her to pack it up, but she didn't want to. I was prepared to leave and take the car, but after dabbling myself, I didn't think it was a good idea to drive. Desperate to get out of there, I called Silvia.

Silvia came, and as I was walking toward the car and about to open the door, Whitney yelled, "Who the fuck do you think you work for? I pay you!" Michael and Donna were standing in the window as Whitney railed, "Oh, so you're a chauffeur now. I pay you to be a damn chauffeur, huh? That's okay. You and I are gonna talk when I get home. Take Robyn's ass home before I kill her." As I sat in the passenger seat like a lost puppy, Silvia looked at me as if to say, "What the hell? Now I'm in big trouble," but I just looked ahead and said, "Drive off. She doesn't know what she's saying."

Cocaine was making me feel isolated and off my game. I was growing concerned again about our increased drug use. By nature, I awakened with the birds, but if I was up late partying, I dreaded the morning. It wasn't that I felt I couldn't stop; it was the fact that I was using at all, even casually. My brother rarely used drugs, and Bina never did. My mother wasn't even a smoker, and as far as I knew, my father didn't indulge in anything besides beer and Tareyton cigarettes. I was the only one in my family who was athletic (other than my father), and before I'd started messing around with drugs I'd typically refused to take any medicine, even aspirin.

Wanting to understand why I was getting high, I called a meeting with my family: I asked my mother, my brother, and my sister to come to my mother's home. I also called my father. Mom wasn't too happy about that. Having survived his violence and raised my siblings and me solo, she didn't feel he deserved to be in her space. I was coming down when I made the call, coming out of being up all night. And Whitney was still at home getting high.

"Where is this coming from?" I asked them, wondering if they had done similar things when they were young but hadn't told me. Did either of them struggle with alcohol or drugs? I wanted them to know I needed help.

"And you felt you had to call your father here," my mother said resentfully.

I wanted to stop doing what I was doing and was looking for some kind of guidance. I felt like I was failing. After my father left the meeting, Mom told me, "Don't ever call your father to my house again. You need to take better care of yourself and think more about who you are."

Meanwhile, a little separation was starting to develop between Nip and me. No matter what rules we came up with around responsible drug use, she kept breaking them and using whenever she wanted to. Her career was in high gear, and my hands were full at the office and the calls didn't stop when I was at home, either. I was juggling what the record company needed her to do, performances, interviews, recording schedules, and ongoing business opportunities that came to the office, by mail, so I had to be on. I couldn't be rolling out of bed feeling like shit.

The real issue was that we'd agreed that cocaine could not go with us, and once again she was finding it difficult to fulfill her part of that agreement. That's when I knew she wasn't having fun. She liked this stuff too much, even at the expense of the dreams we were aspiring to reach. When I suggested that things were getting out of hand and that she might have a problem, she responded, "Don't worry about me. Whitney can take care of herself."

It wasn't long before I told Cissy about the cocaine use yet again. This time, I called and told on Whitney, Michael, Donna, and myself. But nothing ever came of it, except my having to deal with Michael, Donna, and a somewhat chilly Whitney. Donna told me, "The next time you feel like telling on someone, tell on your damned self!" We were all around the same age, and you know what happens when one person chooses not to go along—that person usually gets pushed out. Nippy never said anything about my telling her mom directly, but it was clear that she wasn't listening to my warnings about drugs. A week or so later, Whitney was in her room at the house when Cissy came over. She approached me near the pool and confronted me about what I'd said over the phone. "She likes it too much," I said. "I can stop, but she can't." Cissy said, "I appreciate you telling me," and went on her way.

....

Despite how well *Whitney* was selling, there was a backlash about the album's crossover appeal. I'll admit the look was at the other end of the spectrum—from short, slicked-back hair on the cover of album one to the big hair on *Whitney*. And just maybe her skin looked a bit lighter than it did on the first album, but then the image was taken under studio lights.

Though the artwork for the highly anticipated sophomore album did go along with the product, Jon Pareles in the *New York Times* wrote a harsh review with the headline "She's Singing by Formula." Another reviewer wrote that she was too controlled by the strategic Clive Davis and wasn't taking any chances, sarcastically referring to "I Wanna Dance with Somebody" as "How Will I Know II." In any case, none of the criticism stopped *Whitney* from climbing the charts. "Didn't We Almost Have It All," "So Emotional," and "Where Do Broken Hearts Go" would all reach number 1, making seven consecutive number 1 hits by February 1988 and breaking the record set by the Beatles and Elvis.

There was no way anyone could say the unprecedented success

of her debut was a fluke, but there was a great deal of anticipation and scrutiny from the press, along with the expectations of her label. I was acutely aware of how many days she was singing consecutively, what territories had heavy press attendance, her set list, and how hard her voice would be working. By this time, there were lots of people who thought they knew what was best, but as long as I had Whitney's ear, things were good.

On the other hand, I already knew that Cissy and John's relationship was putting a lot of pressure on Nip, and I didn't want to get caught up in it. I tried to keep out of the line of fire and do my best for their daughter. In my opinion, Whitney's mother was someone who really cared about what other people thought, but sometimes I felt her obsession with the gay rumors masked her concern about something else: the depth of our friendship. It had crossed my mind that perhaps Cissy was angry because Whitney was living farther away and I was there. She was bitter about not having a closer relationship with her daughter, and that wasn't my fault. On Mother's Day, Whitney and her brothers weren't picking up Cissy and taking her out like Marty, Bina, and I did for our mom.

I felt bad for Cissy, because when Nippy needed her mother to talk to, she couldn't, and when Cissy needed or wanted the closeness of her daughter, by that point Whitney didn't want to be bothered with her. One afternoon at the house, Cissy buzzed at the gate and Whitney said, "Don't answer it." On the video monitor, I watched Cissy back away from the gate. More often, her mother would come unannounced and sit in the kitchen with Aunt Bae.

"Where's Nippy?" Cissy would ask me.

"She's in her room. Go knock on her door," I'd say. If Cissy chose to knock, often there was no answer.

Twelve

Moving Fast at Twice the Speed

Just seven months after we returned home from the Greatest Love World Tour, *Whitney* was out and it was time to go back on the road again, this time for the Moment of Truth World Tour. Starting in July 1987 and running all the way through November 1988, we had sixty-one North American dates, followed by Europe, Japan, Australia, and Hong Kong. It wound up being the highest-grossing tour by a female artist in 1987.

This tour, we traveled in higher style than we had on the Greatest Love Tour: The bus was deluxe, and Whitney had a full bed, though she usually opted for a bunk like the rest of us. We now had two security guards, so Whit could have security escort her everywhere.

Also new was the addition of dancers, including Khandi Alexander, partway through the tour. Khandi and dancer-turned-choreographer Damita Jo Freeman were in the audience at the

1988 American Music Awards, where Whitney performed and took home three trophies. After the show, Damita penned a detailed letter to Cissy making the case for the inclusion of dancers in Whitney's act. Up until that point, the belief was that people came to hear Whitney's vocals, which were so extraordinary she didn't need any enhancement. Damita's pitch was that while this was true, Whit was young and had the energy and talent to do both. Slated to open the 1988 Grammy Awards, Whitney decided to give it a try on the Recording Academy's dime. She agreed to have Damita and Khandi choreograph a number and hire several dancers, and they went to work. Sitting in the audience at Radio City Music Hall on the day of the ceremony, I watched Nip sing and dance her way through a six-minute version of "I Wanna Dance with Somebody" that included all kinds of moves from the Hustle to the Cabbage Patch—all in sling-back stilettos. The next day, Janet Jackson called the house to congratulate Whitney on her dance moves. Whitney enjoyed the interaction with the dancers and doing the choreography so much that she decided to add dancers for the second leg of the tour.

A lot of the critics at home reviewed her shows like they knew better than she did about what songs she should sing and how they should be sung! On the first tour, people would comment on her hair or say that her clothing was matronly, which was true. On the second tour, chatter about her appearance wasn't so much in the air, but they would always find something to pick at, even though she and her albums were breaking records and her tours were sold out. It seemed as if the critics were only looking for what she didn't have and didn't do!

Whitney was singing her tail off, and it never even crossed her mind to lip-sync anything, not even during a video. Still, the feedback was: "She doesn't dance, she's as stiff as a cardboard box." But

I didn't see them call out performers who danced with such high energy and elaborate choreography that there was no way to avoid singing to a track. At some point, a critic has to take a seat and acknowledge that millions of people the world over can't be wrong. The audience bought the tickets, and people of all ages and demographics enjoyed themselves. I know because I was out there.

When I watched Whitney working so hard onstage, I just wanted to give her a hug. That was my friend and I wanted her to know that I understood. In the earlier years, if she spotted me in the crowd, she might wink, but for the most part when she saw me, her gaze would linger, almost as if she was looking for something. Like she was trying to see herself through my eyes, and I became her mirror in that moment.

As Nip and I packed our bags for Europe in spring 1988, it was time to look for a responsible person to not only care for our pets, MisteBlu, Marilyn, and the new Akitas, Lucy and Ethel, but also to respect and protect our home. Since Silvia was joining us and Whitney didn't trust her brothers with the task, she asked me if I knew of someone. I said, "The only person I know is *my* brother." Marty still was living down south, after having been honorably discharged from the service. So Michelle and I drove Whitney's silver Range Rover to North Carolina to bring him back up. Other than being a little thin, Marty looked great, was full of energy, and was excited to come up to the house.

....

Before we flew out for the European tour, I again tried to broach the subject of substance use. I was growing increasingly worried about cocaine and didn't like what it did to us, but Nip was fearless and fine getting high without me. I suggested that we put rules in place, like "No getting high when there's work to do" or "No getting high after a certain time," and definitely "No getting high in groups!" This was particularly dangerous, because those sessions could go on all night with no one keeping track of what was going on. She appeared to be on board because she knew it was in our best interest, but I wasn't sure the commitment would hold while she was on the road.

I wasn't the only one who was concerned. My mom had some words of wisdom for me. Recently she'd sat me down and rubbed her hands together as she always did when something was on her mind. "Robyn," she said, "I thought that you would take better care of your body. You surprise me. You know, Whitney has her brothers to be there for her if something happens. But if something happens to you, they'll be sending you home to me in a box." Those words, and the way she looked at me while saying them, reverberated through my body. Mom knew me so well, and somehow she understood what I was up against.

....

On tour, Whitney was facing down nine sold-out shows at London's Wembley Arena, which meant we'd be there for weeks, with all the temptation that came with a long stay in a big city. I knew we'd have access to anything we wanted. That was the nature of traveling with an entourage. Just like on the last tour, people were expecting us and knew where we were staying. So if anybody was looking for trouble, it wouldn't be long before they found it, or it found them. Late at night, doors would open and close, footsteps would creak down the hall, voices would whisper. I didn't want any of that trouble, so as soon as we landed, I decided to play it safe, stay in my room, and listen to music.

Gary had been in rehab for most of the US leg of the tour. He joined us in London, but he was far from healed. Because Cissy was on this tour, he was a bit more visible than he'd been on the last one, but there were still times when he would disappear or engage in strange behavior. He tried to cozy up to me once as I sat on a bench in catering. "Hey, hey, Rob, come here," he said, putting his arm around me. "Why don't we go grab a bite to eat or something?" I didn't want to go anywhere with him, let alone break bread alone with him. He had a jealous spirit. Gary's whole delivery and con-man lingo gave me the creeps.

Michael was funny, sensitive, and caring, but he was in trouble, too. Before we had first left for the tour, most days he would park in the back of the underground parking garage of Nippy Inc. for hours, getting high. On tour, he was Whitney's main source for coke.

When we reached London, it was a good thing I decided to keep my head down for the most part, because Big Cuda was on the prowl. So as the days stacked up, I stayed away from the scene, listened to music, and tried to keep to myself. Now when Michael asked me, "You in?" my answer was, "No."

....

One morning in London, I got a call from Joy, one of Whitney's dancers, inviting me out for a day of sightseeing. I love London, especially the parks, and it was an absolutely gorgeous sunny day, so I accepted. It wasn't an issue if anyone in the executive crew spent time with someone in the band or crew—unless that person was me, as it turned out.

I hadn't seen Whitney for at least a day and could imagine what she and Michael had been doing. I checked in with Silvia, who confirmed that Whitney was catching up on some much-needed sleep, and I told her that I was going out. Then I hit the town with Joy. She was tall, with curly, long bushy hair and fair skin— attractive. I didn't know her well, having spent time around her only during rehearsals, but I thought she was cool.

I was glad to be out and about for most of the day, but when I returned to the hotel, I learned that all hell had broken loose while I was gone. It turned out that Silvia had decided to go out and grab a bite with one of the crew. She'd taken her walkie-talkie but didn't realize it wouldn't work once she got out of range. When Nippy awakened and realized everyone was gone, she was pissed. Enter Big Cuda, to the rescue!

For years, I'd tried to accept Cissy and follow Whitney's advice: "You know how my mother is. You have to ignore her." So I never took her attacks personally. That is, until that day.

I was standing in the bedroom of Nip's Four Seasons suite, be-tween the television and the bed, and Nip was standing off to the side, crying. Big Cuda walked up to me, about half an arm's length away, berating me as though I was somehow responsible for her daughter's unhappiness.

"What do you think you're doing going off like that? You should be where she can find you. Do you know what you're supposed to be doing? You're working!"

I snapped and told Cissy, "I don't have to listen to this. You should save this talk for your children," then I made the mistake of attempting to step past her and walk away. She went to grab me but was so angry and unfocused that her hands snatched at my clothing, like a cat in a fight. When I turned back, she slapped me across the face. Nippy screamed, "No, Mommy, stop!" and she did.

Later that day, I went to talk to Carol, and with my luck found her doing Cissy's hair. Carol gave me a sympathetic look, periodically shaking her head as she continued working.

"You all right, Robyn?" Cissy asked, breaking the thick silence.

"Yeah," I answered. "I got a few scratches, but I'm fine." This was the closest thing to an apology I would ever get from her. But I knew she was sorry.

That evening I would find out that Nippy had been feeling weak and alone. And when I told her about my day, she asked, "Did you sleep with her? Don't lie to me."

I told her, "We kissed. We didn't take off our clothes—" Then, out of nowhere, Whitney slapped me—my second slap of the day, for those keeping count, but at least this one was followed by a hug and an apology. She then picked up a few little pieces of black hash with a bobby pin and started lighting each one with a match. As we inhaled the floating smoke, our mood mellowed, becoming light and easy.

Later that night, Whitney opened up, telling me that for the first time, she was feeling as if she had no voice to do what she needed to do. She felt the beginnings of a cold, and the show at Wembley was the next day. She was worn down, feeling pressure from everywhere. "I'm letting all the people down. I can't cancel!"

"Yes, you can," I said. "Yes, you can. Even Muhammad Ali had to have someone to throw in the towel." I often told Nip that she was like a champion boxer, and that boxers don't know when they've had enough. Instead, they just keep taking jab after jab, hit after hit, and need someone in their corner to give them an out before they crumble. I went into the bathroom, brought out a white hand towel, and threw it on the floor, saying, "There. I did it for you." I could feel her relief as she pulled me in for a big hug before falling fast asleep. I settled in the bed next to her, exhausted from all the drama.

....

1 thought that the issue with Joy had been resolved until we came home for a break in July and Whitney told me she was going to fire her. I countered that there was no reason for her to do that and that Joy didn't do anything to deserve it. But Nip had made up her mind. After Joy found out she was being let go, she called me to say that she wanted to talk to Whitney and have the chance to clear things up. I was with Nip, so I put Joy on speakerphone. She said that it wasn't her intent to cause any disturbances or problems; she just wanted to be friends with me, and with Whitney, too.

Whit responded, "But I don't need any more friends. I hired you to dance, not to make friends, and that's all you had to do." *Wow.* I sat there listening as Nippy ended the call. For the rest of the tour, I felt as if I was tagged: "If you plan on hanging out with Robyn, best think again."

....

It was early 1988, and Whitney was working, working, and working. Around this time, we had been on the road so long that being home around the holidays felt like a vacation. Nonetheless, there were back-to-back award shows and interviews, so our lives were still a blur. And although I was by her side, working with her, I decided that if I was going to continue to grow professionally, I needed her to respect me not only as her friend but as a business partner, too. I thought getting my own place would go a long way toward achieving that. She and I discussed it, and the verdict was that I would look for a place not too far from the house after the tour, later in the year. We found a condo for me thirty minutes away and hired the same interior decorator who designed the house we currently shared. Whitney paid for it all.

A few days before moving into the new condo, I was there checking out the décor when I got a call from Joy, who was in town and wanted to speak face-to-face about what had happened back on the tour. I told Whitney, and she seemed indifferent, until she showed up at the front door of the condo shortly after Joy's arrival. Whitney asked, "Did you two sleep together?" I told her we hadn't, which was the truth, but she was upset and not hearing me. Whitney demanded that I tell my guest (who had managed to discreetly slip onto the back patio) to leave, and when I refused, she abruptly turned around and walked out. Needless to say, the meeting between Joy and me was short and sour, even after I suggested that we go for a drive somewhere and maybe stay overnight at a hotel. She was pretty shaken by all the drama and figured it was best to cut ties and move on. We never saw each other again.

Later that evening, I called Silvia, who'd been waiting in the car, and she told me that Whitney was very upset and had cried the whole drive home.

The next day, Whitney came back to the condo and marched straight to my bedroom. The blue Bible she'd given me was in its place on my headboard. She grabbed it, ripped out the back pages on which we'd both written our messages to each other, and began tearing them into pieces. She forbade me from ever again having Joy come to the condo when I moved in, and I capitulated. She owned the place, after all.

Whitney could be possessive and jealous, but she hadn't stood in my way when I briefly dated a male video director. When she detected a potential situation with another female backup singer, she commented, "Okay, Robyn, remember she's a church girl." I never thought about if I wanted to be with men or women. I was doing just fine. I could attract both.

But I thought Joy had the potential to be more than just a fling, and though I hadn't communicated this to Nip, she was perceptive and must have sensed something different.

Though my new condo was fully furnished, I never actually moved in. I was still so emotionally connected to Whitney and committed to my work that being away from her felt odd. We both admitted we weren't ready to live apart from each other, so after just a night or two away I agreed to stay at the house. Nip sold the condo, taking a loss of $20,000 on the sale, which meant that there was now one more thing that Cissy wouldn't let me forget.

Thirteen

Can I Be Me?

By the end of the eighties, Whitney, Silvia, and I were a team, strategizing our roles and how best to play them. The three of us vacationed together in Antigua and at Whitney's beautiful three-bedroom condo on Williams Island in Fort Lauderdale. Whitney still loved getting away to the beach and running into the water. While she relaxed, I took care of everything career related, with the exception of negotiating the deals.

We each found our role in our little unit, but Nip's family was determined to cause chaos. Cissy and Gary never stopped pushing, picking, poking, elbowing, and shoving—never once looking at how hard we were working or what Whitney wanted. John still didn't like my knowing what was going on with the money. It didn't necessarily mean he was doing something bad, but he didn't like it when I asked questions. I didn't have to do much to get into trouble. One time, when I asked Mr. Houston how I'd upset him, he responded, "You're just breathing, baby."

Silvia had it the worst. Aunt Bae, Cissy, and Michael's wife, Donna, looked down on Silvia, when in fact she was the one who was always there for Whitney. It was Silvia who made sure she'd eaten, rubbed her feet, bathed and massaged her in the wee hours, and held on to her jewelry and wallet, all at Whit's request. She was the one whom Whitney asked to sign her will. Silvia was by her side, honest and loyal, through it all, a task that would become more daunting once Bobby Brown came into the picture.

....

Whitney first met Bobby in 1989 at the Soul Train Music Awards. She was giddy that night, bouncing around, unusually animated. She spotted her dear friends BeBe and CeCe Winans sitting a few rows away from us. Nip went over to say hello, hugging them and laughing. All the while, she kept knocking her bum into the man in the row directly in front of her.

He leaned forward slightly, adjusting himself to try to avoid contact. When that didn't work, he turned to the side and then turned halfway around. It was Bobby Brown. Bobby tuned in while Nip, BeBe, and CeCe continued talking, oblivious. I finally said, "Nip, you keep bumping into Bobby Brown's head." She took notice and said with a smile, "I'm sorry, Bobby." He was cool about it all. He introduced himself to Whitney, she introduced him to BeBe and CeCe, and it was on.

At the time, Nip was interested in Eddie Murphy—whom she'd met in LA at a photo op for "We Are the World" and had spent time with him in New Jersey—but that didn't stop her from testing the waters with Bobby. A few hours before Bobby was supposed to swing by the hotel in Los Angeles, Whitney asked Silvia and me to come to her room. She told us that she and Bobby were going out for a bite and that he might return afterward—which meant that we should disappear or hang out together elsewhere. She also asked us to go to the pharmacy for condoms.

Off we went to the pharmacy to purchase protection for the boss. When we returned, Nippy was still in her bathrobe, listening to music, and we could smell her signature fragrance, Worth. She could never put on too much of that scent, and now it filled the room. After we made the drop, Bobby arrived. Whitney introduced him to Sil and me, and we said hello with a handshake. That was it. Silvia and I disappeared to my room and ordered a room-service dinner, complete with wine and my favorite dessert, crème brûlée with raspberries.

Early the next morning, Whitney called us and asked us to come over to her room. She was strewn across the bed, and we plopped down next to her, eager to hear how the night went.

"We had a good time," she said. She told us he was cool and sexy, smelled really good, and treated her nicely. But he kept saying, "I can't believe I'm with Whitney Houston!"

"I had to tell him to just call me Nippy, please," she said. We all laughed at that one. And then she told us that she didn't use the condoms.

Sil and I stopped laughing and looked at her as if she was nuts. "Geez, Nip," I said. "That was dumb." She didn't say anything, just nodded her head in agreement. Then she said that she wasn't going to get serious with him. I didn't press, but that condom thing really threw me for a loop. I hoped it wouldn't come back to bite her.

Whitney's twenty-sixth birthday was fast approaching, and she got to work planning a big celebration at her house in August 1989. A lot of folks thought it was odd that she hadn't marked her twenty-fifth birthday instead, but she and I often talked about what we'd dubbed "Dumb 25," which was shorthand for all the stupid things we had done just after hitting the quarter-century mark. With that logic, making it to twenty-six was the real milestone. Truthfully, she'd been touring so much that even if she'd wanted a party the year before, she wouldn't have had the time.

Lots of people showed up in the backyard to enjoy music, food, and drinks. Eddie made an entrance with a posse of six dudes but didn't stay longer than twenty minutes. He ventured in only as far from the threshold as was necessary, posting himself near the sliding doors that led to the kitchen, where he and Whitney spoke briefly. Of course, everyone wanted time with the birthday girl, so when she turned around from a brief exchange with another guest, Eddie was gone.

Bobby, on the other hand, came with his brother and mingled with the crowd. His sophomore solo album was burning up the charts, but he seemed relaxed and happy to be there. He looked a bit like a teenager with his Gumby cut, flashy blue outfit, and mischievous smile. Bobby stayed for the duration, drifting outside to the pool and back indoors, looking pleased when he captured Whitney's attention.

Much to my surprise, after the party, Whitney definitely still had her eyes and heart set on Eddie; Bobby was the backup guy. She had managed in that brief encounter to invite Eddie to come back over for dinner the next week.

On the surface, I could see why she was into Eddie. In simple terms, he was Eddie Murphy and she was Whitney Houston. He was a star like her, and he was wealthy like her, and Whitney was smitten. But based on his hot-and-cold behavior, I didn't see any indication of his thinking of her in the same way.

On the day Eddie was supposed to come to the house for dinner, I stopped by the kitchen to grab a plate to take with me, and just before leaving the house, I caught a glimpse of Whitney. She was wearing a classic black dress to the knee and low-heeled slingbacks. She was radiant and beautiful as she circled the intimate table set for two.

I was outside and could see her through the large glass windows. For a moment I thought, *Boy, I wish that she was doing that for me*, but she wasn't. I knew that would never be me with her in that way. Never ever again. And that was the last time I had a thought like that.

The next day, I asked Silvia how the dinner went. Eddie had never shown. He didn't even call. Whitney stayed in her room for the next two days. The house was quiet. You could feel the sadness throughout. I wanted to see her and tell her, "That guy doesn't deserve you."

In spite of this, Whit chose to give Eddie another go. I don't know who called whom, but next thing I knew, she was heading over to his posh house in the gated section of Englewood, New Jersey. This push-and-pull went on for months, and when Eddie's birthday came around in April, Nip decided to surprise him by showing up at his house with a cake, wearing nothing but lingerie and a fur coat, per Aunt Bae's advice. After she waited fifteen minutes outside his gate, one of Eddie's boys came out and told Whitney that she couldn't come in because Eddie was "busy."

Nippy didn't return home that day, or the next. When she finally did, she was a wreck, shaking and barely able to stand up.

Silvia and I took her to her room, and I held her while Sil ran a bath. Whitney was crying and asking, "Why don't they like me?" She'd been on a drug binge and hadn't slept or eaten.

The next time we saw Eddie was on the Paramount lot, where he was filming. Once again, she was chasing Mr. Ed. I kept my distance. Then I heard Whitney shout, "Hey, Robyn! We're going bowling. Wanna go?"

I replied, "No, thanks."

"What's wrong with you?" Eddie said. "You don't like bowling?"

To which I said, "Sure, I like bowling. I just don't want to go bowling with you."

Silvia and I believe that Eddie did a number on Nip's self-worth. He cracked jokes about her, made fun of her weave. He would say, "Whitney and I are just friends." I don't know what they were, but friends they definitely were not.

Whitney was able to speak her mind to me, but she didn't have that same backbone with men. She lost herself in the pursuit of Eddie in spite of how he discarded her and her feelings. Whit really wanted the thing with Eddie to work, and I don't know what he did or didn't promise her behind closed doors. What I do know is that he gave Whitney a diamond ring that looked an awful lot like an engagement ring, but he never showed any intention of bringing her to a church.

....

At the same time that Whitney was dealing with disappointments in her romantic life, she was also facing challenges in her relationship with black audiences. At the Soul Train Music Awards in

1989, I heard jeers coming from the balcony when her name was announced as a nominee for Best R&B / Urban Contemporary Single by a female. Whitney had just performed, and we were standing backstage in the holding area, so we could hear what was going on in the house. "Robyn, are they booing me?" she asked. Unfortunately, this was the second year in a row that she'd been booed at this show.

She didn't like it, of course, but contrary to popular belief, being insulted at the Soul Train Awards did not knock Whitney too hard. However, she wasn't entirely able to dismiss those fools. It was clear that she was at a point in her career where some changes needed to be made.

I spent a lot of time talking to Tony Anderson, Arista's vice president of R&B promotion, who confided that critics were making his job hard. Some people in black radio were feeling disrespected and as if they'd been used to build Whitney up. She wasn't the first black artist to cross over, but the speed with which she did so and the critical response to the material on the second album made things even more difficult. Tony defended himself in an opinion piece in *Billboard* magazine, revealing that he routinely had to convince black radio stations to play Whitney's music "over the objections that the record was 'too pop' (or worse, 'too white') only to see that record go on the air and invariably go to the very top of their playlists." Tony also insisted that it was up to Whitney as an artist to define what "black" music meant.

Whitney met with Clive, and he agreed that her third studio album needed to give more than a nod to contemporary black listeners. Nip wanted to work with producer and arranger Arif Mardin. I encouraged her to follow her instincts because I believed she would finally get to make more of the music she always wanted to. But when Whitney spoke with Clive, he said Arif was dated. Arif had embraced rap and hip-hop, which he displayed on Chaka Khan's 1984 remake of Prince's "I Feel for You," which won Grammys for Best R&B Song and Best Female R&B Vocal. His production of Bette Midler's "Wind Beneath My Wings" for the *Beaches* soundtrack would go on to win Grammys for Record of the Year and Song of the Year.

....

Around Christmastime Whitney and I had gone to see *Beaches*, a movie about two girls who meet on their family vacations in Atlantic City and become lifelong friends. Whitney's film agent, Nicole David, had told us that it was pretty good, and Nip and I were curious to check it out. We were interested in seeing Bette act and, more important, how her music was featured in the film.

It sounded like the perfect movie for us, and I found myself remembering the early days of loading a cooler and boom box on a luggage cart on our trips down the shore. But more than that, as adults, levelheaded Hillary Whitney (Barbara Hershey) and feisty singer/actress C. C. Bloom (Bette Midler) reminded Nippy and me of our own bond. Through romantic relationships, breakups, and their own conflicts, the characters in *Beaches* always found their way back to each other, and Nippy and I assumed it would always be the same with us. While we were earlier in the lifelong journey we planned to share, the on-screen portrait of enduring female friendship allowed us to see a reflection of the kind of love we had for each other. Nippy called me the sister she never had, her best friend, her dog, her nigga. Looking back, I realize that she just wanted someone with whom she could share ideas and confidences, someone to love, trust, count on—someone who would listen and not judge. Someone who understood what it was to be a friend.

Our tissues came out when gravely ill Hillary says, "I waited for you," as C.C. rushes to her dear friend's bedside. After convincing the hospital to discharge her, C.C. watches Hillary embrace her daughter, who then goes off to play, leaving the two women sitting side by side watching a glorious sunset as "Wind Beneath My Wings" begins to play. The next shot is at the cemetery, where C.C. takes Hillary's young daughter by the hand, leading her away from her mother's graveside. Then, as the camera pans right, the screen is filled with a gray tombstone that reads "WHITNEY," and there was no way for us to escape the fifty-foot projection. Nippy and I gasped, grabbing each other's hands. We wept as the image hung there for what felt like an eternity. When we came home to Silvia, both still a mess, we tried to explain the story to her as we bawled. I pulled myself together long enough to call Nicole to request a VHS copy, and when we showed the film to Silvia it wrecked us again. Once we finally managed to compose ourselves, Whitney said, "If I should die, please don't have a whole lot of flowers. You know how the smell gets to me. I want CeCe to sing 'Don't Cry for Me' and celebrate my life with music."

I had just turned twenty-eight and Whitney was twenty-five, but our sense of immortality was gone with that scene. It was unthinkable that one of us could lose the other under any scenario, and certainly not due to early death. We were making a life for ourselves, a life that grew out of a dream, first given wings by Whitney, her dedication to her craft, her faith in God, and her belief that her savior would support our flight.

....

After they met, Clive wrote Whitney a long letter, and she agreed to work with Antonio "L.A." Reid and Kenneth "Babyface" Edmonds. The duo was at the forefront of new jack swing, which combined hip-hop music with R&B vocals.

In early 1990, we made a trip to Atlanta for Whitney's first recording sessions with them, and she was totally looking forward to getting down in the studio with the R&B hit makers of LaFace Records. Whitney, Silvia, and I landed, and L.A. was there to meet us. Whitney got in the car; Silvia and I stayed behind to pick up the luggage and rental car.

L.A. had offered to put us up at his guesthouse and had a studio on his property. When Sil and I finally made our way there, Whitney and L.A. were sitting in the house talking. All the houses in that part of Atlanta looked similar to me, with fake golf course grass and artificial stone or brick facing. But L.A.'s house felt warm, spacious, and welcoming. The garage door was raised to expose bicycles, toys, and the black Mercedes-Benz that earlier had whisked Nippy away.

The recording happened at the private studio adjacent to the house. Babyface lived just up the road in the same development in a redbrick-faced house with his then wife, who was low-key and sweet. It was time to work! "My Name Is Not Susan," "Anymore," and "I'm Your Baby Tonight" came out of those sessions.

Whitney and 'Face, who did most if not all of the writing and tracking of vocals, spent most of the studio time together. At one point 'Face said that "I'm Your Baby Tonight" needed a bridge, and that Nip should take a break for an hour or two so he could write it. I suggested we grab the bikes from the garage and go for a ride around the complex, and she was game. So off we went, with me leading Whitney and Silvia all the way up and down the first hill, around a bend, over a little bridge, straight, down another hill, and then along a flat stretch where we all coasted. Soon it was time for us to turn back.

Nip and I were both very competitive and often talked shit to each other. One of us got it in her head that we'd race back, and within an instant, we were off. Because I have a good sense of direction, I'd typically be in the lead, but Whitney always tried to keep up. The two hills we had sped down earlier now had to be tackled going uphill! Pedaling strenuously up the hill, she somehow managed to talk trash: "Hey, Robyn, remember when Michael asked how you could possibly dribble a basketball with your tiny arms and small hands?" As she gained ground, she added, "Well, I'm trying to figure out how you're managing this hill with those tiny legs." I did my best to tune her out, but my stride broke and she managed to pull ahead, crossing the finish line by a hair.

It wasn't until we got off the bikes that we realized Silvia wasn't with us. We waited and waited and waited. Finally, we returned to the studio to find that 'Face was finished writing. We told him that we thought Silvia had gotten lost. He responded, "Yeah, probably. It's really easy to take a wrong turn around here." So the three of us got into 'Face's car and went searching for Sil. As we approached the second hill, there she was, hot and sweaty from pushing the bike uphill.

Furious, Silvia started running her mouth immediately: "I was yelling for you guys to wait for me, but you just ignored me and kept going! I couldn't pedal up this hill. It's too hard for me!"

In typical fashion, Whitney replied, "Get in, Silvia. Robyn, you get out. You lost, so you ride the bike back."

Recording resumed, with 'Face and Whit sitting at the board. He held a handwritten paper in his hand and said, "Can you sing this?" Whitney got up from the chair, playfully snatching the paper from 'Face's hand, saying, "Gimme that." In the booth, with headphones on, the racehorse zapped right through the freshly written bridge.

> *Looks like I'm fatal it's all on the table*
> *And baby you hold the cards . . .*

I watched him listening intently, head bopping gently as Whitney sang the hook out until the track was no more. Whitney ultimately gave L.A. Reid and Babyface their first number 1 pop hit with "I'm Your Baby Tonight."

....

In 1989, Whitney was asked to present Michael Jackson with the World Music Award in a video that would be taped at Michael's estate. So Whitney, her publicist Regina, and I clambered onto a helicopter on the rooftop of an office building in Los Angeles, and the whole ride—the swaying side to side and bouncing up and down—made me sick to my stomach. But I didn't say much about it. If we'd had to go by rowboat and swim a mile, and Nip was on board, I'd have been there. After forty-five minutes in the clear and sunny skies, we approached Santa Barbara, where the treetops looked like huge marijuana buds ripe for the picking. Everything we could see, for miles and miles, belonged to Michael Jackson. This dude owned the mountains, valleys, and hills.

We landed in a circle outlined on the blacktop, and before the helicopter door opened there was a cameraperson or two ready to document the arrival of Whitney Houston. No one had given us a heads-up or asked permission, and they weren't asking for it now. Whitney didn't say a word and neither did I. We were in

Neverland, and that's exactly how it felt—like being in the midst of magic.

A young man greeted us and escorted us to our quarters so we could freshen up before lunch with Michael and Bubbles, his pet chimpanzee. As we walked past the main entrance, we could see the sign displaying the name *Neverland*, along with a statue of Peter Pan. I was totally blown away. I was at Michael Jackson's house! The little-boy singing sensation every girl on the entire planet wanted to date and one day marry—including Whitney and me.

The house was a large, two-level Tudor with an English-country-farm charm. The second level had lots of windows, which I couldn't see into, though it felt as though eyes were watching us. We were led to one of two bungalow-style buildings with a safari theme and told to make ourselves comfortable. But we couldn't ignore the enormous trampoline situated just in back of the main house, adjacent to where we were staying. As soon as the young man left, Nip and I ran back outside together, and we jumped, careful not to get hurt. We giggled, thinking that Michael was probably watching us; we'd been told that his room was located just above.

After about an hour of downtime, we were asked if we wanted a tour of the house, and off we went. A young woman took us from room to room, and they all had a feeling of comfort, of being lived in. Then she stopped and, with her hand on the knob of a door, just before opening it, said ominously, "This is the dolls' room, and sometimes you can hear them walking about at night." We looked at each other, eyebrows raised, and then stepped inside the doorway. Sure enough, from wall to wall, ceiling to floor, there were thousands of porcelain, cloth, and plastic dolls with a gazillion long-lashed eyeballs staring straight at us! I remember thinking, *That's way, way too many dolls for my nerves.*

As we backed up out of the room, Whitney leaned in and whispered to me, "Why would she say something creepy like that?"

"Well maybe it's true," I said. "All of those damn dolls in one room. Anything could happen."

We never got around to asking about the doll collection, because that concluded the house tour, and it was time to eat. We were led into a kitchen filled with pots clanging, the sounds of dishes, and the scent of baking bread. There was a picnic-style table, a mix of chairs, and a bench. And there, at the head of the table, sat Michael. He was soft spoken but warm, seeming to want to accommodate us and make us comfortable. He included us all in the relaxed conversation, but his attention was on Whitney. Bubbles was seated in an elevated chair next to her, enjoying some finger food.

After lunch, Michael showed us the rest of the house, including his private wing. Standing at his window, I could see the entire property—as well as anyone having a blast on the trampoline. Michael took us to see the animals in the barn—he had llamas, peacocks, snakes, and animals I didn't even recognize—and then asked if we'd like to ride horses.

Whitney was all in. She was dressed for the occasion, wearing jeans and boots, while I, on the other hand, was wearing a white nylon running suit with running shoes and booties for socks. It was the worst possible outfit for riding a horse. But the train had already left the station—literally! We rode in an old-fashioned red train until we got to the stables. Whitney mounted a large, dark brown horse, then Regina got on hers, and then a man walked another one over, which he positioned so that I could jump on. I glanced over and saw Michael sitting on a golf cart, watching. He had this wide ear-to-ear grin plastered across his face.

A few hours later, after we showered and dressed, it was time for the award presentation. We gathered in the main part of the house, and I was off to the side until Nip called me over to listen as she practiced reading through the script. I couldn't help but notice that Michael was staring at me. I didn't want him to know that I knew, but it seemed that he had absolutely no problem staring directly at me for minutes on end. Finally, someone called his name and he stepped away. Nip turned to me: "You see the way that Michael was staring at you, Rob? I think it was your eyes. He must really love your eyes."

....

We were in Europe a few months before the release of Whitney's third album, *I'm Your Baby Tonight*, when Arista called, saying they wanted her to do an interview for the cover story of a magazine called *Fame* to support the release. Reporter Roger Friedman began asking Whitney about my role, so I joined the conversation. We shared our plans for Whitney's acting career, producing movies, television, and representing artists. We opened up to him, excited about presenting our vision to someone who seemed honest. Friedman didn't probe us with questions about our relationship or Whitney's dating. We knew this article was going to come out featuring us as two successful, business-minded women.

When the October 1990 issue of *Fame* hit the stands, nothing on the page reflected our conversation. *Fame*'s headline, "Secret Life of Whitney Houston," said it all. Nearly every word was slanted toward building evidence that we were lovers. She felt violated, and the fact that the request had come through her record company made it even worse. At that time, I had heard rumors about Clive Davis's being with men, but it wasn't confirmed beyond speculation until he revealed that he was bisexual a decade later.

After she finished reading and the shock wore off, Nippy said, "This is what my mother meant when she said, 'They build you up to tear you down.' You know what? They will never, ever get anything from me again." And she meant it. That story altered the professional landscape for Whitney and me, and forever changed the way she felt about doing interviews.

Cissy insisted that I no longer walk next to Whitney in public. I couldn't ride in the car with her or sit next to her at most award shows. "You're playing right into their hands," I said, but they were unmoved. There were times when we both could feel the persistent chatter, and Whitney might hold my face in her hands and say, "Robyn, you know I love you immensely," while advising me to ignore her mother if she said anything mean or pushed me aside.

Whitney was only twenty-seven years old, and already she was tired. It wasn't just the unethical reporters or not being "black enough"; it wasn't just her mother and the rest of her family or the industry's demands. And it wasn't just the rumors. It was all those things that responded with a resounding no when she frequently asked, "Can I be me?"

Family night out in NYC, 1971: Marty, Mom, Bina, and me.

My father running hurdles at Ironbound Stadium, East Side High School.

1978: Clifford J. Scott High School vs. rival East Orange High School girls basketball game. Me (#22) and Janice Walker.

All photographs courtesy the author unless otherwise noted.

The Greatest Love World Tour, 1986, in Italy at the Vatican: Nip and me.

Backstage at the Moment of Truth Tour in 1987: Whitney, Silvia, and me.

Whitney and me on a yacht in 1987, during a tour break in Australia.

Mendham house party in late 1987. *Left to right:* Houston family friends unknown, myself, John, and Wade.

John Simmons, Whitney, and me at Disney World, 1989.

Awaiting the bullet train in Japan on the Feel So Right Tour, 1990:
Back row, standing left to right: Tony Bulluck (tour manager), Shozo Katsuta (Kyoto promoter), Bashiri Johnson (percussion), Ray Fuller (guitar), Bette Sussman (keys), Rickey Minor (bass). *Middle row, standing:* Silvia Vejar (personal assistant), Michael Houston, me, Wayne Lidsey (keys), Whitney, Kirk Whalum (sax) (*bending down*), Billy Baker (background vocalist), David Roberts (security).
Front row, kneeling: Troy Burgess (dancer), Wade Perry (tour accountant).

Aruba, 1990: Whitney befriended a stray, who waited for her on the beach near the hotel. She brought food from her room for the dog every day.

Me and Nip on the beach in Aruba.

On the *Bodyguard* set in 1991. Whitney, wearing her "Queen of the Night" floor-length coat, stops production to sing "Happy Birthday" to me.

Marty, captured by Marc Bryan-Brown in 1991. He's sitting on the patio steps of Whitney's house, unaware that his photo was taken.

Marc Bryan-Brown

Whitney's bridal shower, 1992: Robina, my cousin Dollie, me, mom, and Whitney.

Another bridal shower photo. *Back row, standing left to right:* Michelle, Whit, and me. *Second row:* Regina, Silvia, CeCe, Nip's cousin Michelle Drinkard, Donna, and Perri. *Seated:* Whitney's aunt Marion Houston and two cousins Jill and Sharon Houston, Carol Brown, Cissy, LaLa, Aunt Bae, and Monique. *Kneeling:* Rose, Laurie, and Maria.

Attending a Vegas show in 1992: Tiawana Rawls, Khandi Alexander, David, Silvia, Whitney, Anne Blanchard (security), Ellin, me, Bette, Carol, and Luca Tommassini.

Nip and me playing Ping-Pong doubles on the I'm Your Baby Tonight Tour, 1993.

Dana Lixenberg agreed to photograph Robina, Mom, and me at our home in 1994. Our last family portrait together.
© *Dana Lixenberg, 1994*

My credentials on tour in 1994.

WHEREVER I NEED TO GO

ROBYN CRAWFORD
NAME
CREATIVE DIRECTOR NIPPY INC.
TITLE

Me, holding Bobbi Kristina in a Polaroid given to me from the *Ebony* cover shoot in Mendham, 1995.

One day in 1997, after she sang me a song, I asked Krissi for her autograph.

The Beverly Hills Hotel
and Bungalows

Krissi Brown

The Beverly Hills Hotel
9641 Sunset Boulevard Beverly Hills, California 90210
310. 276. 2251

71ST ANNUAL ACADEMY AWARDS
B
SUNDAY AT THE OSCARS
ROBYN CRAWFORD
PRODUCTION B
* 0 2 7 5 7 *

My laminate from the 1999 Academy Awards rehearsal.

Lisa and me in Croton-on-Hudson, 2019.

Annual two-week vacation in Blue Hill, Maine,
on the ferris wheel at the Blue Hill Fair, 2016.

Fourteen

From Sea to Shining Sea

Despite the turmoil behind the scenes, we couldn't help but be excited about Whitney's upcoming performance of the national anthem at Super Bowl XXV in Tampa, Florida. In the lead-up to the event in early 1991, we kept hearing that security was going to be unusually tight. The United States was in the midst of Desert Storm and there had been numerous security threats, so a feeling of unease hung over the stadium and blanketed the entire country.

Our NFL contact alerted us that there would be a number of safeguards in place, including the presence of the National Guard, plainclothes police, several security checkpoints, and more. We were permitted a limited number of guests and told that the group had to stay together and that once we entered the stadium, we would not be able to leave and reenter.

Once we cleared security, we were ushered to the side to wait for our escort down to midfield, where John and Donna awaited us. Whitney looked around and asked, "Where's Gary?" Nobody had seen him since we approached security, and we would not see him again for the rest of the day and night.

We were anticipating sunny and warm weather in Florida, but this was Tampa, which is farther north than we realized, and as the clouds rolled in it got progressively cooler. Whitney, who had traveled in a lightweight brown suede car coat, now had her coat fastened to the neck, and had fished gloves and a hat out of her bag.

The plan was for her to stand on a podium backed by a full orchestra all dressed in black tie, and she was to wear a sleeveless black cocktail dress and heels. But after sound check, when we were back at the hotel with a few hours to kill, Whitney came into my room, plopped down on my bed, and said, "What am I going to do? I'm going to be freezing in that dress!"

I remembered being in the room watching Silvia packing her bags, and I said, "Why don't you wear the tracksuit that's in your suitcase?"

"What tracksuit?" she asked.

I led Nip to her room, opened her bag, and pulled out a white Le Coq Sportif tracksuit. "You won't be out of place. It's appropriate for the occasion, and no one is going to be looking at the orchestra anyway—all eyes are going to be on you."

For some reason I cannot fathom, Whitney did her own hair and makeup that day. Then she added a white headband, suited up, and slipped on a pair of white Nike Cortez sneakers with a red swoosh, and Whitney Houston was ready to astound the world with her national anthem.

As soon as she began, the packed Tampa Stadium went quiet and remained that way until she reached the final line. When she hit the word *free*, those people who were still sitting began to rise. And by the time she reached *brave*, which she amazingly held for nearly eight seconds, the eighty thousand people who filled the stadium were either cheering or tearful. It was breathtaking. It was extraordinary.

Standing on the sidelines listening to her, I just drifted away. I heard the words she was singing but lost myself in the feeling. A feeling of pride. And it wasn't only that I felt proud to be an American. I felt proud to be witnessing an incredible moment of unity. But that's what Whitney did to a song. That's what she did with "The Greatest Love of All," "I'm Every Woman," and "I Will Always Love You." Her interpretations made you feel something you'd never felt before. That evening Whitney took our minds off fear and gave us something beautiful to hold on to.

"How was it?" Nip asked me after jumping down from the stage.

"You killed it," I answered.

The Giants beat the Buffalo Bills by one point, but on January 27, 1991, the real victory belonged to Whitney Houston, who forever raised the bar for the US national anthem. Her gospel inflections claimed it for African Americans, many of whom felt a connection to it for the first time. When Whitney sang it, you forgot about all the other renditions of the song you'd ever heard.

As I predicted, no one questioned the tracksuit. No one said Whitney wasn't black enough. Everyone claimed that black girl from East Orange that day. We later learned that Arista wanted to release Whitney's anthem as a single. Folks were calling into radio stations asking DJs to play it, and similar calls flooded the Nippy Inc. and Arista lines. After it came out, Whitney's anthem became Arista's fastest-selling single, and she donated all the proceeds to the Red Cross.

And yet, within a few days, a rumor spread that she hadn't sung live but instead had lip-synced.

After John Simmons passed, Whitney first thought his replacement should be a pianist, as he had been. Keyboardist and pianist Bette Sussman was a killer player who began her career as the musical director for the touring company of the Broadway musical *Godspell* when she was just nineteen. The only woman in the band, she had also worked with Cissy, which seemed to make her a natural choice. But Whitney's bass player Rickey Minor called on the phone declaring, "I'm your MD."

"No, you're not," Whitney said.

"Yes, I am," Rickey insisted.

"No, you're not," Whitney replied as they went back and forth like an old comedy routine. In the meantime, back in the office, John Houston was also pushing for Bette. But Rickey was hungry and relentless and seemed ready to completely devote himself, so Whitney said, "Give him a shot and see how he handles it." When Rickey first became musical director, he was stressed out to the max, even losing patches of hair. But he saved himself; he started practicing yoga and soon became adept at handling the whirlwind. Whitney had trusted her gut, and their collaboration was to last for ten years.

A few months before the Super Bowl, Nip told Rickey the only version of "The Star-Spangled Banner" she found inspiring was Marvin Gaye's rendition, which he sang before a 1983 All-Star basketball game. Rickey had the blueprint for the arrangement: Keep it simple. I'd watched that game at home and sat mesmerized as Marvin performed accompanied by only a simple drum machine. Nip's approach also was to keep it straightforward. But what was a "simple" delivery for Whitney Houston was a jaw-dropper for the millions who heard it.

I was with Whitney the day Rickey told us that per our NFL contact Bob Best, the league required that a "safety" version of the anthem be recorded in case of a glitch or technical difficulty during the live broadcast. Rickey made it clear that that was the protocol. So we met him at an L.A. studio to record it. He asked Nip if she had listened to the track and she told him no. He played it for her once and then again halfway through when Nip said, "Okay, let's do it." She went inside the booth, tracked her vocal in one take, and we were out of there. She never listened to the recording again.

But on that most memorable day, all eyes in Tampa Stadium and around the entire world were on her. Now, I have heard Whitney sing everywhere, and I mean everywhere! In the car, in the pool, in the elevator, in the studio, from the bathroom, in the kitchen, at someone else's house, at a restaurant, in church. I know that voice so well that from the very start of a song I can tell by how she sings the first few words where she's going to take the next line. These ears of mine are seasoned. In any case, I don't recall any Super Bowl performance of the national anthem being similarly scrutinized before Whitney's, even though artists like Neil Diamond and Diana Ross had sung to tracks in prior years. That January evening I stood twelve yards from her. And she *sang*.

At a tour rehearsal the following week, John, attorneys Sheldon Platt and Roy Barnes, and Rickey were discussing all the speculation. I looked up at Whitney, who was just sitting there listening to all the chatter about whether she sang live. Before my lips could even move, the look on her face said, "I know you ain't about to ask me." And believe me, I wasn't. I didn't need to. I couldn't believe what I was hearing. It was maddening.

"I know you were singing," I said.

Whitney replied, "I was singing my heart out."

....

But behind the scenes, things weren't all so triumphant. One day around this time, Whitney was rehearsing at a soundstage, warming up, singing a favorite Stevie tune, "If It's Magic," and her voice did something it had *never* done before. It was like when you're walking down the street and you suddenly trip over an uneven sidewalk and then look back as if to say, "What was that?" The beauty of Whitney's vocal instrument was her ability to downshift and then elevate smoothly, soaring upward to her head voice, where the sweetness of her top resided. But this time the sweetness wasn't there and Whit was brought to an unexpected stop. Sitting on her stool, now lengthening her torso, Nip gave it another try—but no go. She knew it wasn't good. I watched her stand up and walk off to one of the closed lounges. I knew something was wrong with her voice but didn't understand what exactly had happened.

We needed to call a doctor.

The doctor diagnosed a torn vocal cord and gave Whitney a mask and inhaler to breathe into. He said there was no reason why the vocal cord wouldn't heal, but she would have to allow her voice to recover. Whit needed to shut that voice down, and quick. This was her first-ever sign of vocal injury, and Whitney Houston was wounded.

After the doctor's visit, Nip returned to rehearsal and took her seat center stage. The band played as Whitney sat, listening. Then she turned and glanced over her shoulder at her singers and turned back, moving closer to the mic.

....

Whitney's first televised concert was scheduled to broadcast live on March 31, 1991, from an airplane hangar at the naval air station in Norfolk, Virginia. We traveled there by helicopter, and despite placing three or four Dramamine patches on my skin, I was still sick to my stomach. Nippy thought that was hilarious. She was in stitches when we were up in the military helicopter and I almost lost it. She laughed heartily, watching me cringe as we floated our way up and down, swaying left and right, until blessedly we landed on the USS *Saratoga*. When we landed on the carrier, it was windy and loud, but I couldn't have been happier to be off that helicopter. Though I never quite got my sea legs on the carrier, I fell in love with the naval uniforms, so much so that not long after, I would design black flight suits for the I'm Your Baby Tonight World Tour.

Since it was a performance for the troops, opening with "The Star-Spangled Banner" made sense. Wearing her new blue military flight suit, Whitney sang a cappella for over thirty seconds before the band joined in, delivering a rendition second only to her Super Bowl version.

Whitney quickly shed the flight suit to perform "I Wanna Dance with Somebody," revealing the cute yellow long-sleeve tunic and shorts set she had on underneath.

I don't know why, but Nip had decided to include "A Song for You" in that night's set list. It was the first time she performed it. In fact, it was the first time I heard her sing it. We'd listened to the song before; I remembered the nights Whitney and I often spent playing music, putting one album after another on the turntable, looking at the artwork, reading liner notes and discussing them. One night at our first apartment, we lay side by side on the floor, our heads propped on pillows, the only light coming from the stereo we faced. I selected the Temptations' "A Song for You," an album I treasured. We relaxed, silently enjoying the tracks that preceded "A Song for You," the sixth song on the record. And then it started. The piano intro filled the darkness before Dennis Edwards's soulful voice emerged:

> *I've been so many places in my life and time.*
> *I've sung a lot of songs,*
> *I've made some bad rhymes.*
> *I've acted out my life on stages*
> *With ten thousand people watching.*
>
> *But we're alone yeah,*
> *And I'm singing this song for you.*

The song ended, and we lay motionless until I spoke. "I'd love to hear you sing that song."

"It's a great song," she agreed, "but I haven't lived enough to sing it."

Now she was twenty-seven, only seven years older than when she'd declared herself too young. Why had she decided to sing it now? What had happened? What had changed? I watched from the sound booth as she perched on a stool and belted the song, her own interpretation, which sounded to me like a plea. I never heard her sing it live again.

....

It felt as though Whitney, Silvia, and I were always on a plane to somewhere, an endless circuit of planet Earth. But during a short break from our jet-setting in 1991, Mom and Bina told me they had taken a good look at Marty. He was thin, so thin, and they realized he was wearing two or three pairs of pants at a time. They told me they believed he was really sick. That maybe he had AIDS. My mother had done her research and had come to this conclusion. *This can't be happening,* I thought. Marty had never said a word.

We never knew for certain how Marty became infected with AIDS, but he told me it was from either a blood transfusion after his car accident (they weren't testing blood then) or his "lifestyle." My brother never told me he was gay, and I never saw him with a male partner, but of course I assumed. We all did.

The news left me speechless.

....

A few months before I found out he was sick, Marty had called saying he wanted to come over to my place. He had a hacking cough, so I gave him cough syrup, then set him up in my spare room. The next morning I asked about his cough, which I had heard throughout much of the night, and I noticed a raw wound on his face. "What's that?" I asked. "Put some vitamin E on it."

Marty came into the bathroom and was standing there while I brushed my teeth. "Maybe you have what I have," he said sarcastically.

His tone made me snap back, "I don't have what you have." I wasn't reading between the lines then. Maybe he wanted me to, but I did not. I needed him to say, "Robyn, I have something to tell you," but he never talked to me like that. I asked him to walk my dog, but Marty didn't want to, which was unusual given that he was always happy to help. Why wasn't I able to tell that he didn't have the strength?

....

Marty was still working for Whitney, looking after the house when we were away, and now we were finally coming home. Snow was falling heavily that night. Driving through the gates approaching our huge circular driveway, we were greeted by dozens of snow angels. There were too many to count, each one meticulously created with perfect spacing between them. They looked magical, shimmering as the headlights illuminated the scene.

"Did Marty do all that?" Whitney asked.

"Yep," I said, smiling, knowing that was just like something Marty would do.

We got out of the car, looked around, and saw nothing but angels.

Fifteen

....

I Will Always Love You

For years, Kevin Costner had been phoning Whitney hoping to persuade her to take the starring role opposite him in *The Bodyguard*. The courtship went all the way back to our days living in our first apartment together. I was usually the person who answered our phone. So he'd gotten to know my voice, and whenever I picked up, he was polite, asked how I was, and engaged in sincere small talk. But each time I attempted to tell Nippy who it was, she waved her hand and said, "I know who it is."

Nippy would tell me softly but clearly, "I don't want to be an actress. All I was looking for was a small part, and now he's offering me a big role, and that's not what I want to do. What makes them think I'd be good at it anyway? It's going to be a lot of work, and I don't really want to do it." I totally understood her reticence. It *was* going to be a lot of work, she wouldn't have control, and she already was tired.

That didn't mean she wasn't getting asked to do other movie projects. *Disappearing Acts, Dorothy Dandridge*, and even *A Star Is Born* came her way, too. Whitney and I made trips to LA, meeting with writers and directors who would pitch various projects. I was reviewing scripts sent to my attention and now had my own assistant, Maria Padula, who helped juggle our meeting schedules, including with producers who wanted Whitney for the title role of a remake of *Cinderella*. I ran lines with Whitney before an audition for the role of Jodie Foster's roommate in *The Silence of the Lambs*, but when we met with Jonathan Demme, he didn't ask her to read anything. "You're too nice," he said.

One day we were lounging at home in soft leather chairs, feet propped on ottomans, facing the Hudson River. The phone rang, and it was Kevin. Whitney told me to tell him that she'd call him back. I'd heard that before. Kevin understood that if he was ever going to get Nip to do the project, he would have to give her the space she needed to decide. But it was clear he wasn't going to allow it to slip out of her mind, and he was perceptive, knowing just how persistently to pursue without pressuring her.

Well, that day, Whitney really did call him back. I sat next to her as she spoke to Kevin on speakerphone, and I listened as he assured her that she could do it and that she would be good. He also gave her his word that he would be there to hold her hand and guide her through the process. Finally, Whitney agreed.

....

Prior to beginning work on the film, Whitney decided to surprise Bobby by showing up at one of his concerts. As she, Silvia, and I were escorted backstage to his dressing room, he came out and met us in the hallway—followed immediately by the mother of his children. The woman was pissed, and as she exited the room, she pushed Bobby hard in the chest with both hands. And then it was on: bap, bap, bap—the two of them exchanging blows. "Whoa, she can fight!" Silvia exclaimed.

Bobby's brother Tommy broke them up, and Bobby said, "Get her out of here—take her back to the hotel."

"This isn't right. You know this isn't right, Tommy!" she shouted. Then, just as Tommy was escorting her away from us, she stopped, turned around, looked directly at Whit, and said, "I don't care if you *are* Whitney Houston. If he would do this to me, he'll do it to you," and walked away with Tommy by her side. Throughout the entire bout, we hadn't said a word or moved from our spot just outside the dressing room. We were frozen. I glanced over at Whitney, who stood there stock still, her eyes a bit wider than usual. I didn't like it and suspected that baby mama was right.

I didn't have much to say to Nip about Bobby, because she didn't tell me much. All I had were the rumors—that he was dating Janet Jackson, had a bunch of children, and slept around here, and there, and way over there, too! There was no point mentioning the gossip to Nip; she also heard it. But over the course of a year, she moved on from Eddie and got wrapped up in Bobby. I noticed that Nip started using drugs a lot more when Bobby was around. She wasn't putting on the brakes. I reminded her that drugs should be over now, and she said, "I know. I admire that you were able to stop, and I will put it down, but I'm not ready to just yet."

....

When we went out to start work on *The Bodyguard*, Kevin proved just as lovely in person as he had been on the phone: down-to-earth and easygoing, with an appealing sparkle in his eyes. Our first real interaction was when he pulled up on the Warner Bros. lot in a forest-green Nova and I was standing outside the room where a script reading was to take place. The car was probably a 1971 classic, and I was staring at it, waiting for him to get out. As soon as his cream-and-cognac cowboy boot hit the ground, I said, "Kevin, what I wouldn't do to get the keys to that car." His face lit up and he said, "It's beautiful, isn't it? I had it restored." I kept admiring the Nova as he spoke. "You really know your cars," he said.

Later, on the day they were shooting the love scene, Kevin walked up to Whitney's trailer: "I want to talk to her a little. Is she decent?" I waited outside until he left. Nippy said, "Everything is cool. I told him, 'Whatever you do, just don't put your tongue in my mouth.'"

Kevin did what he said he was going to do the day Whitney agreed to do the movie. He was a man of his word as a costar. He held her hand and gave her good advice, such as how to use her eyes in a scene. And he did not put his tongue in her mouth.

One day, music supervisor Maureen Crowe, whom Whit and I dubbed "our Long Island sister," came into the trailer and suggested "I Will Always Love You," and played Linda Ronstadt's version for Whitney and me. Kevin was not on board. Then one day, he showed up at the trailer with Dolly Parton's 1974 original and said, "This is the song." The forty-two-second a cappella opening lines were Kevin's idea. There's a lot of soul in that white boy who grew up Baptist. Over lunch, Kevin told us that he had once pushed a broom at a Hollywood studio. This explained part of why he and Whitney connected—they were both self-made church kids with dreams.

Meanwhile, Whitney was feeling pressure from every angle. Clive was against her doing this movie, but once she'd decided to do it anyway, he was constantly phoning me on the set trying to talk to Whit about the music in the film—something the producers did not appreciate. "Clive, I have to work with these people," she'd tell him. She was drained beyond any reasonable limit. There were times she wondered whether or not she'd be able to make it through the process. But she did. And on the day they said, "It's a wrap," no one was more relieved than Nip. It had been seven or eight months of flying between California, Maine, Florida, and New York, rising in the early hours of the morning, wrapping mostly after dark. It was finally over! The thing about Whitney was that whatever she decided to do, she always did her best. Making movies was not in her DNA. It felt foreign and therefore made her uncomfortable, uncertain of the outcome. As soon as we returned home, I received a call from John Houston and Sheldon Platt saying that Arista said they could not stand behind anything they had not heard. So on July 6, I went to Clive's office and personally hand-delivered a DAT and CD of the six songs Whitney had recorded for the soundtrack. With *The Bodyguard*, her career skyrocketed.

....

A year or so prior to filming, her relationship with Bobby had turned serious. Whitney, Silvia, and I were in Montreal, enjoying the view of Mont-Royal from Nip's hotel suite, when Bobby phoned. Whitney took the call, and we listened as she said, "What? What? How could this happen? And don't tell me it was a mistake." After hanging up, she relayed the conversation in anger and tears: Bobby had gone to Boston, allegedly to tell the mother of his children that he and Whit were together, but instead wound up getting her pregnant again.

Whitney was mad as hell. Bobby called back that night to say that he needed to see her in person to explain. "He's only telling you now because she's pregnant," I said. I fully expected her to give him his walking papers, so I was shocked when she chose to forgive him. There were so many forewarnings in her and Bobby's relationship, but she chose to ignore them all.

A few months earlier, Whitney and I had spent some time together at the house. By this point, we weren't often alone. But when it did happen, it was just like old times, before fame came along and she started allowing others to shape her behavior. When it was just us, she talked differently, looked at me differently, acted differently. In those rare moments, she was real, her honest-to-God self—vulnerable but still determined.

I was in my old room lying on the bed, and she came in and lay down next to me.

She said, "Bobby asked me to marry him, and I think I'm going to do it."

I said, "You're ready for that, huh?"

"Yes," she said with a sparkle in her eyes.

"Do you love him?"

"Yes," she said. "I do. He loves and cares for his children, he's a good father." I looked at her, unsure what to say, and then she asked, "Do you think he loves me?"

I didn't expect that! How would I know? I hadn't spent any significant time with him or spoken with him about anything of consequence. I knew there had been rough patches, like the time Whitney and Bobby were tossed out of the Ritz-Carlton in Atlanta for disturbing guests with their loud altercations. I didn't like what I saw or heard, and I was worried by Whitney's behavior. That said, all I could do was be there for her, and I was.

"I honestly feel like I don't know him at all, Nippy . . . ," I began. "But he should love you. I sure hope he loves you." We looked at each other and I said, "I think he does."

She said, "Thank you," and we just lay there quietly.

A few minutes later, Silvia walked in and joined us. Whitney told us both that she loved us and then tapped me on the shoulder and said, "My maid of honor, remember that I love you immensely."

"I know," I replied.

The next time we were at the Hotel Bel-Air, Bobby showed up with his brother and manager, Tommy. At the time, Bobby was signed to MCA, and I learned that he was supposed to be going into the studio to record his next project. There was a lot of back-and-forth talk about money—he'd already exhausted his entire advance—but I never saw Bobby go into the studio or do any recording. It was rumored that he'd spent some of his advance on an engagement ring. When the insurance appraiser later came to our house to value Whitney's jewelry, we found out that the ring Eddie had given her was more valuable than her engagement ring from Bobby. Whitney shrugged and had Eddie's ring made into earrings.

....

Weeks later, Whitney had a recording to do in Atlanta, and she told Silvia and me that we'd be stopping by Bobby's house. As we pulled into the paved driveway, the first thing I noticed, right out front, was a Jaguar with a visibly flat tire; it looked as if it hadn't been moved in some time. The house had a forgotten quality about it. It clearly wasn't a home where attention was paid to fluffing up pillows or returning items to their proper places.

Whitney, Silvia, and I casually strolled around the main floor, checking things out. We headed toward the back of the house, where a great room overlooked the backyard and pool outside. On the way, we passed the laundry room. Clothes were piled nearly to the ceiling and spread across the floor. Silvia reflexively attempted to create order as she commented on the sight and scent of mildew. Whitney said, "What the hell are you doing? We're not staying here!" Silvia froze with an undershirt in her hand. I guess she felt bad for Whitney, taking up with a man who couldn't keep his house in order. Or maybe she felt bad for herself, or for all of us, and her instinct was to try to make it better.

I excused myself to use the bathroom. Now, my mother always told me that you can tell a lot about a person from the way he keeps his bathroom. Upon entering, the first thing I spotted was a bowl half filled with milk and soggy cereal on the edge of the sink, and a sock soaking in the milk, the dry half draped onto the porcelain. As I squatted, now eye level with the bowl, I tried to determine if the sock belonged to a child or an adult. I washed my hands and noticed there was nothing to dry them with. I headed through the dining room and into the kitchen in hope of finding paper towels, and to my surprise, there stood a nice-looking young man, around my age, wearing a chef's jacket and working at the stove. He looked up at me with a smile, as if he'd been expecting someone. "Hi. I'm Ian. You must be Robyn. Nice to meet you! So, how you like the house?" he asked with a smirk.

Boy, was I glad to see him! The presence of order and cleanliness in the kitchen gave me a glimmer of hope. Ian was put-together, polite, professional, and engaged. I couldn't wait to hear where he came from and how he'd found his way here. He told me he was a blend of black and Jewish, a graduate of Columbia Law School, a jack-of-all-trades, and a lover of cooking. Bobby's mother had asked Ian if he could help Bobby straighten out his finances. She'd also asked him to come by and prepare a meal for Bobby's return from LA. Ian was happy to do both.

I wasn't sure how honestly I should answer Ian's question about the house. "It's fine but not my style. It's okay." I told him about the cereal bowl and asked about the Jaguar. Ian said it belonged to Leolah, Bobby's sister, known as Lea Lea. He went on to say that the house belonged to Bobby, but that his family pretty much lived there and that Bobby provided for them all. While Ian and I were talking, Whitney entered and asked what I was doing.

"Sitting here talking to Ian about some interesting things," I said.

She sat down and said, "Like what?"

"Tell her, Ian," I answered, totally putting him on the spot.

Ian looked at Whitney and without skipping a beat said, "So, have you figured out what you're going to do with Bobby's family?"

Nip said, "What do you mean?" But before he could answer, she continued with, "This is Bobby's house, and this is how things go down here in Atlanta. But at my house in Jersey, things go down differently." Ian managed to maintain a stiff half-smile. And in a beat, the next thing I heard was Whitney saying, "Come on, let's get out of here." I can't say exactly what was behind Nippy's obvious agitation. It was clear she didn't care to hear whatever Ian had to say. Perhaps the house itself said it all.

I slid the chair out, stood up, and said to Ian, "Really nice meeting you, and good luck."

That was our first and last time at that house. The next time Ian and I saw each other was at the wedding.

A Song for You

....

As maid of honor, I threw Whitney a bridal shower at the RIHGA Royal Hotel in Manhattan. We were regulars there, so we were very comfortable and they took good care of us. The hotel is now the London, and even nowadays when I happen to walk by, those valets who are still there from the time of the RIHGA greet me warmly with hugs.

The shower was fairly intimate, as I invited only people who were in her life at that time: Cissy; Michelle; her cousin Felicia; my mother and Bina; makeup artist Kevyn Aucoin; Natalie Cole; Sue Simmons; Rolonda Watts; bridesmaids CeCe, and L.A.'s wife, Perri Reid; and, of course, Dionne Warwick. There was a joyful feeling in that room. We were all laughing, celebrating womanhood. Whitney was beaming. The shower remained private and nothing leaked out to the press. The shower gift was a silver Tiffany frame and I later sent all guests a print of a group photo commemorating the day.

I wasn't involved in the planning of the wedding, but I started hearing about the tents—how many tents and how big they were— and then I received a fax about the enormous cake. I had nothing to do with the guest list. When I saw the design for purple bridesmaid dresses with fluttery sleeves, I told the stylist, "I'd rather not wear that. It's just not me." I preferred a fitted jacket and skirt.

My hair was easy, since I'd cut it quite short while we were on tour. During the stop in New Orleans, where it was hot and sticky, everybody was in the pool at our hotel. I was sitting on the side, my blowout losing shape from the humidity. I was sick of being ruled by my hair and I wanted to swim. I went in search of Carol and said, "Cut it off."

"How short do you want it?" she asked.

"Short enough where I won't have to come back and see you any time soon," was my reply.

When she was done, I felt so free. I came out to the pool and everybody stopped talking. I dove in that cool, exhilarating water, and when I emerged into the sunshine, I felt born again! I wished Whitney could have joined me, but water had a bad effect on her weave, so she wasn't swimming like she used to.

When I got out of the pool, everybody was exclaiming about my new look. I heard Cissy say, "I told you she was crazy! She cut off all that beautiful hair." For the wedding, I wore a clutch of lavender satin flowers in my hair that matched my dress.

....

As Nip sat at her vanity getting ready for the ceremony, her private phone line rang. When Silvia answered, she heard a male voice say, "Whitney?"

She said, "No, this is Silvia. Who's this?"

"Eddie," the man said.

"Eddie who?" Sil asked.

"Eddie Murphy. Is Elizabeth there?"

While Silvia told him she was busy, Whitney mouthed, "Who's that?"

Hearing who it was, she asked, "What the hell does he want? Is he crazy? He's calling me on my wedding day?"

Whit took the phone and Silvia heard her say, "Yes, I am. I am getting married today. Yes, I am." She hung up the phone and told Silvia that Eddie had called to tell her that she was making a mistake and not to marry Bobby.

....

The fabric of my dress wasn't as fussy as the others', and though I felt comfortable, I was still nervous walking out of that gazebo and down the aisle in silk shoes still wet with dye. I didn't want to break down into tears and be messy. Everyone was looking and smiling as I took my position. When I saw Whitney walking with her father, I was very emotional. And then I looked right at her when I took her bouquet filled with Sterling Silver roses. I was looking into her eyes—taking one last look.

I felt our dynamic-duo days fading away. She was doing it. She was connecting her life with someone else's, and I hoped it would be what she wanted it to be. She deserved to have a family of her own. She deserved the freedom to do what she wanted to do with her life. That's all I ever wanted for her.

....

The morning after the biggest celebration of their lives together, Whitney and Bobby flew to Italy for their honeymoon, which they were spending on a private yacht with Whitney's brother Michael and his wife, Donna—the first double-date honeymoon I'd ever heard of. They were going to sail down the Amalfi coast to Capri together. I thought that was weird. If I had tied the knot in front of all those people, I would want to be alone with my new spouse.

A few days into the honeymoon, I heard talk around the office about an altercation between Whitney and Bobby. Someone on the yacht had placed a call to John Houston telling him that something had gone down, and when the lovebirds returned, Whitney had a visible scar on the side of her face. The cut was at least three inches, running in a straight line from the top of her cheek down to the jaw. I asked Nip to tell me what happened, and it went like this: "We had a disagreement. I threw a glass, the glass hit the wall, shattered, and that's how the cut happened. Couples argue all the time and it's never a big deal. Except when it's me."

Did I believe her story? No. Until the scar finally disappeared, Whitney's makeup artist Roxanna Floyd had to work her magic to conceal it. I said, "Roxanna, she says flying glass scraped her face and that's pretty much the story. What do you think?"

Roxanna looked at me, disgusted, shook her head, and said, "I covered it as best I could." Even after it healed, you could still see a faint line.

Sixteen

....

The Bodyguard World Tour

The first time I saw *The Bodyguard* was also the first time I met Lisa Hintelmann. Warner Bros. held a screening in New York, and I was eager to see how the film had turned out. Knowing Whitney would need specialized representation for her burgeoning film career, we had engaged the largest and most prestigious entertainment PR firm in the country. Lisa was a young publicist who worked with Lois Smith, a legendary partner at the firm.

Lisa and I had talked on the phone a number of times, but before the screening, we had yet to meet in person. Already in the city for a meeting, I told her that we could meet outside the Arista building and walk over to the screening together. The Warner Bros. screening room was less than a ten-minute stroll away.

I wore an Armani blazer accessorized with a red beret and a generously sized chenille scarf. Lisa arrived in an eggplant Romeo

Gigli suit. As she and I walked to Warners, she looked chilly, so I offered her my scarf, which she happily accepted.

After the screening, I was eager to hear Lisa's thoughts. After all, movies were her specialty. She saw the film as an entertaining mainstream movie that had the potential to make a lot of money, and also described Whitney's on-screen debut as perfectly respectable. "What did you think?" she asked. I agreed with most of what she said, but what jumped out at me was Whitney's relationship with the camera. In every scene, she just lit up the screen like she was made for it.

Later that week, I met Lisa at Arista for a meeting with the head of publicity. On our way to her office, I asked her how many Whitney records she owned. "None," she replied honestly, "but obviously I'm familiar with her hits and know what a big star she is." In the meeting, we were going to listen to the first single, "I Will Always Love You," which Lisa had yet to hear since the early screening hadn't included the final soundtrack. Whitney's voice filled the room. When the song ended, the publicity director stared at us from behind her desk, looking as proud as if she had sung it herself. For a minute, Lisa was silent. "Wow," she said. And after a long pause, "I'm speechless. That was unbelievable." Now she had *heard* Whitney Houston.

....

A few months later, in the wee hours of Thursday, March 4, 1993, I was asleep in my Fort Lee apartment when I was awakened by a phone call from Silvia: "Whitney is on her way to the hospital. Gotta go!" Click! As I lay in my bed, now wide awake, I wished that I could be there for the birth of her first child, but Whitney hadn't asked me to. So before rolling over, I said blessings for her to have an easy delivery and a healthy baby.

That night, Whitney and Bobby welcomed their little girl into the world, naming her Bobbi Kristina Brown. I was really excited to meet baby girl and experience what it would feel like to hold her in my arms. But I thought it best to delay my visit and give the couple some space to settle into parenting together.

When they came home, Bobbi Kristina's bedroom was on the other side of what had been my room and was now Silvia's. When she was about a week old, I had my chance to rock Krissi in my arms in the glider I'd gifted the family.

Whitney had approximately four months of downtime, toward the end of which she had rehearsals before hitting the road for the Bodyguard World Tour.

When I went to the house, I rarely saw Whitney or Bobby. They spent nearly all their time on lockdown in the bedroom suite. The two of them spent day after day after day at home, and then when he joined her on the road they did the same thing inside her hotel suite. Eventually only Bobby would surface, typically looking one nasty mess, with Whitney still out of sight. Not even the arrival of Bobbi Kristina would alter this pattern. In front of the cameras at award shows, they behaved like Cissy and John, presenting a united front, though really nothing was farther from the truth.

Thankfully there was always plenty of work. My ace assistant Maria and I prepared for the tour, putting together radio and television promo spots, and selecting photographs and licensing them for artwork, tour books, and other merchandise that would be sold at the shows.

Finally, in July 1993, it was time for the tour to kick off in New York. Opening night was buzzing, and it felt to me as if all of New

York City were blazing with excitement. We were poised to enjoy five sold-out shows at the legendary Radio City Music Hall with a long list of celebrities in attendance every night. My room at the Four Seasons Hotel was a few doors down from Whitney's suite. It was my routine to check in on her before and during hair and makeup to ensure that she was comfortable and that everything was on course.

As the show began, I was in the wings on the right, facing the stage. Whitney entered from the back of the house, walking slowly down the aisle then toward me as she approached the stairs to the stage. As people sitting in the darkness caught the energy surging through the theater, one by one, they zeroed in on the single spot burning bright on Whit. Soon everyone rose to their feet, where they remained until she was well into the first verse, center stage, one mic and a spot of light.

Seventeen

Four-Letter Word

Mom received a call from Marty saying he needed her to come pick him up from the hospital in Newark. I went with her, and as directed at the hospital, we took the elevator down to the basement. It felt as if we were being sent to the morgue. As the doors opened, we saw a sign on the wall: *Infectious Diseases*. We pushed through two solid metal doors to an open ward of lined-up cots and hospital beds.

The space was the size of an elementary school gymnasium, but the ceilings weren't very high, which made the air still, and sticky, and sweaty with fever. I don't recall seeing medical staff in white coats or scrubs, and as we moved farther into the room, searching for Marty under yellow fluorescent lights, I realized two things: First, there were no women there. Not one. Second, most of the men were brown. It seemed as if the hospital didn't know what to do with everyone, so they kept them in a makeshift holding area, like refugees. Many of them stayed put in their beds, and some slumped over to one side, staring blankly, while others dragged IV poles across the floor. They looked as if they were already gone. Marty spotted us, and after helping him gather his few belongings, we left in haste. We didn't have to sign him out.

....

Just when I thought things couldn't possibly get any worse, the least expected, most terrible thing happened: My mother collapsed on her way up the stairs at work and had to be rushed to the hospital. Whitney and I were together that day when I got the call, so we immediately drove over. We walked into the room, where she was lying in her hospital bed, eyes wide with fear, wearing an oxygen mask. "I'm here, Mom," I said softly. They kept her there for three weeks, running a series of tests.

Everything came back normal, and the doctors were baffled. After they exhausted all possibilities, they transferred Mom to another hospital. I drove right down and met with the head doctor. They had their own tests to run, which he said included an HIV test. In the three weeks Mom had been at the first hospital, no one had thought to test her for HIV. She didn't fit the profile.

Two weeks later, the doctor called to ask if I could come down and talk with him. Marty and I entered his office, while Bina stayed with Mom in her room. He told us that everything had come back except one test, and that in most cases, when negative, the HIV test comes back quickly. This one took a much longer time, which had raised a red flag. The doctor said, "Your mother has full-blown AIDS."

I sat speechless, in a daze, my brother next to me while the doctor explained the difference between HIV and AIDS. I watched him put an X-ray of my mother's lungs up on the light box. "See these spots right here?" he said, pointing out a series of clusters of little black dots speckling the cloudy gray of her lungs. Marty and now Mommy. I wanted to scream, but I couldn't.

"Do you want to tell your mother, or shall I tell her?" the doctor asked. Marty remained silent, immobile, so it was up to me to go back into the hospital room and listen to the doctor tell our mother his findings. As he spoke, I remember thinking, *Don't you cry, don't you dare cry*. I needed to be strong for her, to let her know somehow that it was all going to be okay. And after he did his doctor thing, that's exactly what I said: "It's okay, Mama. We got you, Mama."

Late that night, I drove home, crying and howling the entire way. I bet you could hear it for miles. Then I was ready to fight.

A couple of months later, I was finally able to drive Mom home. I can still see her in the passenger seat of my Mercedes, crying softly. It was a solemn, heartbreaking victory for us all. When I asked, "Why are you crying, Mama?" she said, "I thought I would never leave that place."

I continued giving her all my kisses and nibbling on her cheeks, even though she was hesitant, worried it might be unsafe. She would say to me, "I want you to keep working. Do your thing, Robyn." Janet Marie Williams Crawford, my biggest fan. I moved my mother and brother into my three-bedroom condo so we were close, and I did whatever I could to make them feel comfortable.

Marty was following conventional medicine and for a time did well on an AZT regimen, but my mother wouldn't touch the drug. She knew that it turned your fingernails black, and her research had indicated that it was toxic. She chose to go the other way, pursuing a holistic route that incorporated juicing, healing hot stone treatments, and vitamin C shots administered in Harlem for

$200 per dose. Not until my mother was prescribed interferon and an inhaled medicine called pentamidine did she begin to improve, and vastly. She bought herself a new car and began attending church, shopping, and living her life. I got first-class plane tickets for her and a health aide to go to Jacksonville, Florida, to visit her brother Robert and his wife, Joyce.

Still, she was now watching her T-cell count while witnessing her son waste away. I didn't have half the strength Mom and Marty had, and they were always citing me as the strong one. I wasn't. They were so much stronger.

I have to say that kissing my mother's cheeks and the other forms of tenderness I showed her were very different from how I cared for my brother. But the way Marty dealt with his illness was also different. He was quite close to my cousin Gayle. In fact, in many ways their relationship was more like brother and sister than ours was, in terms of closeness and spending time together. Nevertheless, Marty never told her he was sick.

Back in the early nineties, AIDS was a heavy load for gay men or men who slept with men. They were labeled and saddled with the disease—and as far as the public was concerned, many felt gay men had gotten what they deserved. The perception was also that they were the only ones who had it, which wasn't true. With its apathetic response to the crisis, it seemed as if the country was punishing gay men. With the focus solely on men, it took a while before it was determined that gay sex wasn't the only way to contract HIV. My mother was proof of that. Women were getting it from men they believed were straight. Because HIV/AIDS was considered a gay men's disease, the research that was being done concentrated on men and their response to various treatments. No thought was given to women's bodies, which often respond differently.

I came home one day to find my brother pretty upset because

my mother would not discuss how she became infected. Instead of sharing her own story, Mom asked him why he'd waited so long to tell us. "I didn't want to be a burden," Marty replied. For me, *how* wasn't really all that important at this point anyway. They both had it, and I wanted them to live.

Sometimes I feared that my family was cursed. For a time, I would not sleep with anyone. I didn't want to be touched. Later, I ran to my doctor's office if I simply kissed someone. I was flipped out. One time, after I showed up at his office to get another HIV test, my doctor said that perhaps I needed to go talk to someone. "You're fine, Robyn. I know it's really unfortunate what has happened to your brother and your mother, but that's not how this virus works. You're fine." I was juggling so much, between what was happening with both my family and Whitney and the demands of my job. But I wasn't ready to talk to a therapist. I didn't feel that I could be honest with a stranger. I'd been so conditioned not to disclose anything about Whitney, and it didn't seem that I could open up without sharing everything. So I kept it all in.

....

That summer, Marty and I wanted to see *Angels in America*, which everybody was talking about, so I got a pair of tickets. We were both big into theater, and as children we had watched television productions of shows like *Gypsy*, *Funny Girl*, *Summer Stock*, and other musicals and classics.

He didn't feel well that evening, but we hoped he could get through it. Sadly, his cough was so persistent we had to leave during the second act. I had the driver I'd hired head toward home, but at the mouth of the Lincoln Tunnel, Marty announced that he didn't want to go through it and breathe the fumes. "Well," I insensitively said, "you're going to have to hold your breath. We can't turn around now."

Patience has never come easily to me. My mother used to say, "You'll never be a teacher," because I didn't have the patience, and Whitney told me I had more patience for strangers than for my own family. Looking back, I wish I'd had more patience with and connection to what was going on. I think I was detached, but Marty was detached, too. We shared that method of self-protection.

I gave my brother shelter and love, but he still was very secretive. His way was quiet and private, and that could have been for a number of reasons. One of them had to be the way men were often treated if they were perceived to be gay—particularly black men. Marty had lived a whole other life when he was down in North Carolina, pursuing straight men he and his friends referred to as "trade." According to his roommates, Marty would return home sharp as could be in his uniform and go straight into the bathroom. Soon after he would emerge in short shorts they called his "little poom-pooms" and a tank top, hair dyed dark brown with Miss Clairol, brows arched, and mustache trimmed. He had beautiful legs. And though he had a car, he chose to walk everywhere in those poom-pooms.

Marty was vain and didn't want anyone to see him not looking his best. One night, he was on the phone with his friend Paul and I overheard him crying. When I asked him what was wrong, Marty said Paul wouldn't come see him. I don't know why not, because he never talked to me about the details, but that's the only time I saw him display emotion while his health was failing. I've never been one to dig for information. If he wanted me to know, he would have told me.

That summer, Marty decided he wanted to talk to my father.

His visit with Dad quickly went south. Marty phoned Mom to pick him up, and when he got in the car, he was trembling. "Just get me out of here, he's disgusting." My father had been rude and evaded any attempt at a real conversation. These were my brother's last days. Shortly after returning home and finding out what happened, I went into his room. Marty said, "I'm not gay. I spent all this time thinking I needed approval from a man, and I didn't need it."

Marty was never who my father thought he should be. He grew up wounded by that, searching for what would make him feel whole. Marty was funny and talented; he knew fashion, how to fix things, how to cook and sew. He was a good writer, he played multiple instruments—so many things. Some people say he was ahead of his time. But he would never be the athlete my father was. Dad saw my brother as soft and weak and not like him, and he couldn't stand that. He was right. Marty *wasn't* like him. He was so much more complex, so much more accomplished.

....

While he was living with me, Marty watched me get ready for work every morning. On September 23, 1993, as I was preparing to leave, I heard the sound of him pushing buttons on the phone. Beep, beep, beep, beep. "What are you doing?" I asked.

"I'm trying to call the doctor."

"Why?"

"I need to go to the hospital." Palisades Medical Center was two minutes from the house, but Marty made it very clear that he didn't want to go back there. A few weeks earlier, he'd checked himself out of there and as he and I were exiting the doctor yelled behind him, "If you leave here you're gonna die."

"Fuck you," Marty had retorted.

My brother preferred Morristown Memorial, an hour away. It was a very forward-thinking institution where they were compassionate and committed to caring for people suffering with AIDS and comforting their families. The rooms were bright and clean, and nurses came in with smiles on their faces. People needed to feel like they had a chance at life and were part of society, and to be treated with dignity, love, and respect. The staff at Morristown understood that. AIDS was a death sentence in 1992, when my mother and Marty got their diagnoses, but they were still among the living and wanted to continue living.

Marty had been in and out of hospitals so regularly that this time, I called him a private ambulance to take him to Morristown and continued getting ready for work. I watched out the window as the attendant secured his wheelchair, and Marty gazed up, a discouraged look on his face.

I was called to the hospital a few hours later, and arrived to find Marty on life support. I so desperately wished that he would get better that I chose to ignore what was right in front of me. To this day, when someone is sick, I refuse to think the worst.

Marty's navy-blue sweatshirt with "Whitney Houston" embroidered in white block letters had been cut right down the middle so electrodes could be attached to his chest. Mom, Bina, and I gathered around the bed, joined by the nurse who was monitoring him. He had been sedated while the nurse hooked him up to a ventilator, and she said it would wear off soon. When Marty woke up, he lifted himself slightly and looked at each of us. His eyes went from my mother to Bina, and then to me. He sucked his teeth a little bit and put his head down in disappointment as if to say, "I'm still here?"

Then Marty closed his eyes and never opened them again.

....

Getting clearance to take him off life support was a struggle, but we were all in agreement, my mother, my sister, and I. We had to wait for the doctors to arrive to make the determination. He had wasted away, and he'd had enough. "Didn't you see his eyes? He doesn't want to be here," I said. The lifeless image of him was searing into my brain, and I didn't want to remember him that way. Bina was steady and quiet as the doctors talked while examining our brother. One of the physicians said his lungs were full but his heart was strong. After a chain of doctors came through, one of them finally removed the cords from the respirator.

My mother stood silently, watching her son go.

I felt relieved he wouldn't have to be in that state any longer. My mother didn't want to see him endure any more, either. But I can't imagine how she felt at that moment. She didn't say a word. When we got home, she said she would have given anything for him to live. She wouldn't have cared what he wanted to do, or be, in his life. Her firstborn was gone.

....

My father showed up late to my brother's funeral. He hadn't made it to the wake. Mom said that as far as she was concerned, my father was dead. Sitting in the car before the funeral, Mom was broken. There was a lengthy, steady procession of cars carrying folks there to pay their respects. "Look at that long line," I said. "Look how many people love him."

On August 31, 1997, almost four years after Marty passed, I was at home in bed when a special report came on the late-night news. Princess Diana had been in a terrible car crash. I left the TV on for updates, drifting in and out of sleep. When I opened my eyes again, Princess Diana's picture was on the screen. To the left was her birthday: July 1, the same as Marty's, and she died at the same age, thirty-six. When I saw the dates, something Marty had said hit me like a revelation. One day out of the blue he'd told me that Diana was just like him. When I asked, "How so?" he said, "Misunderstood and searching for joy—simple happiness."

Eighteen

The Trouble with Angels

The day after I buried my brother, I was at home in the shower, and as the water rained down on me, I wept. Marty wasn't here anymore. I had a lot of mourning to do, but I sheltered myself from it by diving into my work. Mom was doing well on her treatment plan and was safe with Bina, so within days of Marty's funeral I rejoined the Bodyguard World Tour in Tokyo. After Tokyo, which marked the end of a month of dates in multiple cities in Japan, the tour continued on to Italy.

Bobby and Bobbi Kris eventually joined us on the road. Months earlier, before Bobby's own tour jumped off, he had stayed behind. Whitney, out of distrust, tried to monitor his whereabouts from afar. The whole thing was like watching a foreign movie without subtitles. It was difficult and frustrating to see my friend allow herself to be disrespected, demeaned, and then discouraged from doing what she knew was best for herself and her baby: leaving a fool.

....

What circumstances led to Whitney's telling Bobby about our romantic past remains a mystery. During a break in the second leg of the Bodyguard tour, Whitney decided to take her family on a vacation to Bali. Silvia and Shelly, Aunt Bae's youngest daughter, accompanied them. Nippy loved the islands—the humidity, balmy winds, fresh fruit, top-notch comfort, peace, and water that was the bluest blue. Our trips were serene, luxurious, and rejuvenating. It's sad that I can't recall a single trip Whit and Bobby went on without my hearing about some crazy stuff going down. Whatever force was behind this union revealed itself like a ball of confusion. And the fun-loving friend I knew was allowing herself to become someone else.

So I was relieved when I didn't hear one report of drama or bad news from the family's first vacation together. But shortly after they returned home, I was at the house and couldn't ignore the silence in the normally busy kitchen. I hadn't seen or spoken to Whitney since they had left for Bali, and now it was about a week after their return.

I cornered Silvia away from the kitchen and asked, "What the hell?"

Sil replied, agitated, "Come on, Robyn! You see the way Bobby is treating you?"

"What?" I was absolutely clueless.

According to Silvia, she and Whit, Bobby, Shelly, and Krissi (who was about two at this point) were having dinner in the restaurant at the Four Seasons, where they were staying. Silvia could tell right away that something had gone on between the couple, and Bobby was fuming. He abruptly rose from the table and stormed out while the other diners looked on. Whitney, Krissi, Sil, and Shelly followed. Once they were all in the hall, Bobby dragged Silvia by the arm and demanded his passport. He wanted to go back to the United States, solo.

"Give me my passport," he repeated. Then he shouted, "And you knew all this time?"

Sil responded, "Knew what? What are you talking about?"

"You knew about Robyn and Whitney?" Bobby asked, and Sil replied, "I don't know what you're talking about, Bobby."

"Aunt Bae told Whitney to tell me the truth, and she did," said Bobby.

"I still don't know what you're talking about." Silvia truly did not have any idea what he was referring to. It was so long ago, before her time with us.

For some reason, Whitney and I never got around to sitting down and discussing our lives and how we felt about all the gossip and its effect on us. Instead, we just went through life without ever making time to talk about it, though we should have. Back in the early days, Nip and I talked about everything, from our families to retirement and ways to make money other than singing. She had a vision of one day long down the road buying a compound on an island, similar to the famous Kennedy spread in Hyannis Port. In this dream, she, Silvia, and I each would have our own home, but we'd be together.

....

I was tired of being alone, and one evening in the summer of 1993 I thought about Lisa Hintelmann. When we had worked together, that was my focus. While there definitely was something about her, it was a feeling I had not allowed myself to explore because I wanted to stay professional. She had gorgeous long, curly dark brown hair, and was slim and well dressed with a classic French flair—straight out of preppy Boston College to the edgy downtown of New York City in the early nineties. She had a together, no-nonsense way about her that made me a little nervous. I was sure that she wasn't lonely, and I knew that if I made any kind of move and she responded, I had better be sure about what I was doing.

Lisa had moved on from the PR firm to GQ, where she was now special projects editor. I remembered where she said she lived and worked up the nerve to call her from my car on my brick-size early-issue cell phone. When she picked up, I told her that I "happened to be" in her neighborhood. I didn't want to assume she drank, so I said, "I was wondering if you'd like to go out for a hot chocolate." Lisa said she had a really bad cold so she couldn't join me. I felt the sting of rejection but pressed ahead. "Do you have everything you need?" I asked, offering to bring chicken soup.

"I have everything I need, thank you," she said. I was plummeting, but just before I hit the ground, she pulled me back up by saying, "I'll take a rain check." She called me a few days later and we met somewhere in Chelsea for a drink and started getting to know each other better.

....

In February 1994, Whitney threw Bobby a twenty-fifth birthday party at Tavern on the Green in Central Park. She was trying to do everything to make him feel worthy and important. I invited Lisa, and she came dressed head to toe in black, even taller than usual in three-inch-high suede boots. Everybody had a blast—hundreds of guests enjoyed unlimited drinks, plentiful spreads of food, and music that kept everyone moving.

I had a driver, so at the end of the night, I offered Lisa a ride home on our way back to Jersey. When we pulled up in front of her building, I asked if I could use her bathroom, and when I came out, she was standing by the front door of the apartment to see me out. Without allowing myself to give it any thought, I went in for one dynamite kiss! Late the next morning, I tentatively dialed her number, nervous that my big move may have blown everything. But Lisa was warm, and I could hear her smiling through the phone.

We started seeing each other regularly, and one of the first times I spent the night, we awakened to a silent Manhattan street blanketed in two feet of snow. No one knew that I was on the third floor of a charming Chelsea brownstone all snuggled up, cared for, and protected. But it wasn't the apartment that made me feel at ease, it was Lisa. My mother could call, but no one else knew where to find me. Lisa would set the table, cook dinner, and pour us glasses of wine. She introduced me to some of her favorite music. Over candlelit dinners, we talked about life, travel, our families, her, me—and it was just us.

Lisa wasn't intimidated by anything, but I remained hesitant about bringing her into my world. As soon as I entered her space, it felt as if my life with Whitney stopped. We didn't talk about that. But keeping away from the topic of work and Whitney had an effect on me: In that cozy apartment, I felt freer and closer to myself than ever before.

I loved walking around the city with Lisa. She had lived there for years, knew it well, and loved it. She was always flipping through *Time Out* and other magazines, identifying fun places and events for us to experience together—plays, museums, bars, and clubs. She would say, "Guess where we're going today?" I truly enjoyed getting to know the city with her—until she tried to hold my hand. "Please don't do that," I'd say inconsiderately. It made me uncomfortable to do that in public. For so long I'd been conditioned to see myself as an extension of Whitney Houston.

I also wasn't ready to be serious. I was still on the fence about commitment. I needed to figure out where I was and make up my mind.

Nineteen

Exhale

$\mathcal{M}eanwhile$ that winter, Whitney *ruled* the 1994 award shows. She took home three Grammys, five NAACP Image Awards, five World Music Awards, eight American Music Awards, and eleven Billboard Awards. At the Soul Train Music Awards, where she'd been booed five years earlier, she won R&B Song of the Year for "I Will Always Love You" (a decidedly *non*–R&B song) and was honored with the Sammy Davis Jr. Entertainer of the Year Award. Accepting the award that bore his name, she spoke about the racial discrimination Davis experienced and what it was like for black performers in his time. Then, after thanking her family members, she addressed me: "To my dear friend and executive assistant, Robyn Crawford: How do you thank someone for loyalty and devotion and love? Words cannot express. . . . So I say to you, thank you, and I love you. Your vision has not gone overlooked." I don't know what prompted her to single me out that particular evening. But on that night as she won the top Soul Train award, she honored me, too.

In April 1995, while we were out of the country, Bobby, his publicist, and his bodyguard were all arrested after allegedly beating a man at a Walt Disney World nightclub. The man needed six stitches on the back of his head, and part of his ear had to be surgically reattached. Charges were dropped after an undisclosed settlement.

Shortly before Bobby's arrest in Florida, the *National Enquirer* ran an alarming story told by Kevin Ammons, the ex-boyfriend of Whitney's former publicist. Ammons falsely identified himself as Whitney's onetime bodyguard and claimed that John Houston offered him $6,000 to break my kneecaps. He quoted John as telling him he should lay my legs "on the curb and break them with a bat" and saying, "I want her arms and her legs broke." During a television interview, Ammons claimed that John added, "I don't want her murdered. That would devastate Whitney."

My mother was beside herself: "Nothing better happen to you." Mom was a notetaker and kept meticulous records of everything, including what transpired between the Houstons and me. She went on the record with my aunt Marlene, too: "This is Robyn's professional business, so I stay out of it, but nothing better happen to my daughter."

I didn't approach the attorneys or anyone else at Nippy Inc. Everyone knew about the allegations, but with the exception of my assistant, Maria, no one said a word.

I went straight to Whitney.

"What is this?" I asked, holding up the paper. I usually dismissed stories about Whitney and me, but I had to read this one.

Staring at the headline and clearly bothered, she said, "I don't know, Robyn. I'll get to the bottom of it."

The next day, Whitney called. "I spoke to my father. You don't have anything to worry about. Are you all right?"

"I'm fine. Are you all right?"

"Yeah, I'm okay," she said, adding, "Nothing's going to happen to you."

Silvia told me that when her father came to the house to talk, Whitney was emotional, crying as she sat on the ledge of the great room's stone fireplace, her father seated opposite: "No, Daddy! Robyn is my friend." In the press, John denied it all, and he never said a word to me about Ammons's claims.

The truth was, every time Whitney took a hit, I took a hit. Despite her success, the lavish wedding, the flashy rings, and the reassurance from the married couple that all was well, the gay rumors about her persisted. Decades later, Gary admitted in an interview that they just wanted to scare me, but I wonder if it ever crossed their minds that it was hurting Nippy, their sister, their daughter, the one providing for all of them.

Once Nip had spoken to her father, I felt better because at least I knew where she stood. Even after Ammons's book came out a year later, dredging up the whole thing all over again, the threat of bodily harm didn't slow me down. But it did lead me to wonder exactly who was involved with what and who got paid for what role. I began connecting dots.

Although I had moved out long ago, I had kept my key to the house Whitney and I used to share. Some of my belongings remained, like personal video footage I'd taken on tour, and I'd often go up there to swim or just hang out.

One day in late September 1995, I sat at the kitchen table with Silvia, watching the news. Bobby wasn't around because Whitney had put him out once again. In an earlier incident, he'd stormed into the garage and smashed the windows of her white Porsche.

This time, Bobby drove off in her cream-colored Bentley, a gift from Warner Bros. after they'd wrapped production on *The Bodyguard*. Now Bobby was caught up in a shooting in Roxbury, his old Boston neighborhood. As we saw the blood on the seats of the bullet-riddled Bentley, the news reported that someone had died. The camera zoomed in on Bobby sitting on the curb, his head in his hands. Per usual he was uninjured, though everything he put his hands on ended up in ruins.

That October, after being given the choice between jail time for driving under the influence and rehab, Bobby checked into the Betty Ford Center for treatment for alcohol abuse.

That same year Whitney signed on to the film adaptation of Terry McMillan's bestselling novel *Waiting to Exhale*.

At the start of filming in Scottsdale, Arizona, Whitney and Bobby were on the outs again, and she was clean and clearheaded. The women in the cast had built a friendship and support system, and Forest Whitaker was a kind and intuitive director. Whitney's character was Savannah, a television producer who, after years of believing the married man she's in love with will leave his wife, finally stops settling for the fantasy and learns to embrace her life without him. I hoped that Whitney would connect with this strong character and stand up for herself. Around the time she was shooting her love scene with Dennis Haysbert, Bobby showed up in Arizona and spent the night. The next morning, Nip showed up on set exhausted. She looked drawn. It was disappointing.

At the time of the film's release, Oprah did a segment on *Exhale* with the four leads. Oprah talked to Lela Rochon, Loretta Devine, and Angela Bassett about how they were cast and how they connected to their characters. She saved Whitney for last, and when she turned to her, she began by noting that she and Bobby were tabloid fodder. She asked Whit to tell the audience "whatever it is [she] want[ed] us to know."

"My life is none of your business," she replied.

Oprah came right back with, "Tell us how Bobby is doing and how y'all are doing." I stood backstage wishing Nip had spent even five minutes thinking about the film and preparing for the interview. She should have been able to easily turn the conversation to Savannah. But her head was fuzzy and unfocused, and instead she fell back to her default, saying what she thought was safe—talking about her mother. She stuck to that old familiar script rather than come up with something fresh, interesting, or relevant. Every interview that she had, even if it started out with talk about a number 1 song, a great performance, or how many awards she'd garnered, the journalist always wound up turning to gossip, gay rumors, or Bobby's bad behavior.

In August 1996, less than a year after *Exhale*'s premiere and the beginning of another round of awards recognizing Whitney's achievements, Bobby would be arrested yet again for drunk driving after losing control of her leased black Porsche, jumping the curb and crashing into a hedge in Hollywood, Florida. He broke four ribs and a foot. Bobby's blood alcohol level was more than twice the state limit, plus he had drugs in his system.

And I kept waiting for her to get tired of it all.

....

Having spent her entire adulthood in apartments, Mom yearned to live in a house, and while I was on the road for the Moment of Truth Tour, she started looking at real estate. When I returned to the States, Mom told me all about the house she loved the most. So on December 12, 1994, we moved to a new house. I'd loved the condo we shared, but my mom wanted a house, and I would have done anything to make her happy. Whitney generously gifted me $100,000 toward the down payment.

Janet Crawford was beautiful inside and out, and when we moved, she was doing well living with AIDS. She attended church, spent time with family and friends, laughed on the phone, wrote letters, and tended to herself. Her T-cell count elevated considerably to a less vulnerable zone. Mom was feeling well and focused on living. Meanwhile, I was flying back and forth to the West Coast, attending award shows and recording sessions with Whitney. When I was home I would work with some of the artists we were developing at Angelway Artists, the management company we ran together, and on our record label, Better Place.

We needed producers and writers to work with two of the acts we had signed, singer Shanna Wylie from North Carolina and a girl group called Sunday, from Newark and East Orange. Late one night my phone rang and it was Raynelle Swilling, my close friend, whom I often referred to as my West Coast A&R ears. She said, "I'm in the studio with Kenny Ortiz and these producers called The Neptunes, and they are baaaad. You gotta get with them right away." She had her finger on the pulse, so I jumped on it. After several phone conversations, I flew to Virginia Beach with Shanna to meet the production team of Pharrell Williams and Chad Hugo. Twenty-one-year-old Pharrell picked us up at the airport, and as we climbed in I heard Joni Mitchell's "Big Yellow Taxi."

"What you know about Joni?" I asked.

"What? I love Joni Mitchell," he answered.

Relatively unknown at the time, The Neptunes were the first

producing team to work with us. It was a beautiful summer day as Pharrell drove to a large green Victorian house, where upstairs he had his recording essentials. He and Shanna went for a ride to the store together to get to know each other a little bit and shortly after they returned, we got to work. We left with two rough mixes, "Let It Go" and "I Can't Explain." Soon after, I rented a van and drove Sunday back down to Virginia Beach to a new studio The Neptunes had recently purchased and they came up with two hot dance tracks, "A Perfect Love" and "Chess."

Months later, a solo Pharrell came to work at Whitney's studio. Leading up to this opportunity, I had been telling Whitney all about what our label could do with their production, sending her every track and rough mix, attaching memos outlining specifics in order to keep her up to speed. I looked forward to making the introduction. Pharrell was working on a project for Space (a.k.a. Traci Selden), and played three of her songs. He asked me if Whitney would sing the hook on a track called "Message from an Angel":

I would never hurt you,
But what am I supposed to do?

I loved the song, played it for Nip, and left her a copy. I strongly recommended that we enter into a partnership with The Neptunes and sign Space to our management company. A few days later, Nip walked over to Crossway, unfortunately with Bobby tagging along. *Here we go!* I thought. I figured he was sniffing around trying to pick up a scent that could lead to something for him. Pharrell played a few tracks for them, including Space's. Nip was into it, but then for some reason, after roughly twenty minutes, she said,

"I'll be at the house," and they left. Pharrell and I just looked at each other like, "All righty!"

"I'll go over and talk to her in a little bit," I said. After an hour, I strolled over and found the couple in the kitchen making something to eat, TV playing.

"So, what do you think?" I asked.

"Yeah, I like him. His stuff is cool. But I can't do the hook."

"Why Nip?" I asked. "It's just a demo." I told her that we should consider making the producing team an offer to work with us.

Bobby piped up: "I like Chucky. Chucky Thompson is better."

Chucky Thompson was a producer out of DC who worked closely with Sean Combs / Bad Boy Entertainment. I liked Chucky too, but this was The Neptunes and they felt like the future.

....

One day I came home and found Mom shaken. She said that as she was driving home and turned the corner onto our cul-de-sac, the steering wheel suddenly became really hard to turn and she ended up running up onto the curb. It was obvious to both of us that Mom's motor skills had been compromised. Luckily no one was hurt, and she escaped fine, though shaken. After that, her car sat unused in the garage.

Then, near the end of 1995, she suffered a seizure. Fortunately, I was home, and as I passed her room I noticed her body slumped to one side. Her eyes were open but didn't seem to be registering anything. The nearest hospital was less than twelve minutes away and the ambulance arrived quickly. Unconscious, she was taken to the ICU. I felt in my gut that Mom was going to awaken and return to us, and after four days, she opened her eyes to find me sitting at the foot of her bed. She looked at me, bewildered, as if to say, "Where are we and why are you looking at me that way?" She didn't remember what had landed her in the hospital.

After about a week, she was released, but this was the start of a slow, steady decline and I realized she no longer could be left home alone. As we sat poolside at our new home, she began talking about parenthood. She talked about how much she loved Marty— how she loved him exactly as he was. With tears streaming down her cheeks, she said, "I would have given everything to trade places with my child, anything for him to live."

I wondered if Mom was afraid, after watching her firstborn and only son lose a battle that she was now fighting. I didn't ask many questions. For once in my life with her, I did a lot of listening. It was more important to know and remember. I believed that Mom would live as I'd believed Marty would. Bina said I was still in denial. I was terrified of death.

My mother had survived domestic violence when there were no laws to protect women, then put herself through six years of school, earning a bachelor's degree in psychology and a master's in counseling, all while raising three children on her own with no help from our father. I was pissed that this was where life had taken her after all she had sacrificed and accomplished.

Janet Crawford, still in high school when she had her first child and only twenty-six when she had her third, had expectations for a better life for herself and her children. Raising us, she often talked about her disappointment and blamed our father for ruining what our family could have been.

I used to tell her, "Mom, let go of him and that kind of thinking. We made it. We made it because of you. We did it. You can be proud of yourself."

A smile would cross her face. "I am very proud of my children."

....

Mom didn't want to spend any more time in hospitals, and I was glad that for the most part we were able to keep her comfortable and at home with Bina and me. Our goal was to keep the pain under control, but there were many signs that the illness was progressing. I wasn't on the road, so I was able to be there with Bina to care for her. We had time to talk. "Take care of each other," she instructed me. "Look out for your sister and get to know Jesus."

Eventually, we were advised to call hospice. They sent a hospital bed to the house, but when it arrived, my mother told me to get rid of it, so I did. It was difficult to turn her in the bed and help her when she needed a bedpan, and it was painful for her, too. The aide provided morphine as needed, and Bina and I would stay with her late into the night. When we finally went to sleep in the wee hours, we'd ask the aide to rouse us if Mom needed anything or asked for us. And then we'd be back first thing in the morning to check on her. She was no longer able to talk and her eyes were closed, but I continued to talk to her.

On what turned out to be her last night, I sat up talking softly in her ear, my head on her chest.

"Mom, I want you to go. Don't worry about us. Bina and I will be fine. It's okay to let go. You taught us well, and we know what to do. Don't be afraid. Go be with Nana and Marty—they're waiting for you. I love you."

She finally passed on Thursday, April 18, 1996. Bina called most of our family members and the friends in our mother's address book while I focused on the arrangements.

Though my mother attended a small nondenominational church in Orange, I opted to hold her service at New Hope in Newark, which could accommodate a larger crowd and would be relatively easy for folks to get to. Whitney offered to call Pastor Buster Soaries to officiate the service, and I asked my "cousin" Ameena Mateen to deliver the eulogy. We had Mom dressed in cream leggings and a blouse, a cream jacket trimmed in gold, and a matching wrap around her hair. We covered her feet in thick white cotton socks. My sister and I sent Mom off warm and comfortable.

In her absence, I felt alone. I felt as though I could no longer make any mistakes because the person I could always run to was gone. Whatever the circumstances, Mom was in my corner. She knew exactly what to do and not do, what to say, and now there was only silence. The day that Janet Marie Williams Crawford left, I finally had to grow up.

....

As production for *The Preacher's Wife* began, I was still trying to make headway with the label and our partnership with Elektra Records. Shanna had been in the studio working with The Neptunes, Mario Winans, Narada Michael Walden, and another producer suggested by Sylvia Rhone, doing two cuts. Throughout our entire relationship and despite all my efforts, I was never able to capture Sylvia's ear.

One afternoon, I went to the Elektra offices to play Shanna's record for about twelve executives in a large, circular conference room. The heads of each department were there: R&B, Pop Promotions, Marketing, Public Relations, Sales, and then, of course, Sylvia. I was in the center seat. We went through the songs one by one, and each person gave their critique. Most of it was positive, with constructive criticism on tracks where Shanna delivered a solid vocal performance. But it was clear that we still didn't have a lead single or the heat they felt we needed to get them 100 percent behind the project. Afterward, I played rough mixes of two Sunday tracks produced by The Neptunes just for Sylvia, which failed to blow her away. This is how it goes for artists, songwriters, producers, and A&R people. Not everyone's going to hear it and get it. Happens all the time.

Our partnership fell apart after a meeting with Sylvia and Merlin Bobb (Sylvia's A&R man) late one Friday morning. I was there to play some new mixes on tracks Shanna had done. When she and I arrived, Sylvia's assistant Tee, who had been with her for years, welcomed us and directed Shanna to make herself comfortable in Sylvia's office. I made my way to another room a few doors away. Inside the small room were a desk with a few chairs, audio equipment, and speakers. Merlin was already seated but stood to give me a hug and said that Sylvia was on her way. We sat quietly awaiting Rhone, who now was running ten or fifteen minutes late. Then she walked in the door, clearly agitated, picked up the CD I had placed on the table, and threw it at the wall!

I had been in good spirits that day, but when Sylvia entered, clearly disturbed about something else, she picked up the case, and flung it like a Frisbee, I broke. I couldn't stop myself from crying. Shanna heard me and came out to the hall, saying, "Robyn, are you all right?" I hadn't ever cried like that before, and certainly not in a professional setting. The partnership was irreparably destroyed.

Back at Nippy Inc., I headed to Los Angeles to meet with the Disney team on *The Preacher's Wife*. Whitney's third film was already under way, costarring Denzel Washington, who was highly respected for his films *Philadelphia* and *Malcolm X*. But in Whitney's world things really couldn't have been much worse. She was distracted, worn down, manipulated, and too easily taken advantage of. It seemed that no one other than Silvia and me was looking out for what was best for Whitney. Where I had once been the point of entry for everything coming in for Whitney, I was no longer able to effectively support her, because I was spending most of my time navigating the obstacle courses within her own company. Once again, Whitney had signed on to do a movie that she wasn't ready for. Typically, in December Whitney headed to Florida or the islands. But here she was, under pressure, under extreme conditions, enduring a brutally cold winter, and doing a significant number of outdoor scenes. She could have said no and probably wished she had—she could have done a gospel album without doing a movie. Instead, she had another starring role and no growth opportunity within it for her future production goals.

Other than when Whitney and Denzel had scenes together, we didn't spend much time with him while shooting in New Jersey. Whenever he wasn't in a scene, he returned to his trailer. Given the temperature, no one took that personally, and we assumed that was his way of working and keeping his focus. But when we arrived in Maine, where we expected it would be even colder, the weather was balmy and we saw Denzel come alive with his happy, charismatic side. He was the consummate professional.

The shoot rekindled the kinship between Loretta Devine, Gregory Hines, and Whitney, all of whom were in *Waiting to Exhale*, and introduced Whitney to Jenifer Lewis, who was warm, friendly, and crazy hilarious.

Mervyn Warren, of the popular a cappella gospel group Take 6, was the film's music supervisor. Whitney had been a fan of the group since the release of their debut album and wanted Mervyn, who had done a lot of the arranging and production on the group, to be integrally involved. In the studio Whit and Merv's relationship was harmonious and inspiring, which wasn't at all surprising.

She was singing the music she loved the most, and it showed. I focused on the gospel side of the project. I'd spent time traveling with Angie and Debbie Winans on their debut record, *Angie & Debbie*, which introduced me to the world of gospel radio. A company called Gospel Centric had been hired to work the music, ensure radio play, handle marketing, and set up the most important media interviews for Whitney to do.

While we were shooting in Newark, the day came for the church scene to be filmed, and the Georgia Mass Choir arrived. We were outside shooting for most of the day, and if Whitney was outside, I had to be there as well, watching the progress and giving her extra strength by letting her see that I was freezing, too. Finally, we entered Trinity United Methodist Church, and as we thawed, Whitney changed into a gold church robe.

The director was Penny Marshall. Coming from a family of comedic creators, Penny was good-natured and effortlessly funny. The West Coaster moved about in the cold winter of Newark in an oversize parka, the fur-trimmed hood pulled up over her head. Penny came over to give Whitney the breakdown of upcoming scenes, most of which she was in, and with a lot of lines. Knowing Whitney's voice was already going from the earlier outdoor scenes, Penny suggested, "Now, Whitney, you can take it easy. Just lip-sync and let the choir do the singing, okay?"

"Okay, Penny," she replied.

With Penny behind the camera in the back of the church, Whitney, Silvia, and I made our way down the aisle to the front, where the members of Georgia Mass were taking their positions on the stage's risers. I watched Whitney begin to get energized, with the church packed with cast members and extras seated in the pews. Whit strolled over to the podium, quietly rehearsing a few lines to herself. Then her mouth stopped moving as she looked out into the "congregation." Feeling it, too, Jenifer Lewis shouted something like, "It's already heating up in here!"

As the choir did their vocal warm-ups, Whit stood to the side of the stage for last-minute makeup touch-ups. It was a few minutes before cameras were ready to roll. Whitney's ears tuned in as she hummed along, exercising her cords. Turning to me, she stated, "You don't lip-sync with the Georgia Mass Choir in town." Anyone inside that church who had never felt the spirit before sure did that day! Praise and worship filled the entire space with "Joy to the World," "I Go to the Rock," "Help Is on the Way," and "I Love the Lord." The Holy One's presence filled me, too.

I had made my way to the back of the church near Penny and the camera crew. Penny watched the scene on the monitor, her hand raised to say "Cut!" But her body was facing one direction and her head another. She finally yelled the word *cut*, jangled like she'd just finished wrestling a bull. I don't think Penny Marshall had ever been to *that* kind of church before!

We went to Portland for the ice skating scene, and everyone was happy about the unexpectedly mild temperature. All except the poor crew, who then had one heck of a time making snow and ice, as the pond melted.

The *Preacher's Wife* soundtrack was released on November 26, 1996, debuting at the top of the gospel charts and staying there for twenty-six consecutive weeks. It was and still is the most successful gospel album of all time. I kept the lines of communication open with the Gospel Centric team working the project. Meanwhile, Arista was laser focused only on the songs that Clive had a hand in, "I Believe in You and Me," "Somebody Bigger Than You and I," "My Heart Is Calling," two tracks with Shanna's smoky-raspy flavor on backing vocals, and then the Annie Lennox–penned "Step by Step." It was the gospel portion of the album that had the momentum, dominating the charts. Executives working the soundtrack at Gospel Centric said they were receiving zero support from Arista to build on what they had and take it into the mainstream. After all, it was the Christmas season, and who knows what could have happened if they had worked together?

Whitney was executive producer on the soundtrack. Maureen Crowe, who was consulting at Arista, called me to say that she and Roy Lott, Clive's number two, had agreed that I should have an associate producer credit. I thought, *Ain't this some shit.* They wouldn't give me any kind of credit on *The Bodyguard,* but they were happy to attach my name to a gospel record they had no intention of getting behind. But instead I said, "Good looking out, Maureen, and thank you." I had nothin' but love for my Long Island sista. When it was all over Whitney voiced her disappointment in Arista's lack of support, saying, "They buckled at the knees."

Twenty

SOS

One day I was leaving the house for work when my cell rang. It was Silvia. "Robyn, it's me. I can't handle this. Bobby and Whitney are fighting again!" The day before, Whitney and Silvia had flown from Jersey to Atlanta so Whit could surprise her husband, who was on the road with New Edition. It was evening when they arrived at the Ritz-Carlton, and they went straight to his room, knocking and knocking on the door, but no answer. They headed down to the front desk, where Whitney requested a key to her husband's room, but the hotel refused to grant entry. So, she paid for a room on the same floor.

When they returned upstairs, Tommy, Kenny (Bobby's producer/bodyguard), and another guy were in the hallway. Whitney asked where her husband was. Then the door opened and Bobby emerged.

"I don't want you here. This is my thing, my time."

"Why didn't you open the door when I knocked?" Whitney asked. In response, her husband moved closer and hocked a loogie directly in her face. She took off down the hall in tears, Silvia by her side, Bobby following, cursing. He pushed into the room behind them, picked up a glass, and hurled it at Whitney. Reflexively, Sil pushed her out of the way, the glass narrowly missing Whit before smashing into the wall and shattering. Whitney grabbed the hotel phone to dial her father, but before she could finish dialing, Bobby snatched the receiver out of her hand, striking her on the head with it. She screamed before sinking to the floor, head in her hands.

It wasn't an unfamiliar story. Bobby reminded me of my father, who fathered multiple children outside of his marriage and then abused my mother and falsely accused her of cheating on him, erupting into jealous, violent rages in front of us kids.

Soon after, Whitney's security man, who was staying across the street at another hotel, was called to the Ritz-Carlton to ride with Silvia and Whit to the airport. But halfway there, Whitney changed her mind and decided to go back. Making it all even worse, the security guard was fired after Bobby accused Whitney of sleeping with him.

This sort of scenario played out again and again, eventually becoming the norm. It was confusing and sickening to watch. I couldn't figure out why it was taking Whitney so long to come to her senses. Every time something happened, I said to myself, "This is it." Bobby saved his worst behavior for when I wasn't around, but the stories always made their way back to me.

The drugs didn't help, of course. I wish I could say Whitney was focused and aware of the goings-on around her, but she was not. And I was no longer in a position to inform her or prevent any of it. When Whitney would go home, she wasn't catching up on much-needed rest. Why do that when you can go even higher? Her marriage was extinguishing what little self-esteem she had left. She once hired an undercover detective to follow Bobby's every move and confirm what she already knew. That time, her husband was in Los Angeles shaking it up with a well-known musician's daughter. I was at the house when Whit gave Aunt Bae's daughter Laurie a package with the taped evidence inside, telling her to take it downstairs and put it away. I never asked to see the video. I hoped that this time she might finally cut him loose. But again, she did nothing. I knew she was getting deeper and deeper into the drugs and I needed to help her.

....

The next time Whitney joined Bobby on the road, Bobbi Kris, Silvia, and Shelly came along with her. It wasn't long before Silvia called me from her Detroit hotel room, frantic. "Robyn, you have to come. Whitney looks a mess and I can't do anything to help her."

"What's she doing?"

"She's been getting high for days and everybody on this tour is laughing at her. She looks terrible, Robyn. You have to come help her."

In no time, I was boarding a plane.

I arrived at the hotel to find the lobby bustling with tour personnel. There were a few familiar faces, but I kept my eyes low, heading straight to Silvia's room on the first floor, near Nip's. As I walked through, I heard someone call my name. I turned my head and waved to one of the dancers, never breaking my stride. As I neared her door, I saw Silvia's head peek out and then she said softly, "Come in." Aunt Bae's daughter Shelly and Bobbi Kris were watching television on the sofa as Silvia began her update: "Whitney doesn't know that you're here. She doesn't know what she's doing. She's not in her right mind." As we headed back toward the lobby, Silvia relayed that Bobby had gotten another room on a different floor so he could shack up with some woman. Whitney suspected he was messing around, and they'd been arguing.

Silvia knocked on the door to Whitney's room, which oddly was only about twenty feet from the lobby desk. "Whitney, open the door. It's me, Silvia." The door opened, and Nip turned away without noticing me. As I entered the room, she turned back and eyed me, her face defiant. I tried to think of the right thing to say, but no words came to mind. The room was a narrow space, with tacky, second-rate décor—hardly the luxury accommodation to which we had become accustomed. She looked unkempt, drawn, her weave dry and pulled back sloppily.

I wanted to hug her, to pull her to me and take her out of there. I embraced her and she didn't resist, but her body was limp, as though she couldn't really feel me. "Hi, Robyn," she said, drugs in her voice.

"We've been hearing all kinds of stuff so I came to check on you and make sure you were all right. Silvia said she needed help and we should bring you home."

"Really? I need to go home?" she replied, looking at Silvia.

I pulled up a chair and sat, scanning the room, thinking of the best way to move Whitney out of there discreetly. I whispered to Silvia, "Let's take her down to your room."

But before we could move, in walked Bobby, belligerent. "Look at you. You look a mess," he said to Nip. Then, spotting me, he said, "What the fuck is she doing here? You called her?"

Whitney's pathetic response: "No, I didn't call her here."

I jumped in. "I came because I got a call that Nip isn't doing well and needs to go home."

This was a chance for Bobby to show that he cared about his wife, my friend. Or at least an out for him so he could continue practicing his typical behavior unhindered. Instead, he asked, "Nippy, do you need to go home?" It was clear what he wanted her answer to be.

"No, I don't need to go home," she answered, turning to me. "You need to go home, Robyn."

"I flew here because I needed to know that you were all right. I'm looking at you and you are not all right. You need to get out of here, Nip."

She just peered at me and said, "I'm fine." I rose, walked out of the door, and flew back to Jersey.

Upon my return, I filled in Mr. Houston and Donna on Whitney's condition, adding that there was no one there to provide her security other than Bobby's "bodyguard." But after telling them, I didn't hear another word about it.

I stayed in close contact with Silvia, keeping my two-way pager powered on and next to me through the day and night. Sure enough, one morning Silvia phoned me in a panic, saying she couldn't find Whitney. They were at some hotel in a remote part of the country and now Whitney was missing. I asked, "Where's Bobby?" She told me that he, along with the rest of the tour, had already left that location, taking Krissi and Shelly with them. I stayed on the phone while Sil asked the front desk staff if they had seen Whitney Houston.

Silvia said that she would call back. When she did, it was from a taxi on her way to the airport. She had learned that Whitney had had the hotel book her a flight to Miami and arrange a car to take her to the airport. Silvia immediately phoned the airline, asking them to hold the flight. When Silvia arrived at the airport, they had isolated Whitney safely in a private room. Silvia took her into the bathroom, cleaned her up, helped her change into fresh clothes, and added a touch of color to her lips. The next time I heard from her, they were back on the tour bus. Bobby's brother Tommy had picked them up from the airport. In hindsight, Silvia was sorry she hadn't tried harder to get Whitney to Florida, away from the madness.

When Whitney, Krissi, Shelly, and Silvia returned, Sil was determined to tell Whitney's parents about what had gone on. She was at the end of her rope and tired of being stuck in the middle of the Whitney and Bobby show. She was stressed to the max, uncomfortable around Bobby, and afraid for Whit. Most important, she felt it was her duty to inform John and Cissy of the gravity of their daughter's drug problem.

The thing is, we all heard the noise from the tour. The tabloids ensured that, and John had even gotten a call from someone who had toured with us back in the day who said he had run into Whitney and didn't even realize until afterward that it was her.

Silvia's meeting with Whitney's parents lasted nearly an hour, and when it was over she swung by my area, which now took up the entire length of the back of the building. Silvia plopped down in the chair across from me and said, "I told them everything."

"Good," I replied. "Good." Maybe now they'd finally do something.

That May, Whitney was booked to travel to the Pacific Rim for eight to ten dates in Japan, Thailand, Australia, Taiwan, and Hawaii, which was a total surprise to me. From what I could see, everybody was looped in but me. Then Silvia phoned to tell me the latest developments: Silvia was being placed at the studio (i.e., punished) and was not allowed inside Whitney's house. She also told me that she would not be traveling with Whitney on the Pacific Rim Tour. Silvia wanted to know why this was happening. "What did I do?" she wondered.

My detective hat was on, but honestly, I didn't know where to start. It just didn't make sense. Those responsible for making certain that Sil stayed behind left Whitney without the person who knew exactly what her needs were and how to keep her comfortable. With the tour departure date a few weeks away, I set out to find out whatever I could quietly, without making too much of a fuss. I hung around, looking for a moment when I could speak to Whitney privately. I didn't trust anybody.

Meanwhile, Whitney remained out of sight and silent. I decided that in solidarity with Silvia, I, too, would stay behind. When I finally saw Whitney, she already knew that I wasn't going. "So you're not coming, Rob?"

"No," I said. "We have a couple of sessions lined up at the studio and it's best I be there."

Sitting on the sofa, she nodded in agreement. Bae, Carol, and a few others moved about in the kitchen. Plopping down next to Nip, I asked how she was feeling.

"Ready to get this shit over with and get people out of my ass."

"Why isn't Silvia going?" I asked.

"Donna and the lawyers told me it was best for her not to go." Then she was interrupted and that was the end of our conversation. Before leaving for the airport, Whitney walked over to the studio and told Silvia, "I wish that I could take you with me, but I can't. They say that I can't trust you."

"Who told you that?" asked Silvia.

"Everybody. The attorneys, my parents, Donna. It's not me, it's them." She gave Silvia a hug, telling her to take care of herself and that she'd see her when she returned in a month.

Silvia had been demoted from being assistant to Whitney Houston to being the bag packer and studio cleaner. While Whitney was away, Silvia was sent to the main house to clean the cat litter boxes and do whatever else needed to be done. Humiliated, she told me she was sick and tired of it and wanted to quit. I reassured her that Whitney would be back soon and we'd figure something out. She just needed to hold on a little longer. But she was bored out of her mind. If no one came up to the studio, she still had to be there. The only good part was that she could bounce at five o'clock on the nose, which was never possible while she was on Whitney watch.

One morning after the tour ended, pulling into the driveway toward the studio, Silvia spotted Bobby dragging Whitney off the porch. She parked and jumped out of her car, running over to intervene. Managing to get between the two of them, she yelled to Whitney to run. Bobby grabbed and pushed Silvia, and she, too, began running across the lawn, past the tennis courts, toward the house, following Whit. The guardhouse was next to the entrance to the main house and Donna's brother Darren, whom she had managed to get employed as a "guard," saw what was going down but chose to look the other way.

Silvia directed Whitney to go inside, yelling to Aunt Bae, "Open the door for Whitney!" while simultaneously trying to distract Bobby until Whitney could make it inside the house. Bobby spotted Nip's black Porsche parked in front of the garage and took his anger out on it, jumping on the roof until it was crushed.

The Porsche drama took place in the morning, and by early afternoon Whit finally had clarity. She told Bae to call the studio and tell Silvia to come to the house. Nip was lying on the sofa when she arrived and asked her to sit down. Instinctively, Silvia began to rub her feet. Nippy expressed how much she missed her and promised that she wasn't going to leave her behind again. In the middle of the conversation, the phone rang. It was Donna calling to speak to Silvia. Aunt Bae must have phoned her to relay that Sil was back on the premises.

Silvia picked up the phone and said, "Whitney asked me to come over here."

And just like that, Whitney rose from the sofa, grabbed the phone, and said, "I don't give a damn what you or they say. She's not going back. She's staying with me. I pay the bills around here." Returning to the sofa, Whitney eyed Silvia with a smile. "I know you love me."

....

More and more, Whitney's career was taking over her life, leaving the things that really mattered to her on the back burner. Whitney got busier and busier doing all the things that others said she should do instead of following her instincts.

The pressures of her career also kept her from spending much quality time with her daughter. All Kristina ever wanted was to have her mom's attention one-on-one, and the majority of the time that just didn't happen. She never really made friends of her own, had sleepovers, or got invited to birthday parties. She spent the majority of her time with adults. And when nieces, nephews, stepbrothers, and stepsisters came to her house, she had to share her mom with them. At the end of each week, she was typically packed up and sent to Donna's or Aunt Bae's for the weekend.

So it was primarily in the recording studio or during live performances that mother and daughter bonded. When Whitney called Krissi to the mic and gave her the cue, her daughter delivered every time. Like her mother, she wished to sing, and even at age four she had the confidence to do so.

Decades later, my therapist pointed out that I had to behave like a grown-up when I was only a child. I was very connected to my mother and feared for her safety—I remembered the time I had to come home from summer camp to make sure she wasn't alone. I'd get all tangled up in my parents' fights, trying to intervene and settle them. I wondered what Krissi witnessed in her own home, how much her parents' volatile relationship affected her. By the age of five, she was regularly being told that her mother was tired or asleep. She must have recognized that that was abnormal.

Kids know. Still, when you watch footage of the two of them onstage together, the love they shared is undeniable.

Months after the Pacific Rim Tour, we were staying in a Manhattan hotel. Though she had agreed to make an afternoon appearance with Clive the next day, Whitney stayed up all night partying with Michael. I knew Whitney wasn't going to make it, and I felt bad for her. I figured there was no point in delaying the inevitable call and dialed Clive to cancel. It took three different tries to get him to accept the news: "She can't do it." "She's not feeling well." And then finally, "Clive—she can't get dressed. She's not in any shape to go."

I immediately phoned John Houston and told him that I believed Clive knew that Whitney had a serious problem, sharing the conversation I'd just had with him. I checked out of the hotel and headed straight to the office, where Mr. Houston was waiting for me. I told him that something had to be done immediately or I didn't know how long Whitney was going to last. Mr. Houston told me that he had spoken to Clive and that he'd suggested a rehab center, Silver Hill. He said that I would have to come to the consultation so I could tell the experts everything I knew and why I felt Whitney was a candidate for their facility. The hospital had an excellent reputation in treating addiction and was discreet in their handling of high-profile personalities. It was rumored that Michael Jackson had been there a few months earlier.

It was a beautiful sunny day when John and I made the trip up to Connecticut and met with the medical director, Dr. Richard Frances. After introducing ourselves, I sat down and told him everything I felt he needed to know, including that Nip told me she had first tried cocaine at age fourteen; that she and I had used the drug together; and that since getting married, her use had clearly escalated. Her behavior had changed: She had become increasingly isolated. She was thin and didn't look well. We were having to cancel some commitments due to her condition.

On the way back from Connecticut, John assured me that I had done the right thing, and now all he had to do was get Whitney to agree to go to rehab. We returned to the office to find an angry Cissy there waiting for us. She was upset about the fact that I had gone with John to Silver Hill and she hadn't come with us. "Why didn't I know this was happening? That's my daughter, too." I could hear them arguing in his office as I walked away.

Later, John peeked into my office to say he was going to the house to speak to Nip. Bobby wasn't there, which gave John the opportunity to talk to his daughter alone. That evening, when I didn't hear from him, I called him at home. "She doesn't want to go," he said.

I had to be certain he actually did talk to Whitney, so I went up to the house myself. I can still see her face when she said, "Yes, my father spoke to me. I'm not ready to go to rehab. I don't want to go." I was so disappointed I had no response. Then she said, "I have the doctor's card. My father gave it to me. I'll call when I'm ready." We'd had so many conversations around the use of cocaine. But now her using had turned into something much deeper and meaner than I had seen before. Whitney knew she was in trouble.

A week or so later, I drove Whitney to Clive's Westchester home. Later that night, Clive called to tell me that Whitney had admitted to her drug use. "She likes it. She told me that she likes it," he said. He offered his home in the Hamptons to Whitney, suggested she bring two people she trusted along with her, and said that he would arrange for a private nurse to be there. The next day, Whitney considered going, but by the end of that day, Michael came up to the house, and he and his sister disappeared into the back room for two days. The Hamptons never came up again.

Twenty-One

My Love Is Your Love

Cindy Madnick, the bookkeeper at Nippy Inc., was a no-nonsense woman in her early sixties, with dark cherry-red hair. If you wanted to know what was going on with the company financially, Cindy was your gal. She hated all of us.

I don't know if Cindy was like this with everyone, but with me, she'd vent. I'd walk in cheerfully greeting her and asking how she was doing. She'd take my receipts and talk: "This poor girl isn't going to have a dime left when you people are finished with her. Bobby's mother calls up here like we're an ATM machine. 'I need my cable, my electricity, my heat paid.'"

She'd go on. "I feel sorry for this girl. It's a shame. She works so hard, and at this rate, she won't have anything left for herself." Then, after questioning the generous tips that I'd bestowed upon porters and doormen, she'd apologize for venting and hand me cash or a check.

The first time that I heard Whitney was out of money—meaning she had assets but no cash flow—was in 1987. We had toured the world for eleven months in a single year. We'd celebrated Thanksgiving in Australia and had just two weeks off for Christmas. I told Nip, "If you want to know where your money is going and who's buying what or why, ask Cindy. You don't even have to go to the office. You can go to her house. She lives about fifteen minutes from the office. Or just call her up."

When she did get in touch with Cindy, she quickly learned that she was paying for a number of family members' homes, car insurance, gas, and more. Nip even learned she was bankrolling one senior employee's condo, car, and living expenses. She also learned that her father had set up a Nippy Inc. account at the Mobil station around the corner from the office, and a number of people were taking advantage of it. "My mother makes enough money! Why am I paying for all of her stuff?" Nip fumed.

She made the decision to have several credit cards taken away from Nippy employees and instructed Cindy to cease paying the Brown family's expenses. She permitted Silvia to keep her corporate card. And yet, no matter how much money Whitney generated with her record-breaking album sales, sold-out tours, successful movies, national and international endorsements, and private engagements, she needed to make even more to continue sustaining everything and everybody.

A few months would go by and her father would say, "Whitney is out of money. Time to hit the road." I tried to slow Whitney's world down by controlling the flow of requests that came in and reminding her how much she was taking on. But still, too much came at her. It felt like a time back when we first met, when we were on one of the rides at a makeshift pop-up amusement park across the street from Nip's church, and I was yelling repeatedly for the operator to make it stop, but he couldn't hear me.

At Whitney's house one afternoon, I was fixing myself something to eat and reached into a drawer for a spoon. I noticed that each had blue and black spots on it, as though it had been burned by a hot flame. I asked, "What's this on the spoons?" In unison, the voices in the kitchen said, "Michael." A light went off in my head. One evening a while before, Michael Houston had come to visit my apartment. I wasn't expecting him but allowed him to come up. This was his first time visiting my place. I opened the door, and as he stepped out of the elevator, he said he was passing through and thought he'd stop by. He pulled out two joints, offering me one. "Sure. I'll have a couple of hits," I said. After taking a full pull and then a smaller one, I began to sweat, as if something was taking me over. I was slipping away, losing myself. A desperate taste filled my mouth, making me thirsty for more as an unpleasant scent hit me.

"What is this?" I asked. He called it a "woolie." I'd never heard the term and began to panic, feeling chilly, vulnerable, and in trouble. Michael told me to relax, that he was there and I'd be okay. I knew I wasn't okay but needed to ride it out. After some time, when I began to feel like myself again, I told him to leave. That night, I phoned Nip and told her that Michael had come by with some bad shit.

"What was it?" Nip asked.

"They look like joints but they're not. One puff separated me from my soul." I later learned that "woolies" are joints laced with crack cocaine.

Now, at Whitney's, I was still examining the spoon in my hands when Silvia said, "Michael was heating something on the spoon and it stunk! Whitney asked if she could try some, and he told her, 'No. You don't want any of this shit. You won't be able to handle it.'"

....

It always bothered me when Whit said, "Clive says it's time for me to get back to work." She had fallen into a pattern of going along with things that were not of her choosing. I sat in Clive's office one day in fall 1998 while he played me potential tracks for Whitney's fourth album. *My Love Is Your Love* came together quickly, in roughly seven weeks, including the creation of the artwork. Lisa's friend Dana Lixenberg, an accomplished photographer, did the cover.

The song "If I Told You That" was submitted as a duet with Michael Jackson. When it came time to make the ask of the King of Pop, Whitney was told to make the call.

After Nip placed the call to Michael, it took nearly a week before she heard anything back, and she felt slighted, and rightfully so. Not only had she presented him with the World Music Award at Neverland nearly ten years before, but she'd also accompanied Michael to an event for the United Negro College Fund.

Michael never did phone. Instead, he communicated through someone else that he didn't want to do the song.

Whitney's feelings were hurt by the fact that she didn't hear back from Michael himself, even if he didn't want to do it. When she was disappointed about something, Nip didn't talk about it much. In most cases, she internalized her feelings and moved on. So, after Michael declined, Whitney simply said, "I'll sing the song myself."

"If I Told You That" had Michael's flavor all over it. On the day she went into the studio to record the track solo, Michael's absence was evident. Nip walked into the vocal room wearing dark sunglasses, put on a pair of professional headphones, and vocally rode that track like she was seated in the saddle of that beautiful beast of a horse galloping over the hills of Neverland. I knew we were going to be in for a real treat after Nip determined she was going to go it alone. I loved watching her record and then perform it live. She had fun performing that song in her shows.

....

$\mathcal{S}$oon after *My Love Is Your Love* was released, John Houston called a meeting in the conference room to discuss details for a world tour. As we got further into the specifics of the shows, I noticed that some of them were back to back. I also noted that *every single one* had already sold out. And because of how quickly the tickets had moved, there was an understanding that more shows would be added. Mr. Houston was beaming with pride; his baby girl had been able to generate hundreds of thousands of dollars per show, numbers unheard of at that time. But before finalizing everything, he needed to get the boss on the phone. John dialed Whitney's number and put her on speaker. I hadn't seen or spoken to her much over the last few weeks, and I had no idea what kind of mental or physical condition to expect. But as soon as she answered the phone, I knew. Her voice was raspy and subdued.

"Hello," she said, finally. And in a beat, "Bobby is also on the line." Mr. Houston started going over the dates, the number of potential additional shows, the amount each show would generate, and the total purse that would be brought home. When finished, he said, "So what do you think, baby?" Whitney was about to say something but then demurred.

"What do you think, Bobby?"

"It's not enough money. Needs to be more money."

After some more back-and-forth, the conference call ended and the meeting continued. As I listened to Mr. Houston read the contractual requirements of the shows we were considering adding, how many there would be and where, I started thinking about what the show might look like and the wear and tear it would inflict upon Nip. This new project included some of the funkiest track-laying producers dominating the charts, so whatever the plan was, I knew that Whitney had to look and feel fresh. I raised the issue of Whitney's wardrobe and was shocked when John responded that she'd have to wear old gear from past tours, as there was no money to purchase anything new.

The need to resuscitate old attire was the last thing I wanted to bring to Whit's attention. I needed to come up with a solution, stat. Instead of making her feel even worse by telling her there was no money for wardrobe, I said, "You've always paid for your own clothing whenever we've toured. How about this time we find a designer who'll agree to outfit you, the dancers, and the band? What do you say?"

Her reply: "Go for it!" On the spot, I asked her to name a few designers that she liked, and she gave me three: Versace, Yves Saint Laurent, and Dolce & Gabbana. There was no time to waste, so with Whitney's blessing, I was off and running. After making some calls, I made the decision to begin with Dolce & Gabbana, and fortunately, they responded immediately.

The agreement we worked out was straightforward: The team would design and supply a wardrobe for the tour, outfitting Whitney as well as the dancers and the band. In exchange, they asked

Whitney to make an appearance during fashion week in Milan, attend the after-party for their show, and wear their clothing exclusively onstage and for all promotional events. I was also assured by the duo that all the clothing they designed for Whitney would be custom-made and would never be advertised or sold. Bobby was going to be traveling with Whitney, so the designers agreed to make clothing for him as well, to complement Whitney at the events that she was required to attend.

....

The US tour kicked off on June 22, 1999, at Chicago's Arie Crown Theater, which has a seating capacity of about four thousand. Whitney wanted to play smaller venues before going abroad, as she preferred to have her relationship with the audience feel up close and personal. But playing smaller venues meant that she needed to do two nights in each city, and in most cases do back-to-back shows. At the time the tour was booked, Whitney did not possess the physical fitness the grueling schedule required. Still, she somehow managed to do sixteen out of twenty shows.

One of the cancellations happened at the last minute, at a venue that accommodated twelve thousand. I was there that evening when my ear caught the code words "P1 is a negative." Instantly I felt the muscles in my belly tighten. I knew her arrival had been delayed, and I had just peeked at the packed lawn full of fans anticipating her arrival on the stage. I made my way back to the production office and was informed that she was not coming.

This was ugly. It was only forty-five minutes before showtime, and all I could do was take notes on how it unraveled. No one in the crowd booed. But there was an unmistakable, disgruntled rumbling of disappointment, disgust, and broken trust from loyal Whitney Houston fans.

....

There were still some bright spots, though. Over the years, we had received requests for Whit to perform during New York City Pride but had never accepted due to conflicting tours, recording, movies, or appearance commitments. But finally, in the summer of 1999, she showed up at the thirteenth annual Lesbian and Gay Pride Dance on a West Side pier. With her remixes burning up radio and the clubs, the timing couldn't have been better, nor could the atmosphere. It was a perfect warm, hazy June night, and the pier was packed with more than seven thousand. Hers was to be an end-of-the-night surprise performance, and the crowd was jumping. I suggested Nip wear a look from Dolce & Gabbana: a black tank and silvery bejeweled capri pants. It was well after midnight when she ran up onto the stage. The already ecstatic crowd went berserk as she launched into an extended version of "Heartbreak Hotel." Whit vibed off the crowd as though they'd lifted her off the ground, jumping up and down joyfully, never showing the slightest sign of fatigue. I'd never seen her like that. She went into "It's Not Right but It's Okay," and the love from the multiracial crowd was undeniable.

It was nearly two A.M. when she came offstage. Climbing into the car, skin glistening with sweat, she said, "Wow—those people were pumped! Folks have a lot of energy."

"Yep," I replied, "they've been waitin' a long time for you."

Agreeing, she said, "I know. I had fun."

The moment she said that, I realized I hadn't heard those words from her in a long time. It seemed that with all Whitney had accomplished on her musical journey, it mostly had become work, work, work. All the platinum records mounted on walls didn't change that. Hearing Nip finally say "I had fun" made me sad.

It had been so long since we had been in a club atmosphere. In fact, the last time Whitney had appeared at a club was in 1987, after the release of "Love Will Save the Day." It was late afternoon the day Whitney went into a recording studio located over the *Late Night with David Letterman* studio on Broadway and Fifty-Fourth Street to work with producer John "Jellybean" Benitez. Jellybean, who initially became known through his work with Madonna, had gorgeous silky black hair past his shoulders, golden Puerto Rican skin, a boyish smile, and a confident demeanor. He wasn't tall, but boy, was he charismatic, with twinkly brown eyes and an unforgettable smile. A young Latina woman who couldn't have been more than twenty-three years old walked in. Jellybean introduced her to us as Toni C., the writer. As he pressed "play," the instrumental track of "Love Will Save the Day" came charging through the speakers, and Whitney moved in close to the mic and never let go. When she finished singing, she sat at the console, next to JB, helping select the best vocal tracks, and then he did a rough mix of the song. When we finally walked out of the studio and into the car, it was six A.M. Whitney popped the tape in the player, blasting "Love" as we zoomed up the West Side Highway and over the George Washington Bridge, the sky blazing orange as the sun began to rise.

After the song was released, Whit showed up one night at NYC's renowned Paradise Garage down on King Street, where Benitez introduced her to the audience, and we jammed alongside him as he mixed that song until folks fell to the floor.

A Song for You

....

$\textit{In}$ late 1999, Whitney did an interview with *Out* magazine, the LGBT monthly with the highest circulation, her first with a gay and lesbian publication. The interview took place in Beverly Hills. Writer Barry Walters, who was black, seemed to like her, and she must have picked up on that because she seemed relaxed and comfortable through most of the conversation. Then Bobby made his entrance and Whit amped up a few notches, bantering back and forth with him. When Walters came around to asking her about "the rumors," her response was uncalled for and wrong:

"I ain't suckin' no dick. I ain't gettin' on my knees. Something must be wrong: I can't just really sing. I can't just be a really talented, gifted person. She's gotta be gay." I was embarrassed. It was the first sign of how the rest of the LA trip would go for her, and for me.

Twenty-Two

2000

With her upcoming Grammy performance, the Academy Awards, the Rock & Roll Hall of Fame, a recording session with George Michael, and then the Soul Train Music Awards, Whitney had yet another jam-packed, high-profile schedule. After what I'd witnessed on tour, I didn't know how she was going to get through it. She needed rest, relaxation, and, most of all, rehabilitation.

At the forty-second annual Grammy Awards, Whitney performed the two songs Clive recommended. She wasn't in great voice that night, and she hadn't been in her prime for a while, but it wasn't bad. Whit was worn out emotionally, physically, and spiritually. The real moment of truth came when, in her acceptance speech for Best Female R&B Vocal Performance for "It's Not Right but It's Okay," Whit walked to the onstage podium and addressed her mother: "You forgot to give me my cards. I'll have to wing it."

I suppose that in that moment she gazed at her husband in the audience, and even in all her own glory, she felt the need to make him shine. She still needed to prove to the world that their love was real, and so from the stage, in *her* moment, she proclaimed, "Honey—this one's for you, the original R&B king." I stood backstage next to the show's producer, both of us looking at the monitor. As he turned to walk away, his eyes met mine and he placed his hand on my shoulder.

On that weekend's *Saturday Night Live*, during "Weekend Update," Tina Fey poked fun at Whitney for not remembering the names of the "real kings of R&B." She went on to say that Whitney and Bobby were performing at the Aladdin casino in Las Vegas and tickets were on sale for "one hundred fifty dollars—two hundred dollars if Whitney and Bobby actually show up."

Whitney obliged when Clive asked her to present him for his induction into the Rock & Roll Hall of Fame on March 6. In the weeks leading up to the event, after she told me she had agreed to do it, I told her that I didn't think she would feel up to it. She had been flying by the seat of her pants, and I knew it took energy to get face, hair, and wardrobe together and then put on a smile when really you wanted to cry. I told her that Clive wouldn't have a hard time getting someone else to do it. But she said she had to do it. And then she no-showed.

I could tell that Whitney shouldn't do the Oscars that year. She should never, ever have shown up for early rehearsals in the state she did, especially not with Bobby. He sat in the front row of the Shrine Auditorium, his legs sprawled out, his coat draped over his head. It was awful. Whitney was onstage wearing a Dr. Seuss–ian hat, dark sunglasses, and a coat. It was clearly the last place she wanted to be. But she had agreed to do it. The drama transpired onstage during the rehearsals. Musical director Burt Bacharach was frustrated but contained. I looked on while he and Whitney talked, and heard her say something about her voice. I guess she had it in her mind that she was going to say she was sick and get out of there. But instead, she came down off the stage and flatly said to me, "I've just been fired."

A failed recording with George Michael followed. Clive never let go of his vision of "If I Told You That" as a duet. He talked to Whitney about going into the studio with George to rerecord her vocal for a dance remix. The day before the session, I called Whitney's hotel room a few times but got no response. Later that day, Silvia told me that Bobby had asked her to place an order for room service, and when she took it in, the suite was a mess and neither Nip nor Bobby came out of the bedroom. I called Clive to give him a heads-up that the session might not happen. Sure enough, later that evening, Bobby called to say that Whitney couldn't do the recording.

Clive called again, telling me that George was going to be in town through Thursday, so we could reschedule. On Wednesday morning, I called Whitney to ask if she could sing late Thursday evening. Bobby answered and relayed the message to her. I heard her say yes, which Bobby repeated, and then he hung up. I should have known better.

Come Thursday morning, there was no word from Nippy. I knew the session wasn't going to happen. I alerted Clive, who asked if I would kindly purchase something nice for George and take it to the studio as a gesture of respect. I asked Clive what he might like, and he said, "A black shirt." So, I hustled over to Fred Segal and picked out an elegant, classic, black button-down shirt. I had it gift wrapped and headed to the studio to meet George and deliver the bad news. He was cool, loved the shirt, and told me he was flying back to the UK the next day.

At the Soul Train Music Awards, Whitney was to present Mary J. Blige with the Sammy Davis Jr. Entertainer of the Year Award. I still hadn't spoken to Whitney about the George Michael situation. When I arrived at the Shrine Auditorium, Whitney was already in her trailer getting ready. The first person I saw was Bobby, then Silvia, then hair stylist Ellin and makeup artist Roxanna, who always gave me a heads-up when it wasn't a good time for me to be around.

After I said hello to everyone, Whitney looked at me and said, "What do you want, Robyn?"

"Nothing," I responded. "Everything's cool. George Michael is back home in the UK. I took care of it." I told her that he loved the shirt I gifted him as an apology on her behalf.

Out of nowhere, Bobby lost it. "Are you fucking out of your mind?" he started yelling. "You don't buy a man a gift from my wife! Are you crazy?"

Then Whitney joined in, saying, "Apology for what?"

I understood exactly why I was getting blasted. They were strung out and out of their minds. There was nothing that I could do to make things any better. I was no longer able to protect Nippy. I had done all I could do, and for the first time I realized that I needed to save myself.

Ignoring Bobby and locking eyes with Whitney, I said my piece: "You know, I'm really sick and tired of this shit. I'm trying to do my job, and you're going to let him speak to me this way? I'm done, Nip. I quit."

I walked out of the trailer, giving the door some help closing behind me. Years later, Silvia would tell me that after I walked out, Whitney said, "She ain't going no-fuckin'-where."

....

1 left Los Angeles on the next plane heading east. Whitney and the rest of the crew returned two days later. I hadn't slept at all, and I was beside myself, replaying the scene over and over, again and again. But I remained steadfast in my decision. I didn't want to leave Nippy, but the circumstances gave me no choice. It was time to go.

I called her on her private line—the same line that Eddie Murphy had used on her wedding day—and Bobby answered. I told him to tell Nip that I needed to talk to her in person. After everything we'd been through together, I felt that we needed to sit down and talk.

Whitney called back and said, "One day this week." Then that week passed. She scheduled another day, and then that day passed. And then a third. Finally, I got a call from Donna, saying, "Whitney told me to tell you that she's decided to accept your resignation."

In a few hours, I was sitting across from Donna at the office, handing over a formal resignation letter. There was no "Robyn, I'm so sorry it went down like this. You two really needed to talk. This just doesn't make any sense." There was none of that. After the two decades that Whitney and I had spent together as friends, lovers, partners in crime, colleagues, after the years of living together, standing up, being there, and looking out for each other, this was it. There was still so much more to accomplish, but instead of taking my hand, she was allowing it to fade away.

Writing my resignation letter was difficult. I didn't know what to write or how to say it. Who was I even writing to—Nippy Inc. or Whitney? This had been my first real job as a young adult and now I was forty. I decided it was best to keep it brief and it wound up being only three sentences, if that.

It was not the place to elaborate on all the reasons why or to explain that I had done all I knew how to do to help her. It wasn't the place to express my frustration and fears. I was hurt and filled with anxiety and couldn't imagine what my life would look and feel like without Nip.

That evening after I handed in my resignation, Whitney phoned me at home. "So, you're really going, huh?" she said.

"Yeah, Nip. That's why I wanted us to meet. We've been through too much together for me not to tell you why I feel it's time I move on, and not to let you know where I see things going. And I need to know what you're thinking, where you are in your head."

"I know," she said. "We'll talk."

Twenty-Three

California Dreamin'

The day after I handed in my resignation, the reality of it all came tumbling down. I was faced with overwhelming questions— *What am I going to do? How much money do I have? Am I staying in Jersey?* I hadn't considered any of them and didn't have answers. The only thing I knew for certain was that my behind was *out*, and I had *no* intention of going backward.

I easily could have allowed the thoughts of feeling sorry for myself to have their moment, along with the words of my mother, which played in my head: "Robyn, you've never finished anything." Oh, how I wished I could run to Mama, but I couldn't. And all of a sudden, I realized that I had no more fouls to give and no more room for mistakes. The combination of my checking account, my savings, and the 401(k) I cashed in, against the advice of Cindy at Nippy Inc. and the outside company accountant, gave me a cushion and the ability to rest easy at night. After that, everything else came step by step.

That summer I packed up the contents of my condo, enlisted a moving company, had my Range Rover serviced, and drove west to California with my chow, Knute, riding shotgun. I chose California partly because I was afraid that if I stayed on the East Coast any longer, I might get cold feet and run back to Nippy.

On the way to Cali, I had a whole lot to think about. I felt alone but was comforted by having Knutie by my side. Driving across the country, we both were bananas. Late one night, I was low on gas and desperate to locate a station. Knute sensed my distress, glancing over at me with those sincere eyes, as if to say, "Oh, shit, Rob." The last thing I wanted to do was run out of gas someplace in the middle of God knows where, a single black woman and her black dog. I had money for hotels, but the ones that looked safe didn't accept animals. I wasn't about to pull into some dive, and certainly not after dark! Instead, I pulled over at a well-lit truck stop, walked around a bit with Knute so we could stretch our legs and get a little exercise, then got back in the car for a few z's and back on the road again. Crossing the United States on wheels is a breathtaking adventure, and though we had moments when we were scared out of our skins, we also enjoyed stretches of awesome beauty.

Still, I was spent, somewhat lost, a weepy mess. I missed Nip terribly. While driving, I listened to a lot of music in an effort to hold on to my mind, trying not to let the feeling I was running from take hold. I never once felt as if my decision to leave meant losing my friend.

On July 6, 2000, I moved into a condo in Sherman Oaks, California. I gave Knute some water and a snack, and then sat down on the gray, shaggy wall-to-wall carpeting, gazing upward at the popcorn ceiling that I hated. Grabbing my duffel bag, I pulled out my pillow, placed it under my head on the floor, and closed my eyes. I said my prayers, gave myself a year in the land of LA, and was ready to roll.

....

One afternoon while getting ready to leave the apartment, my phone rang. It was Silvia.

"Whitney wants to talk to you."

Nip asked if I was all right and if I had everything I needed. I told her that I was fine and that living in Los Angeles was just as we had imagined it would be. Everyone was in their cars, the streets were deserted by eleven o'clock, and the energy was like a flatlined pulse. We were East Coast girls, unaccustomed to feeling like we were the only ones around.

In New Jersey and New York, the energy was always humming. Out in LA, you had to be part of the scene or tight with someone who was. If not, your ass was sidelined and you were bored as shit. I enjoyed my downtime, chilling with a couple of friends. But everyone and everything was so spread out that by the end of the day, the last thing I could see myself doing was getting back in the car.

I would hear from Silvia a few times a month, saying she was calling just to see how I was doing. I wouldn't find out until several years later that Whitney was behind those calls and often cried about my not being nearby. I didn't call her much at all, knowing that everyone around her would get all up in it.

My immediate plan was to focus on the one act our management company still represented: Sunday, the girl group made up of three sisters and two cousins that Nip and I had signed to Better

Place. They ranged in age from fourteen to eighteen and made up the entire choir at their grandmother's church.

During his first year as president of Capitol Records, Roy Lott, Clive's former number two, gave me a deal and Sunday had a label! I made my way to Capitol's headquarters on Hollywood and Vine to discuss the creative approach to the girls' record. Their sound was a funky, upbeat blend of soulful church, and I told Roy that I'd like the girls to collaborate with the producers we chose for them and to have a hand in the writing process. We already had two songs from the sessions I'd had Sunday do with The Neptunes at their Virginia Beach studio before they blew up and everybody became familiar with their sound. I paid $120,000 in order to bring the masters with us to the Capitol.

Other producers lined up for Sunday included Keith Crouch, who was responsible for the success of Brandy's debut album; Soulshock and Karlin, who produced "Heartbreak Hotel" for Whitney; and Warryn Campbell, who was behind the gospel group Mary Mary. Before long, I was traveling around the country with Sunday for live performances and promotional events.

Perhaps it was unrealistic of me to expect the girls to grasp everything that came their way in a relatively short period of time, but they bucked at nearly every turn. They had limited life experience and maybe I expected too much of them. When I arrived to take them on a preplanned LA shopping trip to style them, they emerged from the hotel in rollers and do-rags. "Can you just pull yourselves together a little bit?" They did as I asked but were mad at me for the rest of the day. When they resisted my suggestions and advice, I should have been firmer than I was. We also encountered difficulties with Capitol and I sensed that Roy's enthusiasm had waned, though he never actually told me so.

We went to New York for a *Vibe* magazine shoot of artists with their protégées. As soon as I laid eyes on Whitney I saw she was thinner than usual. I don't remember if she had another engagement that day, but she was in hurry-up mode, so there was no opportunity for the two of us to talk. When the shoot was over, we hugged and she told me to stop by the house.

Sunday's lead single, "I Know," was released in 2000, peaking at number 32 on the R&B charts and at number 98 on the *Billboard* Hot 100. But Capitol never released the album—they shelved it. And we were so close.

....

After our mother left us, it had become obvious that Bina was mentally ill. The signs already had accumulated when she started taping up my televisions by covering the screens with sheets of paper, adamant that the government was surveilling us. She was married, and her husband, Mel, phoned telling me that he'd received a call from an off-duty Port Authority police officer who had spotted Bina walking along the shoulder of the New Jersey Turnpike. We met at the hospital, where Bina was diagnosed with bipolar disorder.

I later learned that bipolar is hereditary, and then I put the pieces together and understood what my mother used to say about the family disposition. She always said that on her side of the family there was an emotional fragility, a "weakness in the neurological system." The youngest of her three brothers, Roland, had spent several years in the army, and his military experience really did a number on him. Uncle Roland didn't appreciate the way he was treated by the white men in charge, and he found himself constantly at odds with them, partly because of his belief in the

Nation of Islam and also due to the color of his skin. In retaliation for not doing what he was told, they punished him by locking him in a small container, lowering it into the ground, and leaving him there until his spirit was broken. It made sense that he referred to those men as "Caucasian devils."

After being discharged, Roland was never the same. He talked to himself a lot, and once, when he was staying with us, he entered my bedroom, pinning my arms down and attempting to get on top of me before I yelled out and my mother and brother came running to my rescue. I was twelve. My mother arranged to drop him with other family in Newark's North Ward. Roland was in the passenger seat and I was in the back. Suddenly he called out, "Look at that building falling right there!" My mother instantly replied, her eyes still on the road, "There's no building falling, Roland."

A number of my mother's other immediate and extended family members also were afflicted with the disorder.

Bina was thirty years old when she was formally diagnosed. They said that the trauma of significant loss had triggered her condition.

One of Mom's last wishes had been that we take care of each other. I decided to move Bina in with me in Los Angeles. She was my family's California baby, born there in 1965. Perhaps being back there would help us find the key to snapping her life back together. While we were there, the two of us agreed that she would stay on her medicine and get regular checkups.

....

The following April, I got a call from Arista Records about a marketing position in their New York office. I said I was interested and was told that I'd hear back from someone at the company with details on next steps. Arista flew me to New York, put me up at a hotel, and brought me in for interviews. I met with L.A. Reid. He talked about Usher and some of his other artists, played me lots of music, tracks from producers he planned to work with, The Neptunes among them. I felt good about everything L.A. played and shared with me about the roster and whose projects I'd be working on. Whitney's name never once came up in the conversation.

Afterward, I returned to Los Angeles, until they brought me back to New York for another series of meetings, this time with key executives on the pop side. I called Whitney and told her I was interviewing at Arista. I wanted to be certain she hadn't pulled any strings. When I asked if she had anything to do with it, she said, "Nope, that was all you." Everyone I met with seemed to be welcoming me aboard. They said an offer would be coming and that I'd hear from the human resources department.

By now it was May, and I was tidying up the apartment, music playing, when the phone rang. It was Donna Houston. We hadn't spoken since I left.

"Listen, Whitney's attorney wants to talk to you. He wants to ask you a couple of questions, okay?"

Whitney's attorney and I knew each other, so I said, "Sure." Next thing I knew, someone whom I'd never known to work with Whit introduced himself.

He began asking a series of questions: "How long have you known Whitney? Did you work for her?" I answered those and then he asked, "How long did you live together? Did you two ever have any sexual relations?"

It felt as if I was being set up for something. I went on the defensive. "Look, I don't have to tell you anything. I don't know what this is about, and I don't appreciate the way you're talking to me. If Whitney wants to know something, tell her to call me."

About twenty minutes later, Whitney did phone, and she wasn't nice. "All you had to do was say no! That's all you had to do," she shouted in my ear. The only thing I was able to say was, "Nip—" before she hung up on me.

Maybe the questions did require only yes or no responses. But the lawyer's interrogation made me uncomfortable. The whole thing bothered me, beginning with Donna's calling me out of the blue when I didn't have a clue what was going on and then putting me on the spot. I tried hard not to dwell on it.

Not long after, I found out that the whole thing was related to a possible *Globe* magazine story. An executive at Capitol told me they had received a call from a tabloid writer who asked them to forward a fax to me, hoping I would answer his questions. They gave me the fax and not surprisingly, it dredged up the same old questions about my relationship with Nip.

Over the years, I'd grown accustomed to reading that story rehashed over and over again. But I didn't want some salacious story running right as I was heading to Arista, so this time, I took it to L. Londell McMillan, a young African American attorney known for his partnership with Prince and credited with successfully orchestrating his release from Warner Bros. Records. He came through, sending a letter to the author of the article.

....

I had learned a lot about myself since leaving New Jersey. There was a life out there to live and new experiences to be had. I could make it on my own, but I still didn't trust myself in a relationship.

I had no idea what it took to be in a healthy one, and I wouldn't allow anyone to get too close. Nor did I know what I wanted. I still didn't even know if I wanted to be with a man or a woman. I had lost my identity working with Whitney, giving all of myself. I came to the alarming realization that I had reached my forties and still didn't really know who I was.

Continuing the conversation with Bina that day, I said, "You know, I'm ready to love, to commit myself." I used to think it was better to be alone, but I had come to feel otherwise. I wanted someone of my own. I felt an urgent need to learn about myself from someone who would be honest with me, telling me both the good and the bad parts about Robyn Crawford.

I knew Lisa cared about me and we'd enjoyed the time we spent together. Although I felt comfortable with her, I hadn't always been totally present. We hadn't spoken in years. I always had my guard up, protecting myself from too much intimacy and vulnerability. I explained all this to my sister and said, "I'm going to call Lisa, and hopefully she'll be willing to talk to me. If she's in a relationship, I'll have to wait, because I know how loyal she is. If she's not, then she's mine. I'm ready to learn how to love."

Bina screeched with laughter. "Robyn, are you kidding? You're so fickle—I wouldn't give you the time of day!" I was surprised to hear her laugh at me, but she did. I went ahead and left a message on Lisa's home phone anyway, and later that night, she returned my call. I told her where I was in my life, that I had changed. I shared where I had been over the years and what I was learning about myself since leaving Nippy Inc. and moving to California. I told her about the possible position at Arista, that I'd be coming to New York soon for another interview and hoped that I could take her to dinner. I was relieved that she agreed to see me. Once we were face-to-face, Lisa listened to me, not like she was looking to rekindle anything, but like someone who understood and cared about me. She could tell I needed help. After that we talked frequently on the phone and I told her that I was ready to flee LA and come back east.

Bina and I were lying on my bed talking about the job and the prospect of moving back when I got the call from Arista telling me the VP of marketing job was mine. They offered a two-year contract and a significant salary. They also offered me another plane ticket back and asked me to come on board and meet the entire team in July. I felt proud and excited about my new career and planned to take this blessing and do the best I could with it.

At the end of June, Lisa flew out to Sherman Oaks to help me pack. There were boxes everywhere! A friend agreed to drive my things back to the East Coast in a U-Haul. Arista had offered to ship my Range Rover back, but since Bina was with me, I figured we'd make the road trip together. I thought it might be a fun adventure. But soon it was apparent that her mental health medicine made Bina sleep—a lot. There were sixteen- to eighteen-hour stretches when I only stopped for bathroom breaks and to pick up food, and my sister remained asleep in the passenger seat the entire time. The medicine knocked her out and still does today, but she needed to be on it.

We made it to Jersey over Fourth of July weekend, giving me enough time to unwind and prepare myself for the new position and career back in the industry. My friend Susan kindly offered to let Bina and me stay with her while I hunted for an apartment.

I thought it was odd that I hadn't heard from anyone at Arista about when to expect my contract, but I kept waiting, assuming that as long as it arrived before July 16, all was fine. I had never been through a job interview process before and didn't know how it typically went. But July 16 arrived and still I hadn't heard a word from the label, so I called my contact there. As soon as he heard my voice, he said, "Robyn, L.A. hasn't called you?"

I said, "No. I haven't heard from anyone."

"L.A. was supposed to call you. Let me call him, sit tight."

"That's what I've *been* doing."

It wasn't long before the phone rang with L.A. on the other end. "Robyn, I'm really sorry. I can't bring you in," he said.

After a long pause, I managed to find the words to ask, "What happened?" He told me that he wasn't able to go into any details just then, but he was really sorry.

Then he said, "If there's anything that you need and I can help you, call me. I will do it."

My head spun and before I knew it, only these words came out of my mouth: "Thank you."

Twenty-Four

Life

After I got the news from Arista, I felt lost. We were still at Susan's place—Bina and I were staying on the top floor of her home. I can still see myself lying in bed, looking at my sister asleep next to me, and wondering, *What's the next step for her, and how am I going to pull myself up out of this? How did I get here?* I was off on planet Pathetic.

Both Mom and Marty had left us life insurance. Jean Riggins, a former record company executive and friend, had generously loaned me $6,000, and those funds had helped hold me together in California. But now, in our second week at Susan's, I had less than $5,000 to my name.

I called my cousin Dollie, who lived outside Atlanta, and updated her on what Bina and I were going through. She said, "Send her to me! I love Bina. And she can help me out with a lot of the things I'm doing—I'll put her tail to work!" I filled Dollie in on her bipolar condition and recent diagnosis of type 2 diabetes. Dollie was well connected, mentioning a doctor friend who she said would refer her to an endocrinologist, and she also said she would contact the mental health department at the local hospital for treatment options.

Dollie and her husband, Larry, kindly welcomed Bina into their home, not as a favor to me, but because Bina was always a pleasure and we were family. My mind lightened now that I had a solid plan. I would send Bina to Dollie's, and then I could turn to helping myself.

....

I'd spoken to Lisa a few times since the move back east but still hadn't seen her. She'd call to ask how I was doing and I'd say I was fine, which I wanted to believe was true. But I wasn't fine enough to let her see my face just yet. I'd be upstairs at Susan's house, reading, writing, or watching something on television, and the minute Lisa called, I just wanted to cry. I felt weak and pathetic and wanted to be held.

Sometimes I drove by my old house to see the trees I had planted: a white pine for my mother and a Colorado blue spruce for Marty, both healthy and growing strong. This became a routine for me, and after a few months, I could feel myself coming around a bit. The next time Lisa invited me over for dinner, I accepted. I loved her cooking, and the company and the conversation. I picked up a bottle of wine and made my way back to her place, and things went on from there.

Lisa inherited a passion for exploration from her mother, who was a travel agent. She loved researching trips big and small, so when we felt an urge to leave the city—which was often—she'd put her research skills to use, finding us interesting and romantic out-of-the-way inns and bed-and-breakfasts in upstate New York. In those pre-GPS days, we'd take off on Fridays, me behind the wheel of the Rover, Lisa next to me with an oversize atlas spread across her lap. We had a rule: If we hit a traffic jam, off-highway we went. Lisa located alternate routes and back roads where we'd often come upon country towns with sweet little places to eat. Eventually, as we pulled up to whatever lodging Lisa had reserved, we'd experience the exciting moment of discovery as we stepped into our latest weekend accommodation. These excursions provided the escape we both craved, and through them, our friendship flourished and we grew closer.

....

Though I still had some of my things at Susan's, I was now spending most of my time at Lisa's. She made me feel welcome but then gave me an ultimatum: She would consider being in a serious partnership with me only if I agreed to go into therapy.

I wasn't sure what to think at first. As I'd told Whitney all those years ago, my mom had brought me to therapy when I was young. She was very concerned about the effect my parents' many arguments had had on me. So, every Saturday morning, we'd visit a Caucasian male therapist who would sit down on the floor with me and let me build with blocks and draw while we talked. Eventually, when I told my mother I didn't want to go anymore, she allowed me to stop.

Having been in therapy herself as an adult, Lisa told me that I would really have to work at it to get the benefits, explaining that it's not simply about talking. In order for it to work, the therapist has to be someone to whom you're able to talk freely and honestly and with whom you can be vulnerable about everything. "How do you know if it's working?" I asked.

"If you haven't cried, it's not working." I agreed to go.

For so many years, I had been conditioned to feel that everything I did or said was a reflection on Whitney. But I had a whole bunch of issues I needed to address, and although the thought of going through the process intimidated me, I knew I needed to do it. I had to face my past to grasp the present and have a future with Lisa.

The thing was, I didn't have insurance or a job that would allow me to pay out of pocket. Lisa stepped back, allowing me all the room I needed to get moving. I wasn't confident enough to even try to land a job. I had to take care of my health, and to do that, I had to go to Bellevue Hospital for insurance.

If you've never been inside this hospital, you should take a tour. My mother was afraid of New York City hospitals, saying they were old, cold, and overcrowded. Bellevue checked all three boxes. The morning I went to sign up, the main floor was filled to capacity. The lines were long, and when I say *long*, I mean like Black Friday quadrupled. I stood in at least three different lines that day: one to register, another to apply for some kind of number, and a third to finally talk to someone. It was an exhausting process, but at least by the end of it I had an insurance card and was able to go to St. Vincent's Hospital for annual checkups and discounted therapy.

....

1 was in a different headspace around that time, just existing, invisible, floating through the day—hardly ever running into anyone I knew or who knew me. A few city blocks away, on September 7, 2001, Michael Jackson's thirtieth anniversary celebration show was held at Madison Square Garden. Whitney performed "Wanna Be Startin' Somethin'" along with Usher and Mýa.

I didn't see the show but couldn't miss the next day's coverage. On my way to buy groceries in Chelsea, I passed more than one newsstand displaying a skeletal image of Whitney Houston plastered across the front pages. Back at Lisa's apartment, I phoned her at home and Silvia answered, telling me Whitney had left days before the show and was still in New York but had canceled the second night's performance. When I wondered why Silvia hadn't gone, she told me that Donna said she had to stay home. I had never seen Nip look anything like that before. I couldn't wrap my head around how in the world folks could dress her, do her hair and makeup, and allow her to step out on the stage in that condition. Her family was there, too.

I tried to keep my attention and focus on myself, finding a therapist and attending Narcotics Anonymous meetings in the evenings. I hadn't had a sniff in years but decided to go because occasionally I had what I called "cocaine urges." Sometimes the thought of getting some would enter my mind, tempting me.

The meetings were an eye-opener. I'd walk up the stairs, then down a narrow hallway into a room where twelve or so chairs were set up in three rows facing a small podium where people got up to speak. People would share testimonials: "My wife and children moved out," and "I lost my job yesterday," and "I haven't had a drink or shot heroin in six months and five days." I never once got up to share. Compared to what I was hearing, my experiences seemed almost trivial. I didn't have an ongoing drug problem.

That's not why I was there. I was trying to understand why I even would think about doing something that I didn't really even want to do.

....

A few days later, on an absolutely gorgeous, sunny September morning, Lisa was in Toronto and I had a plan to Rollerblade downtown. The apartment windows were open, the radio tuned to Hot 97 as I stepped into the shower. Soon as I turned off the water, I heard an uncharacteristically serious tone from the morning DJs: "Whatever you do, stay away from downtown Manhattan." Worried, I turned on the television for more information.

I lotioned my body, eyes riveted on the TV. A plane had just hit the World Trade Center. The commentators were speculating on what possibly could have slammed into the building, leaving a horrific gaping hole in its side.

It was surreal. I ran to the window, forgetting I was naked, then grabbed a T-shirt and leaned out the window. Our apartment faced downtown, and peering up to the skies, I saw thousands of pieces of paper blowing around like tossed confetti within black smoke. An unfamiliar smell filled the air. The sounds of sirens filled the city. I grabbed the phone and dialed Lisa but heard only a rapid busy signal. I tried using my cell and the same thing happened, except that after a few seconds an automated female voice came on to say, "All lines are busy now."

I just needed to make contact with Lisa, hear her voice, tell her I was okay, and then find the safest way for us to reach each other. Then word came: No one was getting into the city and no one was getting out. I was stranded on the island. I don't recall when the phone lines finally opened up, but Susan reached me, asking if I was okay.

Eventually, Lisa was able to get through from Toronto. Of course, all the airports were closed. She said it was mayhem up there and wasn't sure how or when she was going to make it home. She was stranded, too. It took two more days before Lisa walked through the door, back into my arms.

....

Keeping my end of our agreement, I'd had a few sessions with my new therapist, Karen, and it seemed to be helping. After wrapping up an hour of talking her head off, I almost always would leave her office with my face stained from crying. Remembering what Lisa said, I hoped that meant it was working! To a sensitive person like me, crying came fairly easily, especially when I felt frustrated or particularly emotional. But in this situation, I found it awkward.

Karen told me that I was depressed and prescribed a low dose of an antidepressant. Fairly soon, I began to improve. My world looked a tiny bit brighter. I could see more clearly and a little bit of my self-confidence began to return. I spent two years with Karen, and she helped me to see that as a child I had to become an adult far too soon, protecting my mother. I had experienced a lot of loss and hadn't allowed myself to process it. My resignation from Nippy Inc. was a loss, too, even though Whitney was still here.

In September 2001, I wrote a letter to Whitney but never mailed it.

Nip:

I reached out to you 3 days ago, still no word. I wanted to write you a long time ago, but every time I took a pen to paper, no flow. Sad huh? So much to say . . . I'm in NYC, across the water where all the action is, sitting in my car waiting for a space to open up. The rain on my windows looks like tears. It's beautiful. You know, I love life! It's filled with many things, some joyful, some painful. For a long while, my heart was heavy. Very heavy. I missed my Mom and Marty every second of the day. My life changed. Sometimes you don't change with it, but then you have to catch up so you can live on. I have plans and lots of 'em to enjoy my life. I've spent too much time taking responsibility for other people's lives. It's time I took responsibility for my own.

How are you? What is important? And what is not? You know you have a friend in me—for life, always. Whenever you decide to pick up the phone or come and see me, I'll be there. I spent a lot of my life with you and I wouldn't change one thing. (Though if I knew then what I know now, perhaps I would have handled things differently.) It's simple, I didn't know. I'm not kicking myself ever again. Life's too short. You know—I love you. You need to know that I'm concerned about you. I want to see you happy, healthy and whole again. You can and must get back up again. I know God gave you that gift too!

Always here, there and everywhere for you,

Robyn

P.S. Oh yeah, can't forget Bina is on a cruise with family. Los Angeles was good for her—her mind is a lot better. I just have to love her more.

....

Finally, I was beginning to feel whole and ready to get out there again and get a job. Lisa invited me to join her for film screenings she attended to scout for coverage in *Esquire*, where she was working. I enjoyed sitting with her in those intimate screening rooms.

Whenever Lisa had a work event and she and her colleagues were invited to bring their significant others, I was by her side. She would often share ideas that the magazine was considering, especially when they involved music, and over dinner, we would discuss them and brainstorm.

One particular story was highlighting the top music executives in the industry; L.A. Reid was on the list. Each executive would be styled and photographed with the hottest artist representing the label's success. Most of the executives and artists were going to be in Los Angeles for the Grammys. Lisa surprised me, saying she thought it was time for me to take a trip to Los Angeles. *Esquire* rented the penthouse suite of a hotel in Century City.

This was my opportunity to see L.A. face-to-face and learn about the job offer he had rescinded. He didn't see me there when he arrived. I gave him space while the fashion team styled him; his grooming was done in a separate room adjacent to the suite. But as soon as he came through the door into the hallway, I was waiting for him. "Hi, Robyn," he said, kissing me on the cheek. If he was surprised to see me, he didn't show it.

I got straight to the point: "Are you able to tell me now? I need to know."

Without hesitation, he said, "Whitney wasn't comfortable with me bringing you in." The words left me numb.

Shortly after, Lisa came into the hall where I was standing. "So, what did he say?" I told her. Needless to say, she was livid, and I spent the rest of the day helping out where needed but not saying too much. Back in our room that night, Lisa railed against Whitney, stunned that she would do that to me. "What kind of friend— what kind of person does that?" she fumed. All I could bring myself to say was that I truly believed it wasn't her.

"She wouldn't do anything to stand in my way," I explained. "She's not in her right mind. It's the people around her."

That spring, Lisa and I began looking for a weekend getaway. We were lucky to be invited to stay on occasion with friends and family in Bucks County, Pennsylvania, and fell in love with the area. We shared the dream of having a historic home. We had a blast going to Bucks on weekends and looking at our options. Lisa became a Realtor.com addict, often scrolling through the site into the early-morning hours.

While our plan was to be on the Pennsylvania side of the Delaware River, late one night she came upon a home on the New Jersey side, in the charming town of Stockton. We called our Realtor the next morning, and a few days later we were standing in front of a magical, two-hundred-fifty-year-old, ivy-covered, stucco-over-stone, slate-roofed farmhouse. On July 20, 2002, Lisa took the hard-earned money she'd saved for years and bought her first house.

There was work to be done. Because I wasn't working, I was the one going out to the house to meet with contractors and figure out what improvements around the house I was able to do myself. One day we decided to tear down the back deck, a project I handled myself. I put on my overalls, grabbed a sledgehammer, and went to work. It was a serious workout that doubled as an effective way to get out my frustrations. By day's end, we were deck-free.

Soon the time came to move in my dog, Knute, and retrieve my things from storage. Among my things was valuable audio and video equipment: four pairs of twelve-inch Tannoy speakers,

Hafler receivers, European and US dual cassette and VHS players, DAT machines, two laser disc players, and two Technics turntables. There were also at least eight wardrobe boxes, and inside one of them was every Whitney Houston tour jacket, along with my collection of vintage leather jackets. On the day that the truck arrived, a friend helping me move told me all my audio equipment wasn't there. And it wasn't until at least a few months later that I discovered all my jackets were missing, too.

For my birthday later that year, Lisa planned an overnight stay at a historic bed-and-breakfast in northern New Jersey. She reserved the Captain's Suite on the top floor overlooking a waterfall. After taking a long hike and changing our clothes, we went to dinner at the truly white-glove Restaurant Latour at the Crystal Springs Resort. At our table for two, we pored over the dizzying six-thousand-label wine list before enjoying an unforgettable, succulent dining experience.

Returning to our suite, we shared a candlelit Jacuzzi bath with shimmering bubbles, a starry winter sky visible through the window at the foot of the tub. These were the times we talked about what mattered to us, what we wanted out of life, and how we might attain our dreams. My mother always said that you don't really start living until you're in your forties. Now I was forty-two and that night I realized I'd finally found the partner I had longed for.

I enjoyed the peace and quiet that came with living in the country, had become friendly with some wonderful neighbors, and got a job at the front desk of a nearby racquet club. Then one day, Lisa called to tell me that Stefano Tonchi, the former fashion creative director at *Esquire*, who had become the editor of *T: The New York Times Style Magazine*, had called her. He wanted to talk with me about working on a special Grammy issue.

Dressed in jeans, a white shirt, a cardigan, and loafers, I made my way to Manhattan, where I met with Kathy Ryan, director of photography, and Kira Pollack, who worked closely with Kathy and Stefano. They wanted to do a story featuring the top producers from the Virginia Beach area. It was my job to contact each artist's representative, make the offer, and hopefully schedule them to be interviewed and photographed.

....

Shortly after the story came out, I was fired from the tennis club for talking too much to clients and watching basketball games. They were right—manning the desk didn't suit me. It wasn't long before I got another job, this one on a farm ten minutes from the house. The owner grew peaches, apples, and plums, but his primary crop was asparagus, and he had rows and rows and rows amounting to several acres of the vegetable. Noting that I was in good shape, the farmer chose me to be one of his pickers and made it clear that I'd better be fast!

It was hot as hell out there, but I learned how to snap those babies with precision and speed. When the farmer asked who knew how to operate a standing lawn mower, I raised my hand, and next thing I knew I was going to town on the peach orchard. Out in the asparagus field, I wore a canvas jacket covered with pockets that enabled me to pick swiftly with both hands and drop them inside. I would snap a few and eat them as I went row to row. The man in charge didn't seem to mind, asking, "How do they taste?"

"Delicious," I'd say after each bite. He taught me to be discerning, that the thin ones with purple tips were best. After we brought all the baskets to the barn, he would examine a few from each batch to ensure that the look and taste were up to his standards. I stayed there until the end of the season.

Stockton became my hideaway, the place where I could disappear from everything that once was. Our home was situated on a narrow country road. If two cars were trying to cross the small bridge that our yard bordered, one car had to yield to the other. But still, the tabloids, entertainment shows, and news shows found me. Every time something dramatic happened in the Houston family circus, someone wanted my take on it. Reporters would camp outside the house, even pulling into our parking area across the road. Photographers stationed themselves slightly up the hill, focusing their long lenses on the front door. Some writers called repeatedly, others sent FedEx packages, and more than a few offered money for my cooperation. They tried to interview our neighbors, and some even knocked on our door. Lisa advised that whatever I did, I should not take out the trash in my pajamas.

....

1 was bothered by all the bad news I was hearing. I knew Nip didn't deserve it, and I wanted to do something to help her but wasn't sure what more I could do. I'd already told her that my door would always be open to her. She did call a few times, leaving messages on the landline, which we didn't often check.

On my birthday, I picked up a message: "Hi, Robyn. I bet you don't know who this is." Nip laughed. "It's your birthday, right? How old are you, sixty? Give me a call. If you don't know the number, neither do I." Then a giggle and a click. I didn't know her number, and the display said the number was restricted. To be honest, I truly don't think she knew her own telephone number. I don't think she ever knew.

Another time, she called and we talked. It was right on the heels of a 911 call she made to the police in Atlanta after a fight with Bobby. Reportedly, when the police arrived, she was bleeding from the mouth. She asked how I was doing and I stopped her, saying, "I'm fine. I want to hear how you're doing."

She told me that she was okay. I didn't try to push her to share anything, instead allowing her to lead the conversation. I still wanted very much to help Whitney, but my life was different now. I understood that I could help her only when she decided she needed it, not do it all for her. She asked who I was living with. I asked, "You remember Lisa?"

She stopped me and said, "I remember Lisa."

I felt the need to say, "It was all business while we worked together with you."

"I didn't say anything," said Nip.

I don't remember much else about the conversation. But my door remained open for Whitney and her daughter. And Lisa understood this had to be. I gave her my word that I would focus on the life that we were building and the family that we wanted to have. But we also had an understanding that when Whitney called or if she showed up at the door, we would welcome her.

....

In addition to my sporadic contact with Whitney in these years, I'd stayed in touch with her musical director Rickey Minor as well. He lived on the West Coast, but when he came east, we would usually get together. I asked him if he could use me on his team and he said yes. My first gig with Rickey was in a rehearsal space in Manhattan, and it took all day and into the night. My role was to assist Rickey with production schedules and sheet music, ensuring the band had all the details of where and when, whatever he or the band needed—basically, taking care of Rickey and his band.

I was up into the wee hours doing charts for each section: percussion, keyboards, guitar, bass—and if the sheet music was altered during rehearsal, it had to be handwritten in pencil, which also fell to me. Like anything else, it was hard at first, but we had fun, too. I worked closely with Rickey on several shows on both coasts: CBS's *A Home for the Holidays*, the Essence Awards, the BET Awards, the NAACP Image Awards, *Live at the Apollo*, VH1 tributes, and Divas Las Vegas, where I ran into my former boss.

We were staying at the MGM Grand, where the show was taking place, and I'd heard over the walkie-talkie that Whitney Houston was on the premises. I made my way to her dressing room to say hello.

The energy inside Whitney's dressing room was chaotic and unsettling. There were too many people congregating, and when my eyes finally focused in on Whitney, she looked just like everyone else—average. I don't recall what we said to each other, but we hugged and said we'd talk later.

During rehearsal, Whitney mounted the stage wearing a white cone-shaped "mask" over her nose. She sang with this contraption on her face. I was standing onstage next to the singers in front of a monitor while Rickey made corrections, addressing the musicians. Bobby was pacing the stage, exhibiting his usual overly energetic behavior. He came over to me, getting up in my face but saying nothing. "Hi, Bobby," I said, and sat down on top of the monitor, just to get away from him, and he turned and walked away. He used to do the same thing to Whitney—walk up to her and get all up in her face, and then tilt his head to the side, staring at her. I never liked watching him do that to her. It looked aggressive and disrespectful.

I got up and now was standing in front of the stage, off to the side. Whitney was center stage holding the microphone, about to sing a solo, "Try It on My Own." She had very little voice to begin with at that point, and even less trying to keep up with Bobby after both of them hollered through their duet performance. I couldn't stop looking at her with that thing across her nose. What was it? I felt for her and wished we could have a moment where we could sit down and talk, just the two of us.

I must have been in a daze, but I snapped out of it when I heard her call my name: "Robyn! Stop looking at me like I'm crazy." After the show, she invited Rickey and me to dinner at the Bellagio. At the restaurant, Whitney leaned in and looked over to where Bobbi Kristina was sitting and asked, "Are you tired? Do you want Mommy to send your food upstairs?" I felt bad for the kid.

Krissi shrugged, barely answering, but everybody was looking at her, so then she nodded and said, "Yes."

Before I could stop myself, I said, "I think she wants you, Nip. She wants her mama."

As the dinner ended, before getting up from the table, I said, "Nippy, I want to talk to you."

"What do you want to talk to me about, Robyn?" she answered playfully.

"Nothing really, I just want to talk to you," I repeated.

Everybody stood up and she said, "Let me out. Come on, girl, come talk to me." We took three steps away, but before I could say anything significant, out came Bobby to sweep her away. "I'll talk to you later," she said over her shoulder.

....

In May of 2005, Lisa called saying she had something interesting to share with me. *Esquire's* director of photography had told her about a job prospect at *ESPN The Magazine.* They were looking to hire someone with entertainment experience and connections in the music and film industries, plus a knowledge of sports. Familiar with my background, Lisa's contact suggested to her friend, *ESPN's* director of photography, that they interview me for the position.

It seemed almost too perfect. I hung up the phone with Lisa and drove home *claiming* that job. I'd come full circle, and sports was going to bring me the rebirth that I so desperately needed to be me again. Thankfully, I knew this world so well that I nailed the interview and got the job.

I was happy to be back working in the city. Lisa and I would rise at the Chelsea apartment, have breakfast, and depart together for our respective media jobs. I established a routine of walking briskly to and from the office each day, which helped get my body into great shape.

My job involved mixing pop culture personalities with athletes for ESPN's magazine, website, and television. I traveled with the creative team on location, covering photo and video shoots with Shaun White, Misty May and Kerri Walsh, Dwyane Wade, and LeBron James, among others. I would find out which entertainers had a specific athlete they liked and then try to get them together for a photo and conversation. Sometimes the pair made the cover. Ever the advocate for women in sports, I pitched the idea of interviewing actresses who had been athletes for espnW, a new online magazine. The editor liked it, and I was able to conduct interviews with women including Gabrielle Union, Jessica Biel, and Kristen Bell.

The project I enjoyed working on most was *GameNight*, which was special because it appeared on all three platforms. They had been having some difficulty getting cooperation from the talent they were approaching. I pointed out that the problem likely was the amount of time they were asking of them—four hours, which to publicists and managers may as well have been a week. I suggested we reduce the ask to forty-five minutes. Some of my productions paired the creators and cast members of *The Wire* with the Baltimore Ravens, the cast of the movie *Four Brothers* with Brendan Shanahan from the Detroit Red Wings, and WNBA championship team the Seattle Storm with the creators of the basketball documentary *The Heart of the Game*. I stayed at ESPN until 2009.

....

Over those years, I made a conscious decision to focus on my own life and not get sucked back into Whitney World. Early on, Lisa had said I was so involved, so consumed, that I couldn't focus on my own life, what we were doing and where we were going. Ever since my departure from Nippy Inc., every time Whitney walked to the corner, someone would call to tell me about it. So I unplugged. I stopped talking to Whitney's people, including Silvia, and finally I put myself first. Only then was I able to focus on me.

Before dawn on April 9, 2006, I went through my voicemail, deleting old messages. Lisa and I were about to head off for a three-week vacation in Argentina, and I wasn't taking my phone with me, so I was making room in the voice mailbox. I was standing at the window staring into the darkness when I heard her voice. I said, "Nippy?" But I accidentally pressed "7," deleting the message, instead of "4," which would have replayed it. So I didn't hear what she said. I do remember that her tone was different, as if she had something important to say, but she didn't call back, so there was nothing more to do.

It took me a long time to get my life back on track, to realize that I had to focus on me, to create something real with Lisa. I needed to save myself before I could save Whitney. But later, when she needed me and called, I missed it.

....

One of the life goals Lisa and I identified and shared on one of our weekend getaways was to create a family of our own. As a young New Yorker, Lisa hadn't wanted children. But when Lisa was in her midthirties, her sister, Laura, gave birth to a daughter, Helena, and Lisa began to question that decision. She and Helena were close from the jump, and the depth of her love for her niece was so intense that she realized that she wanted a child of her own. When she told me she wanted to have a child, I was all for it. I was ready to have a family with her.

The decision to adopt came to us both simultaneously, and we did a boatload of research on the many options. Though many prospective parents prefer to go through a private adoption attorney, which is said to be a faster process, we didn't feel up to having to vet potential birth mothers ourselves, so we opted to go the agency route. We chose Friends in Adoption, an agency in Vermont that supports open adoption of all kinds, including same-sex and single-parent, and once we had completed mountains of paperwork, a home study, fingerprinting, and reference letters, and created a profile carefully written and designed to showcase who we were to prospective birth mothers, we waited. Early on, I proclaimed, "Wouldn't it be great if we had twins?" I pictured our imaginary family on road trips, me at the wheel, as usual, Lisa beside me navigating, and each of us able to turn her head and see a different child strapped in the backseat. Every few months I delightfully raised the prospect and each time, Lisa rolled her eyes and said, "Robyn, what are the odds of that happening?"

Then on Lisa's birthday, January 23, 2009, our agency called with what they termed "a situation." I was at my ESPN desk when Lisa, from her *Esquire* desk, conferenced me in with our case-worker, who detailed the specifics: The birth mother was due in early May; she and the birth father had met at the University of Georgia and lived in Athens; she had had prenatal care. And then she added, "There's just one thing . . . there's two of them." I let out an elated yelp. Lisa was silent, maybe in shock.

We emailed and talked on the phone, and in mid-March flew to Athens to meet our birth parents. They were thoughtful, funny, and intelligent, and as we got to know one another, they enumerated the many sound reasons they had opted for adoption and why they had chosen us to raise the children. They generously invited us to be there for the birth. But Jeremy and Gillian appeared on this earth March 31, five and a half weeks early, and our birth father called to say, "They're doing everything that they should be doing. They're perfect. They're just small." I had willed my dream to come true. We packed up the brand-new SportCombi Saab wagon we had selected for its size and safety, and headed to Georgia to meet our children.

The next year and a half was a blur of sleepless night shifts, countless diapers, measuring bottles for what felt like constant feeding intervals, grabbing finger foods when we could, and infrequent showers. But we were a family and it was beautiful.

....

February 11, 2012: It was a Saturday morning just like any other sleepy start of the weekend with Lisa and our three-year-old twins, Jeremy and Gillian. Our neighbor and close friend Andy stopped by to say hello and to see the kids, something he did often. He was standing in the doorway talking to Lisa, with his back to me, and I noticed he was wearing a red-and-black jacket from his high school wrestling team, the traditional high school letterman's varsity jacket. I said, "I've never seen you wear that coat!" We'd known each other for a couple of years, and he'd never worn it.

Andy laughed and said, "I know. You can wear it whenever you want." I told him it was okay because I already had one of my own. I decided to get mine out and maybe start wearing it again. It was the only one I hadn't put into storage and lost before I moved in: the red-and-black one I'd designed for Whitney's first world tour. But I couldn't find it.

I wondered if I'd accidentally gotten rid of it. The previous summer, I had decided that it wasn't healthy for me to live with my past literally over my head. So, I cleaned out the attic, where I uncovered many certified gold and platinum mounted records and discs to commemorate Whitney's record-breaking accomplishments, presented to me by Arista Records. I decided to donate them to the Whitney E. Houston Academy in East Orange, the grammar school that Whitney had attended as a little girl, which eventually was named after her. Did the jacket get mixed up in the donation?

That evening, Lisa and I had dinner plans with a couple we'd recently met at a Philadelphia Family Pride event. We were all taking our time, going over the menu and sipping Pinot Noir as we talked. My phone started to ring. Lisa had it on the table near her in case the babysitter called, so she looked at the screen and said it was an old friend and teammate of mine, Paulette. She and I talked often, so I told Lisa I'd call her back.

Two seconds later, it rang again—another friend calling. Then our friend's phone started to ring. She glanced down for a moment and then looked back at the menu. I noticed Lisa picking up my phone, and then she said, "It's Paulette calling again. Oh! Now someone else is calling."

Then our friend looked apologetically across the table and said, "Is it okay with you if I answer this call? It's my sister, and she's called me a few times now. I'd like to see if everything's okay." She called back, and I glanced over at her after a minute. Just as our eyes met, she let out a gasp. I asked if everything was all right, and she immediately held up her index finger to say, "Wait a minute." As soon as she hung up the phone, we were all looking at her, wondering what had just happened. The expression on her face didn't indicate anything bad or good, and then she said it: "My sister is a huge Whitney Houston fan, and they're saying she passed."

I felt my insides shattering. I turned to Lisa, who was still holding my phone and staring at it as yet another call came in. She looked at me and said, "It's Dawanna." Dawanna was the lawyer for Sunday. I grabbed my phone, got up, and walked over to the foyer near the front door of the restaurant.

I answered the phone and quietly asked, "Dawanna—is it true?"

She said, "Unfortunately, I believe so, Robyn. Hold on, I think her publicist is speaking now." I went numb.

When I got back to the table, Lisa said, "We're going home."

I gathered my things, walked outside, and got behind the wheel of the car, but knowing how shaken I was, Lisa insisted that she drive. Thoughts of how my day had started with the red-and-black jacket were playing in my head. It was Whitney—a sign that she was leaving, forever. It was over. Everything was over and gone. I'd thought we had time. And she had, too. Same as the jacket, gone.

....

Whitney's death made me angry. The details and images of her leaving a party in Los Angeles surrounded by handlers a few nights before the fateful day haunted me. The fact that she had several hotel rooms full of people with her on this trip and yet no one was around on a day when her schedule was packed made me even angrier. The assistant said she had gone out for cupcakes for Nip.

Every time someone opened their mouth with alleged details, I didn't believe a word they said. They contradicted themselves over and over. The one thing that I was 100 percent sure of was that the information given by the Whitney team made it seem as if no one came prepared to work, and they were not tending to her needs.

....

I didn't hear from anyone about the funeral, not a word from the Whitney camp. Eventually, her agent called to ask how many tickets I needed, as if we were going to a concert. I told her that I needed five: me, Lisa, Bina, Silvia, and Silvia's daughter, Vanessa.

Then I got a message that Silvia was not welcome at the funeral. "Really?" I asked. "That's mean, and I know that's not the way Whitney would have wanted it."

It didn't matter. Silvia, who remained steadfast and loyal for fourteen years, who saw Nip at her very worst, who regularly rubbed her feet into the wee hours of the morning to help her relax, who knew her so well and who loved her unconditionally, was not allowed to see her off.

When we arrived at Newark's New Hope Baptist Church, the place was packed. Celebrities and other high-profile personalities were on the right side of the church, and family, friends, and employees were on the left side. Though Lisa, Bina, and I arrived early, there were already no available seats. Rickey's wife was on the celebrity side and invited me to sit with her, but I needed three seats. On the family side, seven rows had been marked with white tape, and from the eighth row back, the church was full. Sitting in the eighth row was what remained of the Nippy Inc. staff, and I spotted some old colleagues, but no one said a word.

Finally, I just removed the tape and directed Lisa and Robina to sit down. Then a man came over and told us that we had to move. I pointed out that there was no other place to sit. As things escalated, a publicist working the room came over and told me, "These seats are for the family."

I said, "I'm not family, but I know where Whitney would want me to sit." Then Lisa spotted another publicist, whom she knew and who is a beautiful person. It was she who got them to let us stay there.

A few minutes later, Bobby and his folks came in and experienced the same thing we'd just gone through. They were directly in front of us in row six and we watched it unfold. But this time, a security guard came over to tell them that the seats were reserved for family. Bobby was with nine people and I recognized all of them. I started to tell him to just stay there, but my days of making sure everything was going the way Whitney wanted were over.

Surprisingly, Bobby didn't put up much of a fight. All he had to do was sit down and let them try to remove him and his people. But next thing I knew, they filed out as asked. A few minutes later, I had to use the bathroom and got up to go to the back of the house. When I came out, I saw Bobby standing in the back, talking to a few people by the door. Again, I thought about saying something to him about what happened to us and telling him that Whitney would want him to stay and celebrate her life, but I didn't.

Then I turned my head and saw a producer, Mervyn Warren, sitting alone. This man had produced Whitney's only gospel recordings and even he didn't have a proper seat, and no one cared about that but me. I asked Mervyn if he wanted to come sit with us, near the front, and he said, "That's okay. I'm fine right here."

....

Whitney had told me and Sil that she wanted music but no flowers at her funeral. "You know I can't breathe," she instructed. "Celebrate my life with music." The New Hope Baptist choir; BeBe, CeCe, and Carvin Winans; Alicia Keys; and Stevie Wonder sang their hearts out that day. It really was quite a show. My friend was honored, and I was grateful for that.

As the long service neared its close, there was silence. And then, echoing through the impeccable acoustics of that church, we heard Whitney singing the forty-three-second a cappella intro to "I Will

Always Love You" as the gold casket, covered in a mass of white flowers and Sterling Silver roses, Nip's favorite, was lifted by the pallbearers and walked down the aisle.

We proceeded to the Newark Club for the repast. I saw Cissy seated at the family table having dinner and made my way over. I kneeled to her right so she could hear me. I didn't want to voice any of the clichés, so I simply said, "I thought we had time." She looked at me and replied, "She did, too."

Soon after, my godson, Gary Michael, Michael and Donna Houston's son, grabbed me by my arm and pulled me through the main room to a quiet hallway. "Goddie, Goddie, I gotta tell you. It was like she knew. I was on the road with her for the Nothing but Love Tour doing what my father used to do. I was in the hotel room with her. She was washing her face and I was sitting in the bathroom waiting so I could get her bags and take them out. She said, 'I don't care what they say. Robyn is my nigga.'"

After the service, I realized that I hadn't seen Michael Baker, Whit's music director after Rickey stepped down. I called to find out why he wasn't at the funeral and also what the heck had gone on out there on the final tour. He told me that he'd never received a call from anyone about Whitney's passing. "I probably found out just like you did." He also said that Whitney did not want to do that final tour.

"How was she holding up out there? What was her state of mind?" I asked.

He told me a story from the tour: He had gone out for something to eat and when he returned to the hotel, Donna and Pat, Gary's wife, were in the lobby and told him that Whitney was upset and he needed to go talk to her. Though Baker was hesitant, they made such a big deal about it that he ignored his instinct and went to her room. When he got there, Whitney let him know how disappointed she was by his coming to talk about the show. She asked him, "Whose side are you on?"

I asked him why he thought she asked that and he replied, "She didn't know who to turn to."

I had held on to my Rolodex from my Nippy days and called CeCe Winans. We talked about Whitney and the last time she'd seen and spoken to her. CeCe shared a painful story about being called to Whitney's Atlanta home. When she got there, she found her balled up on the floor in the center of the living room. When she kneeled down and put her arms around Whit's body, she felt like skin and bones. She told her that if she kept on doing that stuff, she was going to kill herself. Eventually, CeCe was able to convince Whitney to return to her Nashville home with her, where she fattened her up a bit and had Bible study, and where Nip prayed for forgiveness for her family. But after a few weeks, Bobby came and took his wife back to Atlanta.

After Whitney and Bobby divorced, CeCe made another visit, but this time to the California rehab facility that Whitney had entered. She arrived at a house that felt to her more like a women's social club than a center for healing. CeCe looked around and said, "This is rehab?"

In the post–Nippy Inc. years, I'd occasionally dial Whitney's in-house publicist, Lynne Volkman, to try to get answers: after Nip's disastrous Diane Sawyer interview, when Nip passed, and the day I heard Bobbi Kristina was rushed to the hospital. In the early days Gene Harvey had snatched Lynne from Arista Records' publicity department and we all worked together for years. Lynne was an important player on our team because she knew the inner workings of the Arista machine.

I can't lie, I did hear Krissi's cries. After her mother was gone, there were people both in the business and outside of it who reached out on Facebook to ask if I was in touch with her or knew how to contact her. I wasn't and didn't, and I expected that trying to get to her by phone would be an ordeal. She was living in Atlanta surrounded by people who were unlikely to welcome my influence. Mainly, I wanted her to know I was there for her, that her mother would have wanted me to look out for her, too, and that I was ready and willing to help. That I would be willing to come down to Georgia, pack her up, and give her a place of refuge in my New Jersey home if she would let me.

I contacted Tommy Brown's ex-wife Carolyn, who lived in Atlanta, to ask if she had seen Krissi and, if so, how she was doing. Carolyn hadn't seen her in a while but also had heard that she wasn't doing well. I tried my godson, Gary, Michael's son, but he said that he couldn't get to her, either. Meanwhile, Silvia was having a recurring nightmare in which Nip's daughter was in trouble. Miki Howard, a singer I hadn't seen in years, tracked me down to say that she'd been having similar dreams and wanted to know if there was anything I could do.

I asked Nicole David to give Kristina my number and email, with a message to call me if she wanted to talk. I also wanted her to explain why anyone had thought it was a good idea for Whitney to go out on that last disastrous tour when clearly, she was in no shape to do so.

Nicole answered, "Because Whitney and her daughter would have been out on the street if she hadn't."

"Is that what you all were telling her?" I snapped.

When the news reported that Whitney's daughter was found facedown in a bathtub and rushed to a Georgia hospital, I called Lynne. She told me that earlier that week Pat had called to ask her to find a rehab facility for Bobbi Kris. What had prompted the call,

Lynne said, was Krissi's showing up at Pat's front door, mouth bleeding, teeth missing, the hood of her car smashed in.

I don't know what or how much Whitney told her daughter about us. I don't know if she shared what life was like when we were inseparable, before fame took everything over. I hope she told her how tight we were, that I would do anything for her mother. It haunts me that I have no way of knowing. At the 2012 Billboard Music Awards show, Krissi said something that continues to disturb me. She accepted a posthumous honor for her mother saying, "I really just wanna say thank you to everyone that's supported us through it all. Not just from when it was good, but when it was bad, too."

"Did someone tell her to say that?" I wondered. "And to whom is she talking?"

....

Years later, while I was writing this book, I felt the need to try to find Dr. Richard Frances, the head doctor I'd met with at the Silver Hill rehab facility. He was no longer there, but I found him and called his practice in Manhattan. I left a message, giving my name and saying that I'd come to see him some time ago with a well-known celebrity's father and that I would love to speak with him. He returned my call and said, "It took thirty seconds for me to remember you. Of course I remember. Who wouldn't?"

I took the train to the city for my meeting with Dr. Frances. I headed to the east side and then decided to walk the forty blocks uptown to his office on East Eighty-Sixth Street. I used the time to relax my mind and think about what I wanted to ask him. Still,

I arrived with time to spare. As I stood on the corner waiting for the light to change, I spotted an old-fashioned pharmacy, and decided to pop in for some for breath mints. A feeling of déjà vu washed over me, and soon I realized why: There were all sorts of cough drops, soothing throat sprays, and a seemingly unlimited selection of lozenges—a singer's candy store! Nippy and I had been there, in that very space, buying boxes and boxes of Luden's Honey Licorice cough drops along with a tin box of Pastilles. I bought some for myself, and headed out to see Dr. Frances, now confident that I was exactly where I needed to be and would learn what I needed to know.

When the time came, I went into his office and we talked about that day. He said that at the time we first met, I seemed to believe that Whitney's husband was not good for her and that her brothers were also heavily into drugs and needed help.

Then he asked, "Were you aware that she called me?" He went on to say that Whitney had called and asked him to come get her. He told her that was not how they did things and offered to send an ambulance. She said no, that she would get a ride there. But she never made it. He didn't recall the exact year but said it was the early 2000s, after 9/11. I had spoken to Whitney around that time and read her parts of the letter I never mailed. I told her that it's really not that hard if she would just stop looking at the mountain and start climbing it. I offered to make the climb with her.

"Maybe I should have gone to get her," Dr. Frances said. "Addiction is tough and she was surrounded, and that made it even more difficult for her to help herself. Look at how many people died last year. Over seventy thousand. If Whitney did get the help she needed, imagine how many lives she could have saved. We cry every day."

Epilogue

The first eight years of our life as a family were spent living in the stucco farmhouse in the country, listening to the soothing sound of water running over rocks in the creek bordering two sides of the yard. Lisa and I wanted our children, Gillian and Jeremy, to have a peaceful start to life, to be able to run out their back door and explore in the woods, to catch salamanders, barefoot and naked in the stream. Their upbringing has been very different from my own. Our yard was home to groundhogs, deer, foxes, snapping turtles, wild turkeys, and blue herons. In early 2010 we decided that after all it required to build our family, it didn't make sense for neither of us to be present when the babies did all their "firsts." So, as unlikely as this once might have seemed, I became a full-time mother. I don't know why I thought that having children meant sharing your life, because those twins ran every moment of each day and every part of my entire world from dawn to dark with only the briefest reprieve at nap time. It was best for the three of us to get out of the house and I felt it would be good for them—even at that young age—to experience all kinds of parks and the different children who played there. So not only did we go to our local playgrounds, I drove us to parks all over Jersey and Pennsylvania and then to the biggie, Central Park, where they interacted with kids of all colors, speaking a multitude of languages. I had those chickens out of their Caboose stroller at two years old. I'd bring them to the city and we'd ride the subways and walk three-across-the-sidewalk holding hands until we could pick Mama up from work and go home together. Lisa thought I was nuts, but our children have some serious walking stamina!

Their early education was Montessori style: focused on nature, play, books, and art. I expose them to all genres of music, hoping it will bring them the same joy it does me. We want them to travel widely and experience the world and other cultures. We hope to bring them to Africa, Japan, South America, and all the other places I saw after Whitney said, "Stick with me, and I'll take you around the world."

Occasionally people would see us together and say, "I bet you can't even remember what life was like without them." I smile, but not in agreement. Of course I remember. I've been blessed with two big lives.

As the children grew, the time came for me to focus on myself again. I decided to become a trainer. I missed caring for my body the way I had as an athlete, and sensed that I could inspire others to do the same. I had spent the last six years focused on my kids, and it was time to get back in the game. I got myself as strong and fit as I had once been. Then I began studying, and in 2015 I earned my certification from the National Academy of Sports Medicine. I landed a position at the Solebury Club, an upscale sports club set in a renovated schoolhouse. My training partner, Colin Kirts, taught me that the key to being a great trainer is the ability to be creative and practice. I continually educate myself, taking classes that allow me to understand more about the brain and how we use it to command the body. I believe that we are all athletes. Some are just elite.

Today we live in a diverse, like-minded community that we love. The four of us hike, bike, skate, and take long family walks together. We have weekly movie nights and evenings where we play all sorts of board games. I taught them Uno, Nip's favorite. We cook together. We're into road trips, especially our annual summer vacation in Maine. My son shares my love of basketball, and although he doesn't know it yet, he is an exceptional pitcher. My daughter is a powerful swimmer and aspires to be a singer.

I cannot put into words just how grateful I am to Lisa, Jeremy, and Gillian for allowing me to detach myself from the present in order to relive the past and share my story. I hope the friendship, respect, and love Lisa and I have for each other has set the bar high for our children. I want them to have an understanding of death, too: We are given only one body in which to live this life. Nothing good ever comes out of drugs. Kindness and empathy are important, but there is a difference between being selfish and being for self. I want them to approach every day happy. To know that true friendship is everlasting. Above all, I want my children to know that there's only one you. People may try to tear you down, stuff you into a box, and slap on labels. They may make up stories and try to own you. But it's your call. You can sing solo, or you can blend; you can grab the spotlight, or you can work the background. The power isn't in one or the other, it's in the deciding. It's in the choosing and the pursuit. It's you and your dream. With the release of this book, I hope there will be no more questions. And that I have honored Whitney, Kristina, Marty, and Mom.

Acknowledgments

....

I would like to thank:

Jill Schwartzman, who believed in me and the value of my story. Thank you for all your encouragement, patience, and guidance.

David Kuhn, for responding immediately and then asking and saying all the right things. Thank you for protecting me, my family, and Whitney.

Kate Mack, for kindly being there throughout the entire process and powering me forward.

Retha Powers, for allowing me to be open and vulnerable as I talked and talked. I was comfortable telling you my story, and I am grateful for the time we spent and what we accomplished. I could not have done this with anyone else.

Acknowledgments

Marya Pasciuto, for all your hard work and for keeping me on track.

Becky Sweren, for your sharp questions, sensitivity, and support in the early days.

Lisa, my nighttime editor and calming voice of reason.

Silvia Vejar, I'm so grateful I recognized your value. Thank you for your deep loyalty, strength, and all the love and tenderness you showed Nip. It pains me to think how much she missed you.

Raynelle Swilling, for putting up with me always and for being there whenever I need you.

Ian Beraunovich, my brother, I can't go to the corner without you.

Khandi Alexander, for extending your friendship to me and Nip. If only there were more time . . .

Michelle Zakee, you know the meaning of true friendship.

Stephen Kirklys, for sharing your extraordinary talent each time we asked, and to Scott Beauchemin for your honest and valued opinions.

Vanessa Brinson, for loving Marty for who he was and for helping me get to know and understand him better.

Anne and Andy Fredericks, for loving us so much.

Usha Gilmore, for keeping my music up to date and me laughing hard!

Tara and Erin, our love for you is infinite.

My family—Mama Glass, Kenny, Derrick, Robert, Joyce, Dollie, Larry, Genie, Joey, Roy, Kyle, Kevin, Kent, and Gayle: All my love.

My dad, whom I never understood or liked, but always loved.

My second family—Maureen Hintelmann, Pat, Mal, Diane, Dann, Uncle Phil, Laura, Scott, Helena, and Kylie: I love you all.

Dr. Richard Frances, for your sensitivity and compassion.

Acknowledgments

Narada Michael Walden, for taking such good care of us when we were so young. Whitney loved you, as do I. Peace, Love, and Happiness.

Marc Hom, what an honor to be photographed by you.

My sis, Nancy Weisman.

D'Arcy Hyde and Kristin Berkvist, for your big hearts and for lending your talents.

Maria Padula, for your meticulous attention to detail and for keeping it all together. You are invaluable.

Michael Baker, I will never forget your calming spirit.

Firoz Hasham, for your honesty and loyalty.

Rose Hunt, for your honesty and integrity.

Carol Clark, for changing the course of my life not once, but twice.

The Nippy Inc. team—Kim, Michelle, Wade, Cindy, Jerry, Steve, Kerry, and Tommy.

Patti Wilson, Randee St. Nicholas, Dana Lixenberg, Kevin Costner, Loretta Divine, Lela Rochon, Lala, Wyclef Jean, Jerry Duplessis, Quincy Jones, Justo Artigas.

Marcelle Banks, for your beautiful friendship.

Special thanks to Emily Canders, Amanda Walker, and the entire Dutton team.

Shakira Atily and Tiffany Squire (my Walter & Scotty), T. C. Carr, Shanna Wylie, and Sunday.

Dionne, David, Damon, and Barry Warwick, for believing "All the Time" that "Love Will Find a Way."

Gene Harvey, for teaching rookie me about artist management and representation, and Ingrid Kvan.

Susan, Jamila, and Kenon Perry, for being such warm, wonderful people.

Acknowledgments

Billy Baker, Carol Porter, John Simmons, Olivia McClurkin, Quiet Fire, Michael Weeks, Roxanna Floyd, Kevyn Aucoin, Luther Vandross, Penny Marshall, Kashif Saleem, Jerry List, Donald Leon, Cynthia Madnick: You are unforgettable.

Benny Whitworth, Ann Blanchard, Tom Lebron.

Paulette Bigelow and family: Friends for the ages.

Coach Joan Martin, Sharon Mitchell, Bonita Spence, Rosie Strutz, Tammy Strutz, Barbara Rapp, and the rest of the Hawk crew.

Sheila and Pierre Coutin: Our Sandbrook family.

Dawanna Williams, Ann Sweeney, Kristian Summerer, Lorrisa Lock, Alisa Tager, Nancee Levin, Gail Deery, Marc Rosenquist, and Abby West, for being there for me.

Andy Ward, for your excellent advice at the start.

Pete Martino and Juliet Weber: So glad to have you as neighbors and friends.

Felicia Morris, for your support.

Carmen, Vonchetta, and Tiajuana Rawls.

The Solebury Club, Rob and Ann Marie DeAngelis, and Colin Kirts, for encouraging me in my new chapter.

Lois Smith: Without you, there would be no Lisa and me.

Eileen Berger: So grateful to know you.

Michelene King, for loving my brother.

The Gittelman family, for the love you gave.

Knute: I miss you.

And, of course, to Whitney's fans around the world. She loved you.

About the Author

....

After a long career in the music industry, Robyn Crawford is now focused on mental and physical wellness and writing. She lives in New Jersey with her wife and children.